Religion Revealed

RELIGION REVEALED

Christianity and Modernity

R. JOHN ELFORD

PETER LANG

Oxford · Bern · Berlin · Bruxelles · Frankfurt am Main · New York · Wien

Bibliographic information published by Die Deutsche Nationalbibliothek
Die Deutsche Nationalbibliothek lists this publication in the Deutsche Nationalbibliografie;
detailed bibliographic data is available on the Internet at http://dnb.d-nb.de.

A catalogue record for this book is available from the British Library.

Library of Congress Control Number: 2013931898

ISBN 978-3-0343-0955-4

Peter Lang AG, International Academic Publishers, Bern 2013
Hochfeldstrasse 32, CH-3012 Bern, Switzerland
info@peterlang.com, www.peterlang.com, www.peterlang.net

All rights reserved.
All parts of this publication are protected by copyright.
Any utilisation outside the strict limits of the copyright law, without the
permission of the publisher, is forbidden and liable to prosecution.
This applies in particular to reproductions, translations, microfilming,
and storage and processing in electronic retrieval systems.

Printed in Germany

To my daughter Emily

Contents

Preface	ix
Acknowledgements	xi
Introduction	1

RELIGION — 7

CHAPTER ONE
Religion in the Modern World — 9

CHAPTER TWO
Its Nature — 19

CHAPTER THREE
Its Problems (1): History, Providence, War, the Environment, Society — 61

CHAPTER FOUR
Its Problems (2): God, God Incarnate, Christian Uniqueness, Evil — 93

CHRISTIANITY — 117

CHAPTER FIVE
With Modern Integrity — 119

CHAPTER SIX
Its Gospel and Truth 135

CHAPTER SEVEN
And Morality 157

CHAPTER EIGHT
Being Christian 177

Notes 197

Index 205

Preface

Parents are familiar with being held to account by their children. It is the reason for this book. Emily, my daughter to whom it is dedicated, asked me if I said what I really think in my books. When I replied that I most certainly did she remained unconvinced and laid down the following veritable gauntlet.

> 'Write a book about religion, Dad, which says exactly what you think and put a laugh in it. Make it sound like you'.

All my following attempts at giving reasons why I need not pick it up failed miserably. So here it is. It is not, I trust, simply a personal indulgence. Emily, a well-educated successful young lawyer, is here understood as being representative of her generation. One, that is, which is unconvinced by the prevailing conventions of religion, largely ignorant of what it actually is and yet sincerely curious about it. Curious enough, that is, to be prepared to make the effort to know more. For this reason, the first half of the book provides the main background information about religion which is necessary for making sense of the second half about Christianity. This information is included because it is no longer that readily available to even educated and busy young people. The jokes might be few and feeble, but I have put them in to be strict to my brief.

Acknowledgements

This book is derived from diverse professional responsibilities; learning, teaching and publishing in the subject, as well as from invaluable friendships and good discussions. Experience of full-time parochial ministry in the Church of England, though now long distant, remains a valued and formative influence. I am profoundly grateful for all this. Some friends have read drafts and I am appreciative of their comments, particularly the more trenchant ones.

For reasons explained in the Preface, much of what follows is a form of a generational accountability. It is unfinished work. Christian theology understands that it will be so until the arrival of the Kingdom of God. It is the vision of that which inspires and sustains Christians in making the most they can of their lives. In this they must share their endeavours with all people of good will. That is why so much of what follows has such regard for insight from wherever it may be found. The vast labour of the search for knowledge which this entails is not simply for its own sake. It is undertaken in the hope of gleaning some practical insight into ways of improving the human lot. I would willingly start this ongoing labour again right from the beginning, if given the opportunity.

There is much imperfection in what follows. For that I remain solely responsible. It will be for others to reply to that in their various ways. Frankness in that, as here, will be welcomed. I ask only that any replies will also embrace the spirit of liberality and inclusiveness which is here intended.

Introduction

This book is about the importance of understanding the world-wide phenomenon of religion and about the positive role Christianity can play in making the most of modern personal and social life.

Religions are the oldest, most enduring and sophisticated ways in which human beings have understood the mystery and purpose of their existence. They are remarkably successful at this as their sheer endurance testifies. They deal with life itself, ethics, aesthetics, happiness, sadness, suffering, mystery and death. This is a list of some of the factors which are protean to human experience.

How do we make the most of life and live responsibly? This is the question all responsible people must ask themselves. The religions perhaps more than any other source of wisdom or insight enable us to answer it. They sustain life and make it bearable, often when all else has failed. They are 'an upholding presence'.[1] Religion achieves all this in the lives of individuals and societies alike. Its practice is, in fact, the most common way in which societies have maintained their coherence and identity. For all these reasons, religions should not be dismissed lightly. They are here to stay. It is our loss if we ignore them. It can even be to our peril if we fail to understand what a power they have in human affairs. All this has never been as important to remember as it is in our own time.

This book recognises that religion is once again and unexpectedly, widely and often adversely reported on in the world's news headlines. These embrace seemingly everything from international and internecine conflict, to education and the minutiae of life such as the propriety of modes of dress. Some of these issues now prompt vast media coverage. All this, in turn, fuels widespread public concern. Little of this could have been anticipated, even in the recent past. Religious controversy is now as prominent in our own life and times as it has been in the past. Furthermore, none of this looks as though it is but a passing phenomenon. It is clearly here to stay.

Thinking people should be asking themselves, therefore, why all this is the case. Why it is that, secular though modern life manifestly is in the greater part, religion remains so predominant, generally intrusive and so often downright disruptive? Why do some religions co-exist peacefully for the greater part and others not? It also needs to be asked whether or not this is most prominently a 'Western' phenomenon and, if so, whether we can identify the reasons for it.

This book is written, primarily, for readers who are curious about religion but have no, or only a patchy, knowledge of it. This is through no fault of their own. In recent mainstream Western education, religious teaching has become increasingly marginalised. Also, the decrease in church attendance has meant that it is no longer the source of instruction that even recently it still was. The result of all this is a vacuum of accurate general knowledge of the subject. It is, however, far too important for this to be allowed to happen. What follows is, therefore, an attempt to inform as much as it is to persuade. It will include reference to innumerable issues in the historic and modern debates about religion. References to these will be given throughout to enable those so interested to follow them up. Chapter Two is included, simply, for those who do not have knowledge of the world's religions. Those who do so might wish to skip it. Without this knowledge it will be difficult for the reader to place the subsequent discussion of Christianity in its wider historical context. It will be shown that this context cannot be ignored because Christianity can only be properly understood as one manifestation of the wider, ancient and ongoing cultural phenomenon of religion.

This understanding will also be conducted in the light of modernity. This will be defined as we proceed. It will involve discussion which ranges from medieval to present day thinkers. Much of this will be philosophical. It will show how important the relationship is between philosophy and theology because of the light the two disciplines throw on each other. We will see how the eighteenth century proved to be a watershed in this relationship and why it is still important for us to understand why. We will also see why new thinking about religion which began to emerge from this period is still relevant to our own life and times.

What will unfold as we proceed is an understanding of religion in general and of Christianity in particular which will enable us to understand better who we are and how best we can fulfil our lives. More than that, it will also show why our ability to achieve these important things is arguably deficient unless it embraces religious understanding. This is as essential to those who are not religious as it obviously is to those who are. All who are earnest about understanding human well-being need to have some proper understanding of religion.

It will also be shown why Christianity can be approached critically and why it is important for us to do this if, as Christians, we want to understand our lives and fulfil them as best we can. Many others will do so with reference to their own religions. Some of their efforts will be parallel to those discussed here and will be referred to. This will show that those who are prepared to think critically about their different religions invariably have much in common with each other. They often share closer affinity with each other than with many of their co-religionists. To experience even something of this is to discover what can be described as a liberating joy. There is nothing self-indulgent about this. With the joy comes the realisation that there is much to be done in the shared pursuit of understanding the contribution religion in general is able to make to global human well-being.

The emerging focus of the book will be on why Christianity needs to be reformed if it is to be practised with integrity. This is nothing new. A major part of North European Christianity went through a transformation in the Protestant Reformation of the sixteenth century. The undertaking there begun is still in process. *Semper Reformanda* is of its essence.[2] Before we can begin to approach the reasons for all this, however, we need to put Christianity in its wider historical and cultural setting. None of the world's religions stand alone. They are all part of the incredible cultural history of the human race. Their manifestation in the modern world derives from this history some understanding of which is, therefore, essential. Without it mistakes can be and are made which adversely affect the personal as well as the social well-being of large numbers of people. The stakes really are that high.

It will here be argued that the reasons for the frequent conflict between the Western religions, Judaism, Christianity and Islam, lie deep in their history. So deep, in fact, that they are invariably taken for granted and hardly ever critically examined. Indeed, it seems as though discussion of the real reasons for the problematic prominence of these religions in some world affairs are invariably tacitly put off-limits by their proponents. It is central to the argument of this book that this state of affairs cannot continue. The interests of the religions themselves, those of wider 'Western' society and, above all, of world peace all demand that we think again and thoroughly about these and other religions.

The contemporary debate about all this has been dominated by some critics of religion who make headlines and who frequently misrepresent it. These have been replied to by a number of writers, particularly Christian ones.[3] What follows is mindful of these criticisms, particularly the one that accuses it of causing violence. In some instances it clearly does, therefore this criticism should not be lightly dismissed. As the argument develops, we will also examine reasons why the Western religions and Christianity in particular must now be subjected to ongoing critical scrutiny. Only after this will we go on to explore why and how Christianity still has so much to contribute to our understanding of the human condition and its welfare.

This book will, therefore, explain why the Western religions, Judaism, Christianity and Islam, are as much a part of the world's contemporary problems as they are the solution to them. It will make uncomfortable reading for those Western religious believers who might believe that *their* religions are not a part of the problem. It will, in fact, be shown why these three religions are all in ideological conflict with each other, in spite of the so many things, indeed the greater part in them all, that they share in common. This conflict is not superficial. It is akin to that which often exists between like biological species which fight with each other more ferociously than with unlike species for scarce resources.

CHAPTER ONE will discuss the place of religion in the modern world. CHAPTER TWO will examine the origin and nature of the major world religions and focus on Judaism, Islam and Christianity. CHAPTER THREE will identify and discuss reasons why these three religions are historically and politically problematic. It will be shown why the roots of so much modern conflict are to be found embedded deep within them and why none of them can be exempted from bearing some responsibility for it. In CHAPTER FOUR we will consider some more abstract, but no less important, problems which apply mainly to Christianity. At this point the ways in which Christianity, specifically, needs to change if it is to maintain credibility in the modern world will begin to emerge. Only after it achieves this will it be able to continue to contribute its wisdom and richness to the world's greater good. CHAPTER FIVE will begin to examine what this wisdom is. CHAPTER SIX will examine what it means to understand Christianity as 'Good News' and something which can be said to be true. CHAPTER SEVEN will examine its relationship to some of life's major public concerns. CHAPTER EIGHT will consider what is principally involved in the practice of Christianity so understood.

Though the book will move, in the ways outlined, from critical examination to affirmation, in the case of just one of the world's religions, Christianity, it is not intended, nor should it be read, as an easy apology for it. Enough such books exist already. There will never be an end to them. This one is neither for the faint-hearted Christian nor for those who are comfortable with the ways things are. It will, rather, show how just much previously cherished belief has to be jettisoned if the vessel containing the real and abiding treasures of Christianity is to remain afloat.

It is for proponents of Judaism and Islam to decide if their religions will need similar reconstruction. Indeed, many of them are already claiming that this is necessary.[4] It would be imprudent of a Christian writer to do anything more than, as here, draw attention to their problems as ones which mirror the problems with Christianity. Nothing which will follow is in any way intended to express anything less than complete respect for those other two religions. If in any way it helps to further constructive thinking about how the three of them can live together peacefully and continue to make their wider contributions to the good of the world, it will have been worthwhile.

For all these reasons, what follows is explicitly written to be read by genuine enquirers into the role religion plays in our understanding of life's meaning and purpose, who are willing to make the effort to increase their knowledge of it and embrace even radical solutions to some of its seemingly intractable problems. As these emerge they might be found to be acceptable or not. It is confidently and sadly expected that many traditional religious believers will find them not so. The reasons for this will, again, be discussed as we proceed.

In the discussion many different subjects will be embraced: history, philosophy, ethics and theology, as well as biblical studies, church history and current affairs. (Even this list is not exhaustive!) None of them will be found to be difficult to follow by patient readers. Guidelines are here given throughout to aid navigation through often turbulent waters. To extend this analogy, the aim will be to show that such a passage is possible for all thinking people who are prepared to set out and put in a little effort. Good sailing!

RELIGION

CHAPTER ONE

Religion in the Modern World

In the comparatively recent past, many people assumed that religion in general had entered a period of terminal decline. The alleged reasons given for this were various. Some, for example, claimed that the long process of cultural secularisation, in which life is understood only from a human point of view, was in the final stages of its displacement of religion. Others pointed to the growth of materialism (whatever was meant by that). Yet others, pointed to the seemingly inexorable overall decline in Church attendance. And so on. Some, or all, of this might yet prove to be true, but at the moment, at least, it is far from self-evidently so. Indeed, 'religion' in general is very much back in the news. One central reason for this is the ever ongoing conflict in the Middle East. There one group of people, who are of identical genetic stock, who occupy two countries and who profess three religions are seemingly incapable of resolving their disagreements. Whilst many, the majority, of those who profess these three religions do so amicably with the other two, there are significant numbers who do not do this. They exacerbate their differences and, invariably, cite them to thwart international peace initiatives thereby hindering peaceful co-existence. As a result, repeated attempts by the United States to get Israel to withdraw to its pre-1967 borders are rebuffed. Neither Israel nor Palestine have formally recognised each other's legitimacy as states and this debate constantly embroils the United Nations Organisation. Significant numbers of Muslims in Lebanon, Syria, Iran and elsewhere think that Israel should not even exist and Christians in all these countries are caught up in the resultant often horrific conflicts. They, equally, insist on their own differences and claims.

None of this is a new phenomenon. Of all the world's religions, Judaism, Christianity and Islam have been in particular conflict with each other throughout history. The wars they have engendered or been involved in have often caused widespread bloodshed and had other horrendous consequences. All this has been and, sadly, still is sometimes the case. This, is in spite of the fact that many people in all these religions do so much to promote mutual and interfaith understanding and toleration. This book will show why such conflict arises directly from interrelated causes which are intrinsic to *each* of the three religions. It will also show why they must *each and equally* share responsibility for it. In the three religions those causes arise directly from the fact that they all claim that their religion is the *only* true one. For example, some Jews, although they theoretically acknowledge the multiplicity of covenants, claim this because the covenant God made with *them* as the chosen people is their exclusive right. They claim that they are, therefore, *the* people of God. Some Christians, claim that theirs is the only true religion because Jesus is the Son of God by whom they alone come to the Father. Some Muslims, claim that their religion is the only true one because Muhammad, the last Prophet, alone makes possible a direct relationship with God. We will examine something of all these claims in Chapter Two. Sadly, the conflict these three religions generate is often now as intense as it ever has been. They all, therefore, need to re-examine their histories and their consciences.

This conflict which centres on the Middle East, now spreads elsewhere. Most poignantly, this was seen in the 11 September 2001 attacks on New York and Washington, as well as subsequent attacks on London, Lisbon, Bali and elsewhere all with clear religious overtones. In 2006 hostilities between Israel and Hezbollah erupted briefly into open warfare with tragic consequences. The continued fragility of the cessation of this conflict alone testifies to the seriousness of the ongoing problem.

More generally, the world finds itself vulnerable in a new way to resurgent nationalism and 'terrorist' attack. This, first use here of the word terrorist, is deliberately inverted. Its current widespread usage is invariably pejorative. This must be avoided if what it refers to is to be properly understood, but this is, perhaps, easier stated than achieved. The reason for this is, of course, because the modern use of the word carries overtones of repugnance which are derived from still powerful memories of the ferocious Jacobin reign of terror in the French Revolution. The Jacobins believed so vehemently in the justice of their cause that they saw themselves as the rightful custodians of the nation's integrity and held that the use of any effective, even draconian, means was legitimate in its defence. The repugnance this then caused, of course, became one of the principal counter-revolutionary forces in the reconstruction of French civil society. It probably also did much to check nascent revolutionary forces elsewhere in Europe at the time. Little wonder that the word is so loaded in European and European-influenced lexicography. We will make but little progress with understanding how to use the word responsibly in the present if we fail to disassociate it from these historically modern origins. It is, therefore, imperative that we do that. We do better to begin by remembering the uncomfortable truth that terrorism as a systematic use of coercive force, is never one sided. Nor is it only the prerogative of minorities. States equally make recourse to terrorist activities. This happens whenever coercive intimidation is used to further a political will by deliberately creating a climate of fear and using the destabilisation that such fear causes as an instrument of capitulation. Nazism is, of course, the most frightening twentieth century example of state terrorism used in this way. Stalinism is another. These examples alone are enough to remind us that neither might nor secularity are preventative of terrorist activity. That said, however, contemporary international terrorism is invariably carried out by minorities against majorities. Such minorities find it a relatively inexpensive and logistically achievable way of exerting an influence on the international order which is often out of all proportion to their actual political or military strength. Here the use of surprise and sensation is of the essence. So too is the targeting of innocent civilians which might well include fellow nationals an co-religionists. So understood, 11 September 2001 was probably the all-time text book terrorist achievement. The idea that probably less than ten people active at one time, armed with nothing but knives could cause such immediate devastation with so much aftermath, was previously only the stuff of fiction. Its possibility was never seriously contemplated in military contingency planning. The use of aircraft as bombs was, seemingly, inconceivable. At 09.05 (New York time) on that date it became a frightening and awesome reality as the never to be forgotten television images were flashed around the world before stunned audiences. It was immediately clear that the date would be culture-defining in the sense that an older generation remembered the assassination of President Kennedy to be. (Few of us will ever forget where we were when that happened.) *The Times* of London leader of the following morning announced 'The Day the World Changed'. This reflected the international mood of that day although, with hindsight, it was not strictly correct. By then the world had already changed. International terrorists had long since been planning meticulously for these events. 11 September was, more precisely, the day we all had to come to terms with the fact that the world had already changed. The immediate actual change was, of course, horrific with thousands dead and dying and others performing unbelievable acts of bravery to rescue the still trapped survivors in the rubble. The consequent symbolic change was no less dramatic. The World Trade Towers were laid waste and the Pentagon attacked, with impending and largely unpredictable economic consequences. However, as the rescue work in New York and Washington heroically proceeded alongside all the concomitant personal and collective grief, the world drew its breath and made immediate contingency plans for the re-establishment of personal, social, political and economic normality. That this happened as quickly as it did, is a testimony to the resilience of the collective human spirit and to the remarkable roles played by individuals and groups who helped to bring it about. New York and Washington miraculously came back to life, the financial markets re-opened and soon began to show signs of more rapid recovery than was expected.

More widely, the nations of the free world looked afresh at their relations with each other and began to pledge renewed co-operation in the fight against international terrorism. President Bush repeatedly referred to this as nothing less than a 'war' against terrorism. Other nations, such as the UK, were less bellicose and chose, rather, to confront the phenomenon as a breach of everyday law and order. Both of these approaches have their credibility. The second increasingly and wisely prevails. International terrorist activity is here to stay for the foreseeable future and it can be expected to re-define the international strategic order every bit as much as previous other events, such as the collapse of Communism in the USSR, have also done.

None of this can be analysed as a simple conflict between the East and the West. Eastern and Western countries are equally as horrified when finding extremist elements in their midst. What is now increasingly self-evident, however, is the fact that there are some radical Muslims as well as some Jews, Christians and others who are opposed to them who will go to any length to thwart peace processes particularly those in the Middle East. In response to this the West, for example, often makes resort to desperate measures such as the summary killing of Osama Bin Laden. One commentator previously wrote of this conflict as follows. 'Since 2001 the region has been turned into an ideological battle ground between two rival camps with global ambitions. One camp, led by the United States, claims to represent the modern global system of open markets and sexual equality. The other camp is represented by radical Islam which regards the Western model as not only decadent but dangerous for the future of mankind. It hopes to unite the world under the banner of Islam, which holds to be the "The only True Faith"'.[1] If this chilling analysis is correct, what is now happening in the Middle East cannot be separated from the wider phenomenon of global terrorism for these obvious reasons.

What is now equally clear is that no analysis of the Middle East problem or proposals for its solution will be adequate unless it addresses the religious causes at its roots.

We have already begun to identify these. They are what enable the three related religions, with otherwise so much in common, to compete often vehemently with each other. Their co-existence is often tenuous. Of course, as we have already noted, many of their proponents do this and do so to their credit. They are decent spiritual people with an immense respect for and toleration of each other. If this were not the case the problem of the conflict of these religions would by infinitely worse than it already is.

The point here being stressed here is that apologists for these three religions can no longer go on claiming that their religions, as such, are not part of the problem. They all are in their different ways. It is unhelpful to react to the modern conflict between them by saying that they are all virtuously equal in every respect. They are not. We need to look at each of them critically. Only in this way will we be able to discover where they do not serve the general good as well as where they do. What follows is an attempt to do that in the Christian tradition.

An argument of this book is, therefore, that it is fundamentally dishonest to claim that the three religions are not part of the problem. Those elements of these religions which are the manifest cause of so much death and distress must be identified. Only when this is done will the abiding beauty and value of these religions again become credible. We will examine what this abiding value is in the Christian tradition in the second half of this book.

Little wonder, is it not then, that the nature of 'religion' is high on the agenda of civilised concerns? This, for reasons we began by mentioning, would have been impossible to foresee in even the recent past. Religion is now often perceived as not always serving the greater good. One reason for this is because it so often turns people into fanatics who will go to any length to pursue their ideological ends. Its renewed critical examination is, therefore, imperative. Such an examination must be unconditional from the outset, if it is to get at all close to the truth about the undesirability and desirability of the roles religion plays in human affairs.

This raises, immediately, questions about the point of view from which this enquiry can be conducted. Some have held that those who espouse religion are unsuited for this because they are incapable of exercising the necessarily objective criteria. This charge has much force and must not be taken lightly. Too ready apology for this aspect, or that, of this religion, or that, has and will continue to stifle the debate. For this reason alone, it has to be eschewed by religious believers who want to participate in it.

An example of such a too ready apology can be found in the writings of Richard Harries. His *God Outside the Box: Why Spiritual People Object to Christianity* is an eloquent defence of Christian orthodoxy against perceived reasons for its widespread current rejection.[2] It will appeal to the converted. For the following reasons, it is doubtful if it will do so to the wavering and the unconvinced. As an able apologist, Harries is clearly aware of the weakness of his position. He recalls that Donald Mackinnon once pointed out that '...apologetics is the lowest form of Christian life', but tries to escape the censure by claiming that what this opposes is '...any attempt at propaganda – Christianity at the level of the party political broadcast.'[3] With this awareness, the book promises to deliver '...uncomfortable truths'. On reading it they are not that easy to find. One central uncomfortable truth, about God's election of the Jewish people is discussed but not at all rigorously examined.

God's election of the Jews as God's chosen people is, of course, an unquestioned assumption in Christianity as well as Judaism. If this is a 'truth' of these religions, then it is certainly an uncomfortable one. The still unresolved conflict this has caused for almost three millennia makes that, sadly, all too clear. Harries is, of course, well aware of this, but defends it on the grounds that God also gave God's chosen people great responsibility. He writes, '...in the Hebrew scriptures the people of Israel are chosen not for privilege but for responsibility; not because of their moral qualities but simply because God has chosen them for a particular task – to reveal the knowledge of himself [sic] and his purpose to the whole of humanity'.[4]

This is the classic defence of what is probably one of the most uncomfortable religious 'truths' of all. Its strength is that it emphasises that such election bears responsibility as well as privilege. It is most distorted when inordinate emphasis is put on the latter. Can we, therefore, seriously go on believing that an all loving and all knowing God would have bestowed privileges on one group of people which would cause so much mayhem in human history? 'No' is the only honest and uncomfortable answer to this question. Harries does not even contemplate it. Nor is it contemplated either, of course, elsewhere in the mainstream Western Christian establishment. Palestinian Christians and others know this uncomfortable truth all too well. They deserve more sympathy. It is rightly inconceivable to them that God, their God of Abraham and Isaac, historically gave such, then almost uniquely fertile, land to anybody. Harries, however, is convinced that such orthodox Jewish doctrine, which is also a part of Christianity, need not be compromised in any way when replying to sceptics. That self-confidence is reflected more or less throughout the narrative.

The thrust of Donald Mackinnon's point is, surely, that this confidence must be more sensitive and even be prepared to admit its own vulnerability. He concluded his Inaugural Lecture as Norris-Hulse Professor of Divinity in the University of Cambridge by saying that philosophers of religion *cannot* be apologists because they 'may perhaps feel a peculiar kinship with those who, from similarly situated territory, make protesting raids upon the theologian's cherished homeland'.[5] Guarding the gates thereof is the assumed mission of the apologist. On Mackinnon's view, it is clearly a mistaken one. Criticisms of Christianity have to be listened to more carefully. Sadly, Harries' sort of argument which makes too ready recourse to orthodoxy will probably not do that much to convince the ever growing majority of religious sceptics. On the contrary, it might make the orthodox more complacent and, in the longer run, thereby become counterproductive in its otherwise laudable aim. Orthodoxy has to listen to religious scepticism more carefully than this and respond with more contrition. That is, surely, the deeper profundity of Donald McKinnon's point. We will, at least, try to heed that in what follows.

This is easy enough to promise, but it is also painful to deliver for those of us who find it necessary to re-examine some of our most cherished beliefs and practices. Religious believers can no longer shirk the responsibility of doing this. Simply leaving it to others is not an option. It has to be done, so to speak, from the inside. This is because religion involves the passions and feelings if it involves anything. They are, in fact, a key to its proper understanding. Its allegedly 'objective' analysis and criticism might well serve some useful purposes, but there is far more to religion than this, alone, can discern. In the discussion about religion, therefore, religious believers have to participate. To do this acceptably, however, they will have to learn new rules. As we proceed we will try to discover, at least in part, what some of these are.

One such will require the disengagement, for the purposes of enquiry at least, of religion from individual and group self-interest. Since, as we shall see, such self interest is writ large in religious belief and activity, this will probably be the most difficult thing of all to achieve. Indeed, it is probably true to say that those of us who are religious believers can never be entirely sure about the way in which what we believe and practise actually serves our self-interest. This is, simply, because religion is so closely bound up with personal and social identity that we can scarce separate the many elements involved. We might well be able to observe the relationship of a religious profession of self interest in others, particularly when it goes wrong and when the social consequences are unacceptable. It is more difficult for us always to be aware of when we are caught up in what we criticise in others. This alone can hamper our objectivity. However, all this should not be taken as reason for not trying to be critically analytical about religion from within. This has to be attempted in ways which demonstrate both religious and intellectual integrity. The aim must be for nothing less than an understanding of religion from within which has faced and survived the most strident of criticisms. This does not mean that, whatever that understanding turns out to be, is necessarily some 'reductionist' account of religion in the sense that religion is reduced to something else, such as morality or whatever. The historically most common way in which religion has been so 'reduced' is to reduce it to whatever can be reasonably accepted, according, that is, to whatever the prevailing canons of reason might be. The well-known and obvious weakness of this is that religion, so understood, becomes immediately marginalised and unintelligible once the contemporary canons of reason shift, as they inexorably do. An example of this happened at the end of the eighteenth century when the by then centuries old confluence of reason and religion came under the devastating attacks of thinkers such as David Hume and Immanuel Kant. It need not detain us for the moment, beyond noting that the view here taken is that this attack was and remains a successful one. In its aftermath, thinkers like Friedrich Schleiermacher began a process of reconstruction which still continues and of which what follows can be seen to be a latter day part. This process will always need to continue as ever new challenges to religious belief and practice come to the fore, just as they do in every other area of human activity and understanding.

There are no assured results in all this from the outset and such as there are cannot be expected to make any immediate difference. Entrenched religious attitudes and customs can take generations to change. This will all take a very long time. But, if we really are at a re-defining crux in the history of Western culture, none of this can be shirked. In area after area of our community, national and international lives we have no choice but to think again. What follows can be read as a contribution to such thinking again about religion in general and Christianity in particular.

We will see as we proceed why religion is a powerful source of what we will describe as 'practical' wisdom. This can be said of all religions. After describing these in the next chapter we will then begin to concentrate our discussion on Christianity. Chapters Three and Four will discuss 'problems' of Christianity and of its Jewish origins. Here we will see, in more detail, why these problems, some of which we have already identified, cannot be shrugged aside or apologised for too easily. Only after that, in Chapters Five to Eight, will be able to consider in more detail why it is that a religion like Christianity has so much to contribute to the betterment of the human condition both individually and collectively.

CHAPTER TWO

The Nature of Religion

In this chapter we will look at the major world religions, concluding with Christianity. Before we commence that proper, however, it will be necessary to remind ourselves why it is that Christianity has to be understood as part of the wider religious history and experience of humankind and not as a unique religion in its own right which can be understood without reference to that history. There is a particular reason why this needs to be pointed out.

One powerful modern idea has caused many to accept the uniqueness and supremacy of Christianity over other religions. It is evolutionary biology. This was famously established in the nineteenth century and remains all pervasive in its field. It holds, simply, that organic processes cause ever new forms of specie to appear which become by process of subtle change ever more fit for purpose, particularly the purpose of survival. Charles Darwin called this the process of 'natural selection' and he illustrated it from his painstaking observation of chosen species. Before he demonstrated this scientifically in the 1850s, the basic idea had, in fact, already been widely postulated.

The famous nineteenth century controversy between science and religion arose for the simple reason that the observed specie evolution required a longer timescale than the literal interpretation of the biblical account of creation allowed for. According to that the earth was not yet 6,000 years old. This dispute was, in fact, soon resolved. The evolutionists won the day, though creationist thinking does still, of course, survive among some Christian believers who cling to their interpretation of the literal meaning of the biblical text. Very soon, the idea of evolution not only came to be accepted by religious believers and this is our point, they actually turned it to their advantage. In 1894, for example, Edward Caird published his Gifford Lectures entitled, *The Evolution of Religion*.[1]

He distinguished the lower forms of primitive religion from the '...higher forms of religion which may still be said to survive as recognisable influences in modern life'.[2] By this simple expedient, Caird, like others, used the idea of evolution to establish the superiority of Judaism and Christianity over all other forms of religion as well as of the latter over the former. He also went on to trace the evolution of Christianity itself from New Testament to modern times. His conclusion is that this '...long, unhasting, unresting process of the evolution of religion is itself the best evidence we can have that there is a divine meaning in the world'.[3] Ever evolving Christianity stood at the apex of this process because it revealed the divine spirit in all its fullness. It, '...thus took up into itself all the religious life of humanity that existed before, brought it to a higher unity, and started it on a new course of development'.[4] Christianity in general and modern Christianity in particular was seen as the most evolved form of religion the world had ever seen.

Appropriation of the idea of evolution in this way was, in fact, then widespread. By the end of the nineteenth century it became such an influential idea that the suitability of its application to non-organic areas of life and thought, such as this, was taken for granted. Even a cursory browse through book titles of the late nineteenth and early twentieth centuries will show what widespread and inappropriate use was made of the idea.

Such views about the evolved superiority of modern Christianity became so widespread that they lasted well into the second half of the twentieth century and can still be heard at least by implication in the way some Christians speak and behave. It was considered to be axiomatic by many biblical scholars and theological educators. Seldom in the history of thought has a single idea in one subject area been so widely and for so long been so misapplied in this way to others. Though evolution in biology might well, in surviving species, be inexorable it is not self-evidently so elsewhere. Things do not necessarily always improve everywhere for the better. Least of all, perhaps, can we suppose this of religious beliefs and general social arrangements. The wars of the last century and emergent international terrorisms of the present one illustrate this all too sadly and self-evidently. The place of religion in human history and culture, as well

The Nature of Religion

as its manifestation in the present is both more complex and more interesting that these inappropriate evolutionary views of it ever allowed for.

Were it not for the fact that such a view of the evolved superiority of Christianity still partly prevails, it would not have been necessary to begin this chapter with such a caution. The rejection of this view opens the possibility, at least, of understanding the place of religion in human history and culture in a more open-minded way. This requires that we eschew any notion that some religions, *per se*, are higher or more evolved than others. The use of the term 'primitive' to dismiss some religions pejoratively, such as the so-called nature religions, is on this view not to be allowed. So, the way religions compare with each is more complex than the now invalidated claim that some religions like Christianity are more evolved ever allowed. The more profound approach to the phenomenon of religion from the beginning of human history requires that we observe it with an open mindedness which does not permit us to start by supposing that 'our' religion is in any way superior to that of others.

Before the world's great religions came to be identified, in ways we will consider below, the phenomenon of religion was evident in earliest human history. It is notoriously difficult to define. For our purpose, however, we use the word here to mean *any evidence of the fact that human beings have shown an awareness of any powers, whatever they may be, other than their own which affect their well-being*. Evidences for this are artefacts, paintings and above all burial customs. These latter clearly show that even the earliest traceable evidences of religious consciousness embraced the belief in immortality, that humans were destined for other and higher things which were not thwarted by their mortality. Burial decorations from the earliest Palaeolithic times show that magic played a central role in all this, as did animals and other life forms. This became central to the sophistication the funerary customs of Egypt and so many other of the world's first great civilisations. The religion of Egypt with its sun worship, animism, polytheism and belief in divine kingship is, perhaps, the first example of religion becoming established as the cult of a highly developed state. We are still as amazed as ever at new discoveries of its extent and extravagance. That so much wealth and human energy was devoted to the erection of the pyramids alone, almost defies comprehension. It cannot be accounted for as entirely the result of slavery since there must have been a voluntary and social commitment to the enterprise involved. The same, incidentally, must have been true of the many other great early religious undertakings which led to massive construction projects. Those of the Maya and Inca cultures of South America are other clear illustrations of this.

Many of these phenomena predated by centuries the sophistication brought to the religious understanding by even the most primitive forms of writing. Indeed, even these were, again, pre-dated by centuries in which religions were preserved and communicated by oral traditions among nomadic tribes.

Evidence of early religious consciousness is also found in the mythologies which provided so-called primitive peoples with their understanding of life. They expressed these in stories which then enabled those who told them to establish their individual and social identity. Creation myths are to be found in most early religious records. Latter day questions about the literal truth or otherwise of such mythologies would not then have occurred and it is inappropriate to ask them retrospectively. The mythologies were accepted as true because they served their purpose. They provided understanding and security by explaining the relationship of everyday human experience to history and the wider world. Moreover, they did this successfully. For this reason they were cherished, preserved and passed on carefully through the centuries. This is one of the main reasons why there always has been and still is such respect for elderly people in primitive societies. They are the custodians of orally and pictorially transmitted wisdom. It is, therefore, wrong to think of such early human communities as being pre-literate. To the contrary, the literacy of primitive societies as their mythologies alone show is extremely sophisticated. Indeed, the greater part of this profundity probably remains hidden from even the most rigorous of our contemporary scholarly methods of enquiry. Mythology was something which had meaning because it was lived by and trusted in. Something, also, which was venerated because of its antiquity and inexhaustible relevance to whatever challenges life presented in ever changing times.

As time passed and different cultures came into contact increasingly with one another their mythologies overlapped and interacted. Recurrent motifs can be observed throughout. Indeed, struggles for cultural superiority can often be traced through the histories of their mythological interaction. Mythical superiority was a powerful social force. It was sought by showing that whatever might be explained in another's myth was better so in one's own. Little wonder that primitive mythologies were so often and so seriously in such competition with each other. The exact history of all this need not detain us apart from noticing as we have done that; (a) religion so defined is as old as the most primitive human cultures we know of, (b) that it passed from the primitive mythologies of nomadic people into their oral tribal traditions and (c) it then, in some cases, came to be expressed in the written forms to which we have access. When we set our careful study of these writings in the context of our other, however scanty, knowledge of primitive peoples we begin to get some insight into the sheer sophistication of their lives and of the important place religion played in them.

Early expressions of religion are difficult to classify, save, perhaps, for one thing. They might all be said to have in common the fact they helped humans *to cope with the mystery of their existence and its vulnerability, as well as provide them with some confidence in the future.* By this simple but profound means, human beings rose above the exigencies of their immediate environment. They did this by contemplating its relationship with eternal values. They, therefore, came to see themselves objectively as parts of a wider scheme of meaning.

Such a view of the origin of religious experience is, of course, noticeably anthropocentric. It focusses on what human beings can be observed as doing and believing about their religion. It does not begin, therefore, with over preoccupation with questions about whether or not such religious beliefs were 'true' in the modern sense of that word. This anthropological approach to religion has, in fact, been tremendously influential in its modern study. It raises, of course, a well-known methodological problem in the study of religion. It can be simply stated. If you begin the study of religion in this way, so to speak, from the human level (below), then you immediately encounter the problem of how to study it from (above), from some divine or other perspective. Similarly, if you begin from this latter point (though how anyone can think that they can do that from a human point of view has always struck me as being of the ultimate arrogance) the first problem you have is how to relate it to all that is human. Many, too many, religious believers such as some Jewish, Christian and Muslim ones claim to know about all that is human in the second place because they know so much about all that is divine in the first.

None of this necessarily reduces what is 'other' about religion to what is human. It does not deny the importance, existence or whatever of that other. Indeed, it even requires a healthy open mindedness about it. This can take the form of an *a*gnosis, a not knowing. This can be lived with. In doing so we are clearly and unambiguously rejecting any understanding of religion which requires, as a precondition of participating in it, that this or that has to be 'believed' in some 'objective', or whatever, sense as being true. That view of religion is, frankly, crude to the, 'nth' degree. It purports that all we lesser mortals have to do is to believe this or that (particularly whatever 'this or that' the religious advocates want us to believe to join their club), and all will be well. Indeed, some forms of evangelical Christian preaching to the young and immature are as crude as this. There are downright dangers here for the obvious reason that they tamper with and even exploit the insecurities of immaturity. This is psychologically dangerous territory. Such notions of religious truth are invariably compounded with forms of social control which can be damaging to the individual. Little wonder that such a crude approach to religion is so appealing to the insecure (which is most of us at some time or other), and also so unappealing to the more self-confident and independently minded (which is most of us most of the time).

There is another important thing to notice about the early religions. They were invariably sensitive towards the natural order. Our widespread recognition of this dates only from the last century. We are now conscious of the fact that human welfare is crucially dependent on that of the natural order. This has not always been the case. It is arguable that the Judaeo/Christian understanding of religion has, in large part, caused the bifurcation between nature and human nature in Western culture. This is mainly because the Hebrew Bible sees humans as a separate creation and encouraged them to 'have dominion' over nature and exploit it for their own interests. Those wishing to reject this claim often counter it by stressing that the same Bible also gives humans responsibility for the 'stewardship' of nature. They also invariably point to the abuse of the natural environment which was caused by the Industrial Revolution. This debate continues and it is important that it does so. Christianity has much to learn from those early religions which focus on the importance of maintaining harmony between nature and human nature. Once we see the former as not being more evolved than the latter it becomes much easier to achieve that.

In the rest of this chapter we will outline the world's major religions and briefly consider one influential account of what they have in common. Some such understanding of these religions is necessary because we need to know how Christianity fits into their history and how it compares and differs from them. As mentioned previously, readers with some knowledge of these religions might wish to proceed to Chapter Three.

The modern religious world map is dominated by the so-called big six; Shintoism, Buddhism, Hinduism, Judaism, Christianity and Islam. These originate, in order, from East Asia, India and the Near East and all have their derivative forms.

Shintoism

Shintoism is the traditional Japanese state religion. Its sacred books, the *Kojiki*, record ancient history. The term Shintoism came into common use to distinguish it from older forms of Buddhism which it displaced. The essence of Shintoism is not at all difficult to grasp. It does not contain, like so many other religions, elaborate theological or moral exposition. It derives, simply, from the belief that elemental natural forces are at work in human life. These are expressed through human impulses. The more intense these are, the more they reflect the deity: *Kami*. This is a religion of the here-and-now which requires a radical purity. The story of how Shintoism accommodated itself to different influences throughout Japanese history is well and briefly told in *Encountering Religion*.[5] Most remarkable, of course, is the fact that it was, rightly or wrongly, identified by the Allied Powers as one of the causes of the fanaticism which prompted the committing of atrocities by some Japanese troops in the Second World War. As a consequence, after the Japanese surrender it was prohibited as the State religion in 1945. Emperor Hirohito was thereby forced to renounce his claim to divinity. With the cessation of state funding, Shintoism thereafter waned (over 100,000 shrines ceased to exist without that support). It came to prominence again in the controversy which surrounded the manner of the Crown Prince's succession on the death of Emperor Hirohito in 1989. Passions about this ran deep. In spite of the 1945 settlement, there was a clear national desire for a Shintoist religious element to the enthronement. An alleged compromise was reached whereby, the Royal Family paid for this themselves. Today, Shintoism has fragmented into innumerable sectarian 'shrine-religions' which seem to cater for the innate spiritual needs of a people who have also become noted for their secular and material achievements. Membership of these shrines runs into millions. In 2006 the Japanese Prime Minister, Junichiro Koizumi, caused controversy by visiting the Yasukuni War Shrine in central Tokyo.

Even this brief reflection on the nature and history of Shintoism, illustrates that such a religion is a collectively powerful force. Its influence can survive for centuries and it becomes seemingly impossible to eradicate it from national consciousness. The continuing place of Shintoism in Japanese life illustrates, if nothing else, the protean nature of such a religion. It now has some four million adherents.[6] Empires may come and go, conquests may be won and lost, but the force which endures is a religion such as this which resonates with the deepest needs of a collective self consciousness. That it can do this as it now seemingly does, not as a unified collective religion, but in so many fragmented forms is all the more remarkable. Furthermore, the way in which it does this in what has been, at least until recently, the world's most accomplished consumer society, again illustrates its survival by adaptability. Like all religions, Shintoism has been susceptible to distortion by fanaticism. Short of that, however, it continues to exert its deeper and more perennial meaning. This is a clear example of the abiding influence and power of religion in a collective self-consciousness.

Buddhism

Buddhism began in the foothills of the Himalayas in 560BCE with the birth of Siddhatha Gotama, who was later known as the Buddha. Its early geographical spread was phenomenal. From India it went principally to Ceylon, Burma, Siam, Cambodia, Tibet, China, Japan, Mongolia and Korea. In these countries it continues to flourish. In its native India, however, it did not survive as a discrete religion. It did so only as part of the Hinduism in which it had its roots. One reason for this is because Hinduism is the name for a portmanteau of religions rather than a single entity. In the third century Buddhism was adopted as the state religion. This enabled it to begin to produce its own religious texts. There is even now no complete and definitive version of them. They exist in both Sanskrit and Pali.

In Buddhism, we encounter a religion which is most appropriately studied 'from below' in the way we considered earlier. The reason for this is because it is, foremost, a religion of personal enlightenment. Unlike all the other of the world's major religions, it does not have a doctrine of God. It is, rather, a religion of personal awakening. Buddha means 'enlightened one'. Mainstream Buddhism, even in its different forms, is unique among the classical religions in its insistence that it does not claim to be about anything else. What it stresses, personal enlightenment, is as important in different ways to other religions as it is to Buddhism, but Buddhism fastens on this as the *single* most important thing about religion. So important, that it claims that this is all-sufficient. Buddhism has no small part to play in the reconstruction of an acceptable world-view of religion.

Buddhism eschews two extremes. The first is the extreme of excessive devotion and the second is the extreme of sensual over-indulgence. It advocates a *via media* between them. Notwithstanding this, early Buddhism at least, was clearly an ascetic and world-denying religion. This is manifest in its simplicity of dress, worship and general behaviour. By tradition, its content came to the Buddha after reflection on old age, sickness and death.[7] Buddhist asceticism is also manifest in the elegance of its temple architecture. This expresses a profound sense of place where enlightenment can be found. Principal among these is The Bodh-gaya temple which marks exactly the spot where the Buddha received enlightenment whilst sitting under the Bodhi-tree. The present 170 foot high temple dates from the eleventh century. The ancient Buddhist settlement in northern Afghanistan with its massive Buddha carved into the rocks by monks through the early centuries was infamously in the news when it was destroyed by members of the Taleban in 2001. The vast number and architectural scale of such temples testifies to the Buddhist belief that the ascetic life needs the support of sensual experience, although it has to be kept in proportion. Enlightenment is achieved through release from suffering in a manner which is unique to Buddhism. It is triggered by meditation on its three causes: old age, sickness and death. By this simple and elegant means, reflection on the objects of distress becomes the source of the eternal release from their tyranny. This release is called Nirvana. Training in the method of securing this release from the barriers to enlightenment by confronting them in meditation is of the essence of the Buddhist spiritual life. This can be perfected by disciplined practice, just as an athlete might improve performance in the same way. None of it was ever thought to be easy, progress is not always assured and frustration can result. There are many stories of those who committed suicide after failing to achieve it. It was recognised, therefore, that not all who sought enlightenment would achieve it in their lifetime This reveals the weakness of Buddhism as a religion of personal enlightenment. Achieving enlightenment and keeping it is all. There is nothing else. No, for example, moral life in which aspiration and achievement can be sought. The religious life of enlightenment is everything. When it fails there is nothing else. When it succeeds, however, *karma*, enlightened peace is achieved. This is preserved and passed on in the *sangha* the spiritual communities. In them, the spiritual disciplines are extremely onerous and even, one would observe, obsessive. This *karma* does not translate itself directly into ethical action. What it does is to provide that action, which is reflected more explicitly in the wider caste system of Asian society, with a right intention. All this is expressed in the famous four 'noble truths' of Buddhist spirituality. The first of these is a personal confrontation with the inescapable fact that individual existence is misery. The second is facing the cause of this misery, the seeking after sensual pleasure. The third is discovered in the recognition that release from such misery is a possibility. The fourth is the attainment of enlightenment according to an eightfold path. This is made up of right understanding, motivation, speech, action, livelihood, effort, mindfulness and contemplation.

Like all religions, Buddhism changed over the centuries. Some three centuries after the death of the Buddha, Mahayana Buddhism radically embraced philosophical speculation. This caused it to split from the older Hinayana Buddhism which remained closer to the original simpler forms of spirituality. Mahayana Buddhists spiritualised the historical Buddha and understood him as part of a wider system of speculative metaphysics. This gave prominence to seeking enlightenment through the contemplation of 'Absolute Being'. This, it was claimed, is what transforms human experience and brings about its redemption: Nirvana. In this human achievement and heavenly bliss are at one.

The geographical spread of Buddhism, over the centuries, continued to produce its many and ever adapting forms. In Burma and Southeast Asia, where it remained under the influence of Hinduism, so-called Theravadin Buddhism maintained the central place of the monk as a holy person, someone who could alone attain the spiritual ideals. These men still live awesomely disciplined spiritual lives. Their daily cycles of devotion are unvarying and end with the avowed intention to do even better tomorrow. Again seemingly under the influence of Hinduism, even this rigorist form of Buddhism, has developed a devotion to shrines which hold replicas of the Buddha. All this has done much to create a more widespread and popular access to Buddhism's stricter spiritual disciplines. Mahayana Buddhism became and remains dominant in central and Western Asia. Its forms are partly derivative from the indigenous religions with which it came into contact as well as from, as we have already seen, its willingness to embrace rational and metaphysical speculation. This had the effect of democratising and popularising the earlier Buddhist ascetic disciplines. Its spirituality is derived from many other Buddhas, such as the Manushi, the Bodhisattvas and the Dhyani. These sustain popular devotion in a more forgiving and less disciplined way than did original Buddhism. These Buddhas are beings who have reached the ultimate states of devotion but who delay the Nirvana which is available to them in order to answer the prayers of the devout, thereby transferring their enlightenment to lesser beings. For them, compassion for others is put before their own salvation.

It is often pointed out that Buddhism is a religion of peace and that no wars have ever been fought in the name of the Buddha. Given that other religions so often have been and still are so often embroiled in war, this is no small thing. However, the commitment to peace is Buddhism arises more from a general lack of engagement with ethical issues as such, than it does from a positive commitment to peace. The focus of the Buddhist monastic spiritual life is an inward one. Lay people are encouraged to join it for its own sake rather than for what they can achieve elsewhere on doing so. This is not to belittle the Buddhist commitment to peace. It is but to point out its difference from the same commitment found elsewhere in the world religions. For example, in the so-called Christian 'Peace Churches', Quaker and Mennonite, where the commitment to peace, by contrast, is both grounded in spirituality and prioritised in social concern.

Buddhism is an influential, colourful and devout religion. Its elements have parallels in other religions, particularly in many of the Christian monastic traditions. What, for many, it lacks is an engagement with the pressing affairs of the wider world which is commensurate with its spiritual aspirations. It fails, it can be argued, to create a spirituality which coheres with and sustains the moral life in all its complexities beyond the purview of Tibetan society. This is the more a pity because it is at this point that religions engage in earnest with the world around us. Other religious traditions, Christianity included, do this more explicitly.

Attempts are now regularly made to unite the many different forms of Buddhism in order to strengthen its position as a religion with a world-wide missionary programme. This is active in North America, Britain and Japan. It is presided over by The World Fellowship of Buddhists for World Buddhism. Missionaries have also now returned to India to try and redress its centuries of Buddhist decline. They have now regained possession of their holiest site, the Bodh-gaya where the Buddha first received enlightenment under the Banyan tree. There are now approximately some 376 million Buddhists in the world.[8] They are more fragmented than ever before. Since the nineteenth century, following the influence of the philosopher Arthur Schopenhauer in the eighteenth, Western intellectual interest in Buddhism has steadily increased though the numbers involved remain small. In the UK a Buddhist Society retains considerable interest and maintains numerous *sangha* which often attract young people to its spiritual life.

Hinduism

The foregoing two religions each have core systems of belief and or practice which more or less remain identifiable even in their diverse manifestations. Hinduism is fundamentally different in this respect. It is better understood as the social designation of the many and diverse religions of India, than it is as a description of what they all share. There are no common practices, beliefs, or organisations which claim to represent the whole. It is the name for what people freely choose to do about religion in the Caste systems which still structure Indian society. It is an open religion and is ever adapting to changing circumstances. It is tolerant of diversity and even promotes it. Hinduism is also noted for its equal embrace of people who are literate and illiterate, those who live amid urban sophistication as well squalor and those who live in primitive rural villages. It marks the triumph of a democratised, popular and immediately accessible religion over the exclusive Brahmanism from which it originated and which still exists. This latter, which dates from the Vedic period (c. 1700–c. 650BCE), was under the tight control of priests who maintained a sacrificial system of religion to which lay people only had access through formal ritual and a strictly hierarchical Caste system. There are no agreed accounts of when Hinduism grew out of Brahmanism in this way.

Understanding Hinduism as social phenomenon in this way, means that we must approach it differently from other mainstream religions. There is no founding figure nor are there universally accepted texts, though there are two great epics. Furthermore, the sheer diversity of contemporary Hinduism is as complex and dynamic as it has ever been. Some four fifths of the billion or so population of India, now one of the world's leading industrial nations, regard themselves as Hindu. There are also thought to be some thirty million Hindus elsewhere in the world.

The two great epics of Hinduism are the *Puranas* and the *Tantras*. The compilation of the former was a long process, completed only some five hundred years ago. It contains ancient Vedic texts. These have been successively re-worked through the centuries to reflect changing interests and goals. This very fact shows that, unlike the use of texts in other religions where they invariably have divine and unalterable status, in the Hindu traditions they are part of the living experience of the religious life. Something to be reflected upon and adapted in ever changing circumstances. (This, in fact, is very much akin to the actual nature of the Jewish/Christian Bible, though few in those traditions understand it in that way.)[9] They are subdivided into major and minor texts and these are further subdivided. They all address creation, the genealogy of the Gods, the reigns of the Manus (lawgivers), and human and lunar history. The *Tantras* are by comparison more philosophical and popular. They contain hymns and poetry. Much of them is in the form of a dialogue between the *Siva* (the major Hindu deity) and the *Devi* (the archetypal Hindu Goddess). These are thought to be of ancient origin and written by divinely inspired authors. Much of what they contain is seemingly intentionally cryptic. This mass of literature is as broad and shapeless as Hinduism itself. It does not focus on single truths. It is, rather, to be perused by the reader in the search for enlightenment which resonates with the reader's experience. What so enlightens, is whatever emerges from this interaction. (A modern and ungainly name for this is the 'hermeneutic circle'.) In this way the Hindu texts directly enable the religious life because their content resonates with the experience of their readers.

Hindus consider life to be illusory. For this reason they are often thought to have a negative attitude towards it. However, this is perhaps more a readiness to accept things as they are in the knowledge that greater realities are to be contemplated elsewhere. In Hinduism the acceptance of diversity is paramount. (So much so, in fact, that it does not lead to the sort of social cohesion which is so often necessary for collective action.) Ironically, the only thing that all Hindus have in common is this acceptance of diversity! Even this does not have fixed points. 'When reading Hindu philosophical analyses of a particular topic, one very often sees a continual displacement of shifting perspectives. Just before a particular or train of thought reaches its conclusion, one is introduced to another way of seeing the issue – another way of speaking about the subject in hand. When one approaches, in turn, the end of a particular analysis, another one is introduced, and the process of analysis is temporarily deferred and extended'.[10] All this is undoubtedly why the Western mind-set, with its preoccupation with logical consistency and clear conclusions, invariably finds it so difficult to understand the Hindu one. Inconclusivity, for the Hindu, is more a consolation than a frustration. Something, it seems, which is to be treasured to the extent that it must be prevented from coming to an end. Hence, the sagic nature of Hindu literature which we have already noted.

Two concepts are central to the Hindu religious life. The first, *karma* has a long history in Hindu tradition and is diverse in its contemporary manifestations. In this way it exemplifies the pluriformity of Hindu religion. In general, *karma* focusses on the creation of a unity between action and spiritual virtue. This action is something dynamic which can be passed on between individuals and groups. It produces a spirituality which enables both a present release from the trammels of the everyday life of illusion, and a means of entering an improved re-birth in the next incarnation. This is *artha*, the goal of life. It culminates in the total release from all that is insufferable. Interestingly, it does have its evidences in this life as well as the next. They are the worldly manifestations of wealth and success. The outer fruits, so to speak, of inner release. Here the link between Hindu devotion and phenomenal commercial enterprise, often wrought by sheer hard work, begins to appear. It is just one of the many paradoxes of Hindu religion. One the one hand it is world rejecting, yet at the same time on the other it is world affirming even to the point of being materialistic. This, of course, goes some way to explain the role Hinduism has played in forming modern India, a country where rapidly emerging industrial might and success co-exists with abject poverty.

Happiness and success in this life are not valued in themselves. They are so only because they promise much spiritual reward in the next. The ways of achieving happiness are diverse. A seeming plethora of religious belief and practice is tolerated. It includes animism (the ascribing of life to inanimate objects), magic of all kinds, mysticism, reverence for the natural elements of fire and water, sun worship, and the ubiquitous reverence for animals of all kinds, particularly the cow. Seemingly nothing in this life is incapable, to the Hindu, of yielding religious significance and value. The spirits abound and are celebrated in the joyous riot of Hindu aesthetics and art. Local deities are sought by pilgrimage and celebrated in carnival. They are the lesser gods, the constant companions and friends of everyday joyous spiritual life. The lives of all these local deities culminate in the lives of the three great Gods *Vishnu, Shiva* and *Brahma*. *Vishnu* is the creator and sustaining God who is identified with the sun. A God who is capable of representation in human form by *avatars*. These are the human manifestations of sublime deity. (Buddhism, as we have seen, grew out of this.) The *Krishna* and the *Rava* are the principal avatars of *Vishnu*. *Krishna* worship is highly celebratory and even erotic. In contrast, *Rava* worship is more austere and every day. Here again, equally valued extremes happily co-exist in one religious tradition. In many other religions, such metaphysical diversity and toleration would alone be enough to produce schism. In Hinduism it produces religious and social harmony. Indeed, the greater this diversity becomes, the more assured the social harmony seems to be. *Shiva*, the second principal deity, is identified with the river Ganges and has a composite identity. This sustains so many varieties of devotion and practice that it becomes difficult for anyone not of the Hindu mind to comprehend the sheer reconciliation of diversity and unity in a single devotional tradition. *Brahma* is the supreme creator god in Hindu tradition who is now known by many names in, again, diverse sects. In Brahmanism many of these sustain rigorous priesthoods which demand and receive lay respect and devotion. These priesthoods and their lay followings are, in turn, part of the fabric of the Indian Caste system. As already noted, in later Hindu traditions the popularity of *Brahma*, does not compare with that of *Vishnu* and *Shiva*.

Even these introductory considerations more than show that the metaphysics of Hindu religion are as diverse as are its spiritualities and practices. They are also, like the latter, dynamic and ever changing. The supreme Gods are no more sacrosanct than their manifestations in the lesser deities. All is flux and endless interaction in the breathtaking religious life of the Indian sub-continent and of Hinduism world-wide. All this is to be admired for many reasons. Chief among them is its inherent toleration and even celebration of difference and acceptance of change. The certainties and even pedantries which mark so many other religious traditions are, refreshingly, absent here. It will remain to be seen what form all this will take when the social, political and economic life of the sub-continent becomes more unified. It may well be, of course, that it will survive in its present diverse forms as a complement to other unifying elements in Indian society. Paradoxically, the two might equally need each other.

Judaism

Judaism is, of course, the parent religion of both Christianity and Islam. It was known as such only from about the beginning of the Christian era when it came to be perceived as a single entity. Its nomadic tribal origins, which reach back at least some four millennia, are largely obscure. They can be understood only by inference from the older oral traditions which are detectable in Israel's earliest writings. These date from about the beginning of the first millennium BCE, at the time of Israel's emergent national identity and settlement in Cana. To be Jewish one had to have a Jewish mother and a genealogy reaching back to the Patriarchs (the founding fathers of the nation). These were Abraham and his sons Isaac and Jacob. According to Jewish scriptures, God made a covenant with Abraham as he did with Noah and Moses and this gave the Jewish people the status of being God's chosen people. In this way, Israel's founding consciousness fuses national identity with divine privilege. It justified the displacement of the Canaanites when it moved into Cana by claiming that God had bestowed the land upon Israel as a gift to them as God's chosen people. This, they further claimed, was proven by the historic acts of divine favour such as the parting of the Red Sea (Deuteronomy 11:04) and tumbling of the walls of Jericho in Joshua's famous battle (Joshua 6:20).

The five earliest books of the Jewish Bible, the Pentateuch, tell the story of Israel's history from the creation. They culminate with the death of Moses who, having led the nation from Egyptian captivity and received God's commandments in the wilderness, died whilst pointing to the promised land of Cana. The Ark which contained the covenant with Moses was made at God's command during the forty years or so of Israel's wandering in the wilderness. All this has been celebrated in Israel's liturgies ever since. The Ark of every Jewish synagogue is its central and holiest place. It faces the Temple Mount in Jerusalem and contains scrolls of the Law given to Moses. It is customary to stand during worship whilst its doors are open.

The history of Israel went through seminal transformations. First. from being a nomadic to a captive people who then became nomadic again before becoming a settled nation. When this settlement first happened Israel urgently required new sorts of central institutions. With no precedents of its own to draw upon, it invariably modelled these on those of the surrounding nations. Central to them was the need for the institution of kingship. Israel had never needed this before. Saul, Israel's first king, was anointed in about 1020BCE, He was succeeded after some twenty years by Israel's famed warrior king, David. Under him Israel became the foremost power in Palestine and Syria. In only forty years or so he consolidated the nation and prepared the way for it to erect its first Temple in Jerusalem. This was completed by his successor Solomon, who reigned for a similar period until 922BCE. These were the high years of Israel's united religious, cultural and economic prosperity. But all this soon became too expensive to maintain. It could only be paid for by ever increasing taxation and this was to be Solomon's downfall. It weakened the empire which Saul and David had bequeathed him. This was exacerbated by the fact that for all the glories of Israel's kings, none of them ever entirely solved the problems created by the remaining tribal loyalties of earlier times. (An all too familiar story, one might muse, in the light of modern day attempts to superimpose national identities and democratic systems of government on tribal loyalties in the Middle East and elsewhere). Only Solomon's person and rule could hold it all together. On his death the nation split between Israel in the North and Judah in the South. The former reverted to older and less expensive ways though it too had to re-invent new state institutions and rituals for itself. It lasted for two hundred years before it fell to Assyrian armies. By this time Judah had also weakened but it lasted until it too fell to Babylonian armies in 586BCE. Solomon's Temple was then destroyed and King Zedekiah fled in terror. He was captured near Jericho and hauled before King Nebuchadnezzar. He was blinded and held in chains until his death. The people of Israel were now again in exile, in Babylon.

None of Israel's central institutions, nor its theology, had prepared it for this catastrophe. Everything was in ruins. Not even its Prophets could save it. Indeed, when King Zedekiah, sought solace from his contemporary the prophet Jeremiah, he received only the message that he was to be delivered into the hand of the king of Babylon. Little wonder that he fled as he did. Jeremiah's only solace was that he believed that there would come a time when God would make a new covenant with the people of Israel. It would be one written in their hearts and not on stone (Jer. 31:31).

The captivity lasted scarce half a century until king Cyrus of the Medes overthrew Babylon which had become destabilised after the preceding death of Nebuchadnezzar. Cyrus is widely regarded as one of the most enlightened national rulers of this period. He immediately issued an edict of toleration which permitted the return of the Jewish people to Jerusalem. The Second Temple was soon built in about 520BCE. The Jewish people then settled into centuries of life under successive conquerors of Jerusalem. This Second Temple was destroyed by the Romans in 70CE.

This brief outline of Jewish history to the first century CE has only touched in passing on the sheer religious genius of the Jewish people. Whether or not one accepts the claims they make for themselves about being the chosen above all others of God, the riches of their religious traditions are among the world's finest and properly understood and used they remain an inexhaustible treasure. The understanding of so-called 'ethical monotheism' is central to this. It emerged in Israel's Northern prophetic traditions in the eighth century BCE. Its exemplar was the prophet Amos whose book is considered to be the earliest of the prophetic writings. He was of obscure origin, probably a herdsman. He inveighed against Israel for failing to understand and honour the obligations which went with its divine privileges and foretold its punishment as a result. His vision was of a God who did not require the sacrifices of endless ritual worship. This

God required, rather, justice and righteousness throughout the social order. This is expressed in one of the Bible's most resonant passages. 'I hate and despise your feasts, I take no pleasure in your solemn festivals when you offer me holocausts. I reject your oblations, and refuse to look at your sacrifices of fattened cattle. Let me hear no more of the din of your chanting, no more of your strumming of harps. But let justice flow like water, and integrity like an unfailing stream' (Amos 5:21–24). Amos applied this vision of the relationship between spirituality and justice to the minutiae of Israel's life. He inveighed, for example, against laziness, cheating at trade, and the indulgence of second homes. The later prophets followed this example and all developed it in their own ways. Jeremiah, as we have briefly seen, interpreted Israel's punishment in a way which enabled it to begin the reconstruction of its religious life. Indeed, it is often observed that Jeremiah's teaching in many ways closely fore-shadowed that of Jesus. Israel's prophetic writings are still an important influence in Jewish and Christian worship and theology.

There are two other equally powerful traditions in the Jewish Bible. The Law and the Wisdom Literature. We will consider both of them briefly. The Law of Leviticus, the Torah, and the summation of all Law (Deuteronomy 4.44). It contained 614 precepts. These were given by God to Moses and were also thought to pre-exist creation. Israel believes that this Law is the means whereby God's will is applied to the minute circumstances of life. Nothing is, therefore, is alien or impervious to God's will. This deep conviction is, to the Jewish mind, a source of profound rejoicing and thanksgiving. Its summary is 'Love your neighbour as yourself' (Leviticus 19:18), it was famously quoted by Jesus (Mark 12:31, Luke 10:27). It is difficult for latter day Western gentile minds, who instinctively see law as prohibition and restraint, to appreciate how liberating and joyous the delight in God's law has always been for Jewish people. It is the means whereby God cares for the whole of creation and promotes its best interests. Little wonder that Jesus subsequently came to be questioned so closely on his attitude to it. St Paul, of course, went to great lengths in his letters to explain how Christianity had succeeded it.

'Wisdom' is another distinctive form of literature in the Jewish Bible. Its principal writings are the books of Job, Proverbs and Ecclesiastes. In recent scholarship ever more biblical literature is identified as such, e.g. the

Joseph saga and some Psalms. It respects the central place of accumulated experience in the religious life. An experience, that is, which is tried, tested and not found wanting. Its attribution to Solomon is an act of pious imagination. Its origins are, in fact, several. It is not even exclusive to Israel and can be found throughout contemporaneous religious literatures. Modern Jesus scholarship has pointed out how influential these wisdom traditions were in his own teaching.[11] These three great literary traditions in Israel's history, prophetic, legal and wisdom, are all complementary. They each throw their own light on the relationship of the knowledge of God to the actual circumstances of life, in tragedy and defeat as well as in joy and triumph.

Modern Judaism is the continuation of centuries of tradition and often traumatic change. The founding of the modern state of Israel in Northern Palestine in 1948 was part of the international response to the horror and unimaginable scale of the tragic loss of Jewish life in the holocaust in the Second World War. This creation of statehood was well intentioned, but it has exacerbated the politics of the Middle East ever since. It has strengthened movements in Israel which longed for its return to Jerusalem ever since the destruction of the second Temple in 70 CE. Zionism is a world-wide Jewish movement which embraces many sects and outlooks. Modern Israel is an admixture of these older aspirations, a variety of more liberal Jewish outlooks and downright secularism. All these interplay in Israeli politics as the nation copes with both international and local, Palestinian, opposition to its resettlements in disputed territories, particularly the West Bank. All this provokes a growing more widespread sympathy for the displaced Palestinian people though not toleration of their use of rocket attacks on Israel. This seemingly intractable problem has a long history, as we have seen. Its solution is sought earnestly by the international community. This has given rise to now decades of peace talks which have invariably foundered for one reason or another. The ones initiated by president Obama with fanfare stalled because of the American and Palestinian insistence that Israel should cease building new settlements in the disputed West Bank and because of Israel's seeming reluctance to comply. Recent political unrest across the Arab world, following the fall of President Mubarak, the turmoil in Syria and the possible aspiration of Iran to the possession of nuclear weapons, is causing Israel to feel further threatened as its existing peace treaties become increasingly fragile. For all these reasons the Middle

East remains a politically and militarily unstable region. No progress will ever be made with this predicament unless all concerned are prepared to go back centuries to re-examine the historic origins of Israel as a nation. This is a very big ask.

For the rest, Jewish people have assimilated themselves throughout the world's nations and particularly so in the Western ones. Here they have made often unequalled contributions to the arts, the sciences, all the professions, politics, commerce and other many other areas which have led to the enrichment of life. Like members of other religions, some Jewish people have become thoroughly secularised, even in Israel itself. Others are to be found across the spectrum of commitments found in most religions. Some are of liberal outlook and have more in common with liberal members of other religious traditions than they do with conservative members of their own. Others are more orthodox, to the point of being near separatist even within their own communities, but these are a minority. Modern Jewish life is as richly diverse as it ever was. It is a major force for good in the international community. However, anti-Semitism is a sadly, to say the least, recurrent theme in Western culture. It too is centuries old, though it only came to be called such at the end of the nineteenth century. Many locate its origins in Christianity. In the New Testament Jews are seemingly held responsible for the crucifixion (Matt. 27:25). Not surprisingly, with the political domination of Christianity in Western Culture, Jewish people understandably felt and clearly were, marginalised. In the Fourth Lateran Council in 1215 they were forced to wear distinct clothing. The Protestant Reformation left all this unreformed. Luther's infamous *Against the Jews and their Lies* (1543) is an incredible prejudice in the mind of an otherwise inspired religious thinker and leader.[12] That some Christians have been anti-Semitic is indisputable. This is why Pope John Paul II formally apologised to the Jewish people for bygone Vatican complicity in the same. Anti-Semitism was, of course, central to the creed of German National Socialism which bred Nazism. It is still an ugly feature of some extremist far-right European politics. Fortunately, those who espouse it are a minority. The majority recognise and are thankful that Jewish people have made and continue to make immense contributions to European culture where, with others, they enjoy the freedoms of open societies.

Islam

Islam is the second of Judaism's offspring religions. It has some 1.5 billion followers world-wide.[13] We will discuss it next simply because we can then focus our considerations on Christianity in the rest of the book.

Islam and Christianity co-exist, for the greater part, peacefully in Western culture. This is witnessed by the widespread good relations which exist between Muslim, Christian and other faith communities in the U.K, North America and elsewhere. This enables the integration of Muslim people in everyday life. Their commitment to family life, for example, is particularly inspiring in some societies where it often seems to be under threat. In these and so many other ways, Islamic people remain true to themselves while at the same time, assimilating into and contributing to their surrounding cultures.

However, centuries old Islamic/Christian/Jewish conflict is an all too common a part of the history of these great religions. Some of this is promulgated by some Islamic fundamentalists who are ranged against others, including Christians. This is a visually vivid conflict because it is often flashed electronically around the world in seconds. Scenes of carnage associated with people of dress which is uniformly strange are powerfully evocative of older religious conflicts. All this makes life extremely difficult for those Muslim people who live peacefully in Western societies and who make the valuable contributions to them as we have noted.

Once again, the international order is having to deal with confrontations which are, rightly or wrongly, associated with ones which reach back for centuries. All this does and will continue to put great strains on religious people of all faiths as well as on the secular societies in which they live. These strains can only be eased by creating societies in which people religious and secular people live at peace with each other. More than this, they need to explore actively together the relevance of their traditions to the wider public good.

Islam is a religion of direct contact with and submission to God through his Prophet Muhammad ibn 'Abd Allah whose ministry is recorded in its holy book, the Koran. He was born in Mecca 570 CE, the central place of Islamic pilgrimage ever since. This was to become the first year in the Islamic calendar. God's revelation came to him through two angels whilst he lived in isolation in caves in about 622 CE. The content of their message became the Koran. Such revelations to individuals are not uncommon in religious history and this would not, therefore, have seemed at all unusual. It caused Muhammad near madness which, had it occurred, would have been an end to the matter. He was encouraged, however, to test the revelations by preaching them. This again, was a common enough pattern in the history of the origin of new religious movements. After meeting initial hostility, the directness of Muhammad's message began to be heard. He fastened on one central issue That there is one God and that that God is emphatically *not* the God of Jews or Christians or of the lesser and many other deities of Mecca. That one God is Allah, the God of Islam alone. This caused immediate conflict between the small but growing number of Muslims and Jews and Christians alike who had previously occupied Mecca peacefully together. After a series of battles, Muhammad captured and held Mecca in 630 CE, eight short years after the initial revelations. He died only two years later without an heir. Caliphs, were then chosen to succeed him. Their first task was to secure the small community which Muhammad has founded in Mecca. The surrounding nations of Persia and Byzantium were militarily weak at this time. This meant that conquerors could expect to proceed largely unopposed. For this reason, Islam achieved phenomenally rapid geographical expansion. Some of this happened, however, by remarkably peaceful means as the masses followed contritely once their key strongholds were held by the invaders. Constantinople (modern Istanbul) was conquered and even the marauding Mongols were eventually embraced. The Muhammadan Empire soon dominated Asia and its sub-continent under the Mogul Emperors. Within only a century of Muhammad's death, it amazingly reached across Western Europe to the Chinese border. This is breathtaking history in the making. It can only be even partially understood by the remarkable fact that the directness of the new Islamic religion had widespread appeal just at the time when its military advance could not be opposed. This phenomenal geographical spread, domination and freedom from external threat meant that Islam had no need to waste its powers on military self-defence. Its name, therefore, became synonymous with political sovereignty and conquest, it was imperial. This, in turn, goes some way to explain why its Empire rapidly became noted for its achievements in the arts, the sciences, mathematics, architecture, philosophy and wider culture. For example, in the early Middle Ages, its philosophers re-discovered the then lost works of Aristotle. This directly and indirectly had a profound and lasting effect on Western culture. It also gelled with the Islamic interest in empirics, the way things are. This, in turn, produced advances in astronomy and the practical arts. For reasons such as these, Islam became one of the world's greatest civilisations and it has produced lasting benefit for all. Of course, no such edifice could last forever. Like all empires, the Muslim one suffered from internal division. The Sunnites (traditionalists) became the largest schismatic group. For them, the minutiae of religious observance based on the Koran remains the focus of the religious life. The Shi'ites then became and remain a second largest separate Islamic sect. They are followers of Ali, the first Imam, the Prophet's cousin and son in law whom they consider to be his successor. Succeeding Imams, they claim, inherit this authority. Today 'Islam' is a generic name for a family of sects. These embrace the spectrum of religious witness from liberalism to fanaticism (much as one finds in most of the world's great religions). So far, we have noted only that Islam is a religion of direct and total obedience to God, a God it sees as Allah, the only God. The brief outline we have given of its history has been necessary only to put a more detailed understanding of Islamic religion in its amazing historical context.

The oneness of God is the most fundamental of all Islamic beliefs. It is followed, as we have seen, by the necessity of total obedience on behalf of the believer. Only this total surrender can bring the peace and security of faith. Five, equally fundamental, elements of faith follow from this. The first is *Shahada*: witness. Profession of this, the total acceptance of Muslim teaching and practice, is the only requirement formally made before admission is granted to the Muslim community life: the *umma*. The simplicity of this underscores the Muslim demand for total obedience. Whatever requirements this profession might subsequently make, they have to be accepted in advance. They are not a matter for negotiation. Obedience to the one God and obedience to the precepts of Islam are one and the same. This is not even affected if those precepts change, or even if they only appear to do so. The Muslim life is a life of total and unconditional present and future obedience. No understanding of the religious life could be simpler, clearer or more all demanding than this. The second element is *salat*: the discipline of prayer. This is required before personal devotion of any kind. It is a duty to be performed at all times. Its weekly focus is at noontime prayer on a Friday. This noticeably involves a variety of posture of male worshippers in serried ranks. Women either observe all this from above (a derivative of Jewish practice), or they worship on their own. The haunting call to this worship and the uniformity of its spectacle is one of the central motifs world-wide Islam. *Zakat*: the tithe for the poor is the third fundamental element of Islam. It is required of all Muslims according to means. Its giving is the discharge of a religious duty. In its turn, it enables the giver to use any remaining wealth freely. This can include further voluntary occasional giving, but does not strictly require it. The fourth is *hajj*: the requirement of pilgrimage to Mecca during the sacred month *Dhow-al-Hajji*. It is to be made at least once in a lifetime by every free adult male Muslim. The *hajj* requires strict ceremonial observance on arrival at Mecca. In this way sins are to be forgiven and blessings received. Equally strict requirements are made about provision for wives and families during this required absence. Uniformity of dress and abstinences are also strictly required. These are juxtaposed by periods of celebration and feasting. The *hajj* is a powerful international symbol which serves among other things to bind all Muslims together. The fifth fundamental element of Islam is the *sawm*: the requirement to fast during the holy month of Ramadan. Healthy and unconstrained males must avoid all food, drink, smoking and sexual activity during the hours of daylight. Provision is made for the constrained, such as those on journeys, to compensate with almsgiving, or extended subsequent observance.

Islamic law, *shari'ah*, is not part of its fundamental precepts. It does, however, follow closely from them. It embodies the daily requirements of the Muslim life. Not unnaturally, there are different schools of such law with varying interpretations of what is required. These differences are accepted as divine blessings which enable Muslims in this situation or that to work out the requirements of law for themselves. Much of the daily life of Islam is preoccupied with all this for the simple reason that, as we have seen, the fundamental precepts of its faith are so simple. These, however, lack the sort of detail necessary for leading the devout life. This is provided by *shari'ah*, which enables Islam to keep abreast of the ever changing circumstances of life. Islam does not secularise easily for the reasons we have been considering. Muslims do, of course, live in secular societies and make immense contributions to them, not the least through the professions. In doing this they also do much to contribute to religious and social toleration in wider plural societies. The separatism of Islam is, however, invariably evident at the same time and this can be a cause of tension. Indeed, in recent times, particularly since 11 September 2001, some Muslims and particularly young ones, have been noticeably turning away from the seductions of non-Islamic cultures such as the Western one, back towards more noticeably Islamic manners of dress and behaviour. At the same time, however, other Muslims in Western societies are doing everything they can to become more integrated within them.

Muslims are required to be assertive in their faith. They also have an intrinsic missionary zeal which is allied to their geographical and political aspirations which we have already noted. Little wonder that Islam always has been and remains, in very large part, a religion with a potential, at least, for territorial and political confrontation. Apart from all this, however, it must never be forgotten that Islam is one of the two great religions derived from Judaism and one with, as we have noted, very great achievements to its credit. By far the greater number of Muslims everywhere, exemplify the spiritual virtues as they celebrate their knowledge of God in the midst of all they do. They invariably do this, moreover, with a quality of self-discipline which is often unequalled by other religions. This alone has much to contribute to the wider understanding of the place of the spiritual disciplines in the modern world.

Christianity

Although Christianity obviously pre-dates Islam we have left its consideration to last in this chapter because it will now be the main focus of the book. Before we proceed with that, however, it is necessary to be clear about the relationship of Christianity to other religions. We will now do this by drawing together threads of discussion which have already begun to appear.

We began this chapter by noting why it is no longer possible to approach Christianity as though it is the most evolved and, therefore, the most perfect of the world's religions. Such presuppositions no longer serve us well as we seek to understand, as we are doing, its place and potential in modern life. Christianity, as we will now see, is an integral part of the wider religious experience of humankind. Unless it disavows claims for itself which set it apart from and 'above' other religions, it will not be able to make its important contributions to modern life. It must be noted, however, that many and probably the majority of Christians will find this unacceptable. They are invariably hindered in their understanding of and relationship to other religions by their assumptions about their religion being different from and superior to them. This Christian approach to other religions is no longer acceptable. Understanding the reasons why will take us to the heart of the debate about the relationship of Christianity to other religions.

Christianity, of course, is not alone in approaching other religions from a position of assumed superiority. Many other religions invariably do the same thing. Jewish people, as we have seen, consider themselves alone to be the chosen of God and the majority of Muslims believe that their relationship to God is more direct and effective than any others. And so on. None of this will do. The world is no longer the sort of place where religions can vie with each other to demonstrate their exclusive superiority. As our discussion continues, it will become clear why it is that religions will only be able to make the unique contribution they can make to human understanding if they first embrace a new collective humility. This as we will see, needs to be one which focusses more on what they have in common rather than on what they do not. For now, therefore, we will discuss Christianity as we have discussed all the foregoing religions. In a way, that is, which enables us to understand its wider place in history as well as some of its essential teachings.

Christianity is a religion of Jewish Messianic fulfilment and future Messianic expectation. Israel expected that God (Yahweh) would send it a Messiah to redeem its misfortunes and it still waits in this way. According to the New Testament, Christians believed, as they still do, that Jesus of Nazareth is that Messiah. For them, in Jesus God has disclosed God's self completely, finally and for the last time before the end of the ages. This belief was held keenly in the early years of the Christian faith, those immediately following the death of Jesus by crucifixion under Pontius Pilate in about 33 CE. We know a lot about this from the Gospel according to St Mark, the earliest of the Gospels which was written only some ten years or so after this time. It enjoins its readers to prepare themselves for the imminent return of the Lord in glory. It reads as though the trumpet, so to speak, announcing this will sound at any moment. Christians must, therefore, do nothing which will jeopardise their salvation when it happens. This was the earliest Christian message – stand by! And then? Nothing, of course, even remotely like this happened. We are all still here and still waiting. The first great change in Christian self-understanding, therefore, came in these early years. First, it had to accept that the return of the Lord in glory would be temporarily delayed. As history continued, it then had to accept the indefinite delay of the Lord's return. Even more, it then also had to accept the ever growing self-evidence of the permanence of history. St Matthew's Gospel reflects part of all this. It clearly thinks that the return will be delayed and that, in the meantime, Christians must look to sorting their lives out as best they can.

Mark's Gospel is also probably constructed to explain why people did not recognise who Jesus was in his lifetime and why he died as he did. St Luke's Gospel was, in all probability, the last to be written, possibly as late as the beginning of the second century CE. It comes to terms completely with the permanence of history. It explains the ongoing place of the Messiah in this, at 'God's right hand in glory' and shows why the Christian message is not at all adversely affected by the fact that the first and greatest expectation of the earliest Christians was unfulfilled. Luke's view is still very much the prevailing one among Christians. This is that the Messiah was Jesus in whom God's self revelation was complete and that, in God's good time, Jesus will return at the end of the ages. Jews, therefore, wait for their Messiah yet to come and Christians wait for theirs to return. Both are religions of waiting. Both, however, so do actively. We have seen how Jews do this and will now see how Christians do so.

The central message of Christianity is that Jesus, the Messiah, brought salvation, first to his own followers and then to the whole world. It is a salvation which triumphs over evil for all time and is effective in spite of human sinfulness. At a time of God's own choosing Jesus will return and the Kingdom of God will be established. This message would not have survived, however, were it not for a remarkable phenomenon which occurred after the death of Jesus. Without it, Christianity would in all probability have become yet another long forgotten unfulfilled religion of mistaken ancient Middle Eastern messianic expectation. That phenomenon was only, in part, the reaction of the disciples to the resurrection. Christian preachers are beloved of claiming that this was the sole reason for the survival of Christianity. It was not. Of its own it would not have been enough to save Christianity from oblivion. It was centrally important, of course, but it only remained so and achieved the huge importance that it did because of the work and ministry of St Paul, the single and by far the most influential of early Christians apart from the Gospel writers themselves. Along with them, Paul was the earliest Christian chronicler. He was also a consummate organiser (some might even say in modern jargon: a control freak).

Seemingly alone, Paul 'invented' the Christian Church. He based it on the vulnerable, insecure and often tiny Christian communities to which wrote and visited. He gave them a collective identity and called it the 'body of Christ'. Under this vision, these early Christian communities became remarkably well organised and disciplined in a very short time. Paul was emphatic on the latter. He had little tolerance for dissent. The communities soon increased in number throughout the then known world. Indeed, it has even been suggested with plausibility that Paul travelled that world as frenetically as he did because he thought that he was actually being instrumental in preparing the emerging Christian Church for the return of its Lord in glory.[14]

The main source of our knowledge of all this is, of course, the writings of Paul himself. We also have a record of his doings in the second part of the only Gospel with a sequel, that to the Gospel of Luke: the Acts of the Apostles. It is notoriously difficult, however, to reconcile the information in these separate sources. There is, for example, amazingly no mention in the Acts that Paul ever wrote any letters. One, in fact, wonders how ever he found the time to do anything else! His many letters, not all of which are attributed to him in the New Testament are actually by him, contain a remarkably similar overall structure. First they proclaim the gospel of salvation. Then they contain reflection and explanation in which Paul develops his own emerging theology. Finally, they explore the implications of all this for the lives of the communities to which they were written. Much of this dealt with disagreements among the communities. In this Paul is often at his most creatively brilliant as a religious thinker *par excellence* in his own right. A central such issue was whether or not Christianity was a religion which brought privilege to the few or salvation to the many. Paul, of course, eloquently held the latter. He stressed throughout that sinful humanity was redeemed by Christ's death on the Cross and by the freely available grace which emanated from it. This grace was independent of the Law of Israel and, indeed, had superseded it. It was an unbounded grace for all, Jew and Gentile alike. With Barnabas, Paul was the architect of the Christian mission to the Gentiles. A new relationship to God was now available to all. Paul brought to this vision a remarkable theological literacy and creativity which soon enabled Christianity to become an increasingly mature religion in its own right. Its early doctrines have survived and they are the means whereby historic Christianity maintains its continuity with these early Christian beginnings. In addition to all this, Paul laid the foundations of the threefold Christian ministry of Bishops, Priests and Deacons, though this did not come into being until over a century later.[15] Yet more, Paul set out the fundamentals of the Christian moral life for individuals, families and their wider communities. In doing all this Paul actually helped to create a new religion with immense potential. It had structure, doctrine and, above all, an incredible energy which was expressed in missionary zeal. The rest, as we say, is history.

Throughout the second century CE the spread of Christianity was rapid. It was noted for the way in which it extended the life of faith and the moral life which went with it, equally to the unlearned and the learned. It democratised virtue by making it freely available to all who repented of their sins. This was something radically new. Hitherto in the wider classical world, with which Christianity was rapidly coming into contact, only the learned were expected to aspire to the virtues. The rapid expansion of Christianity created the need for it to identify what held the many different Christian communities together. Without this it would become fragmented and weakened simply as a consequence of its own success. It did this in two ways. First, it formalised the order of Christian ministry and brought the whole Church thereby under the jurisdiction of Bishops, Priests and Deacons. This structure, as we have seen, was envisioned by St Paul, but not developed by him. It was now made necessary for practical reasons. Second and even more significantly, the Church established its own canon of scripture. The New Testament which had hitherto not existed as such, became just that. It was created by selection from a plethora of Christian writings which were already in circulation. Not all of these made it into what then became the Christian canon of officially recognised writings. The Christian Bible was created in this way. It established the parameters of a Christian orthodoxy which was, in turn, used to refute those it considered to be aberrant.

Christian orthodoxy expressed itself in the early Councils of the Church. These culminated in that at Chalcedon in 451CE when the orthodoxy which still more or less prevails was established. The great divide between the Western and the Eastern Orthodox Church began to emerge at this time. It was caused by central doctrinal differences. By the ninth century Rome and Constantinople had serious disagreements and subsequent attempts to reconcile them have all failed.

Constantine was the first Roman Emperor to accept Christianity when he saw a vision on the eve of a battle at the Milvan Bridge in 312CE. This promised him victory in the name of the Christian cross. He heeded this, converted to Christianity and won the battle. A year later the famous Edict of Milan, ended nearly three centuries of Christian persecution by the Romans.[16] Christianity now became the religion of the state. This brought it the security to develop and broaden its theology. It did this by drawing, on Greek and other learning as well as on its own traditions. This was a major new development which presaged Christianity becoming the predominant religion in Western culture. In this it was so successful that writings from the period entirely dominated Christian orthodoxy for a thousand years and they are still influential. Chief among them were those of St Augustine of Hippo (354–430). He was involved in numerous controversies. Principal among them were the nature of goodness and of freewill and of the Church and its sacraments. His principal work is *The City of God*. This was written in response to the crisis in Christian confidence which occurred after the fall of Rome to the Goths in 410CE. Augustine, famously distinguished the earthly city from the City of God and identified them with two loves, the love of humankind and the love of God. The City of God, he argued, is not affected by the fall of the earthly city.

A dispute about the implications of understanding God as the triune Father, Son and Spirit began to emerge at this time. In the Council of Nicea in 325CE the person of Jesus is identified as the eternal word of God. That of Constantinople in 381CE further defined the divinity of the Holy Spirit and added that it proceeded from the Father and the Son, the so-called *filioque clause*. The Eastern churches progressively objected to this on the ground that it denied the truth that God the Father was the undivided source of all things. One way and another, this difference preoccupied the unity of the Eastern and Western Christian churches for three centuries. It all came to a head at the Synod of Constantinople if 876CE. It condemned the Pope for his political activities and for not correcting what it saw as the heresy of the *filioque*. This made it clear that the universality of the Pope's jurisdiction was seriously qualified. It paved the way for the great separation of Eastern and Western Christianity which occurred in 1054. A Papal legate then condemned the patriarchate of Constantinople. This was vehemently reciprocated and the two great branches of the Christian Church have gone their separate ways ever since. (The English Church was not unaffected through all this. It had already debated and accepted the *filioque* at the first Synod ever held in England at Hatfield in 680CE.) This difference between the Christian East and West still stands. An interesting modern footnote occurred to it when Robert Runcie was installed as the

Archbishop of Canterbury in 1980. He insisted that the *filioque* be dropped in his Installation service as a mark of respect to the Eastern Church. Little do many Christians know of the momentous effect the words '...and from the Son' have had on history when they fall from their lips. Just perhaps, however, they are none the worse for that!

During the early medieval period the Papacy enjoyed its golden days. It was accorded such spiritual allegiance by Western Kings and Princes that it effectively delivered political and economic, as well as religious supremacy. However, as those potentates became increasingly secular throughout Northern Europe in the sixteenth century, they began to resent this and sought their autonomy from Papal control and particularly from the taxation it imposed. This growing independence, of course, lay in large part behind the Protestant Reformation of the sixteenth century. Before we turn to that, however, we need to note something of the incredible intellectual achievements of Western medieval Christianity.

These achievements coincided with the rapid foundation of Universities in Northern Europe. They were dominated by Christian teachers who renewed and carried on the influence of the early Christian thinkers such as St Augustine who were essentially followers of Platonic philosophy. The synthesis this produced between Christian and secular thinking was one of the greatest intellectual achievements the Christian Church has ever experienced. It was presided over at the University of Paris by St Albert the Great, and St Bonaventura. It was. further, embedded in the newly widespread scholastic activities of the religious orders. They dominated both ecclesiastical and secular education which were at one. All this, along with the co-incident supremacy of the Pope over secular as well as religious rulers, was the very stuff of Christendom. The visual realisation of it all was, of course, the building of the great medieval cathedrals throughout Europe. It must all have seemed politically, spiritually and intellectually impregnable. Of course, it was not.

The seeds of intellectual, political and economic discontent were slowly germinating beneath the surface of all this. But, a far more direct challenge to the synthesis of Christianity with classical Platonic learning suddenly appeared. It was confronted by nothing less than the fire of a new learning. Islamic scholars, as we have noted, re-discovered the works of Aristotle which had been effectively unknown in the West for at least half a millennium. These works enabled them to undermine the very foundations of Platonist learning upon which the Catholic intellectual supremacy and political authority had been based. An Islamic philosopher called Averroes was central to all this. He wrote extensive commentaries on Aristotle. These were widely used by European secular philosophers. However, they contravened the prevailing European Platonism to such an extent that they were condemned by the Pope in 1270 and 1277. In obedience to this, St Thomas Aquinas (1225–1274) initially opposed Aristotle's writings. As is well known, however, he soon changed his mind and became the principal medieval interpreter of Aristotle to the Christian Church. This became possible because, as the primary texts of Aristotle became available it was observed that they were not so exclusively favourable to Islam as Averroes and others had claimed. The influence of Aquinas continues and he stands for all time as one of the greatest philosophical theologians of the Christian Church. All this was the more dramatic, because of the then sheer numbers of people, especially the young, who gathered around their fashionable teachers in the seats of learning. The battle for their minds was enjoined and it was won by Aquinas and the Schoolmen, his contemporaries and followers. Roman Catholic philosophy and theology has, effectively, been Aristotelian ever since. What it, in fact, has paradoxically done is to allow freedom of intellect whilst, at the same time, keeping it in check. In this way it proffers the reconciliation of reason, revelation and faith with a plausibility which still commands Roman Catholic orthodoxy. It is such an achievement that it also commands the careful respect of those who wish to differ from it. The achievements of Aquinas, really were that great. The intellectual hegemony of later medieval Aristotelian Christendom came to seem as impregnable as the earlier Platonic hegemony had been. Moreover, it effectively was. However, its challenge, in turn, was soon enough to come from the Italian and then the European Renaissance and its champions such as Erasmus.

The European Renaissance grew out of two things which were different from each other but which in combination proved to be an unstoppable force. The first was the growth of humanistic learning and its offspring, scientific enquiry. Inexorably, the value of observation, enquiry and careful deduction was preferred to the unquestioning acceptance of dogmatic assertion. A marvellous story is often told which epitomises the spirit of this time. A group of Friars had long been engaged in discussion how many teeth there were in a horse's mouth. Scholarly opinion ranged on the matter and debate was intense. Friars disputed the matter in time-honoured fashion. Then one day, a young Friar caused immense consternation. He suggested that the matter could be settled, simply, at once and for all time by a single action – that of looking into the horse's mouth. This superb story will always be told of the period. It epitomises the new spirit of enquiry which was soon to have such dramatic results in philosophy and the sciences. Out of this a new Christian humanism was born. This sought to reconcile faith and the emerging new reason. Many locate the origins of Western philosophical modernity at this time. Though few would have then been aware of it. The intellectual hegemonies of medieval Christendom were being confronted with a force which, as time would show, they could not stop.

We have already noted the second thing that was happening in this period. It was the increasing wish of the Northern European nations to establish their political and economic independence from Rome. Most dramatically, of course, this affected England and Henry the Eighth's desire for a divorce from Catherine of Aragon. Its refusal by Pope Clement VII was cataclysmic for the Papacy and led to the cessation of its control of the English Church. Again, of course, there was much more to this. Henry was surrounded by ecclesiastics and thinkers who were inspired by the new humanism and the Protestant Reformation. They were ready for change. This was soon unstoppable because these reforming currents came together. No single one of them, the divorce included, would have effected such change. They all did. The Papacy, effectively, lost control of religion across swathes of Northern Europe. No other single institution replaced it. The many Churches of the Protestant Reformation were born. They offered an immediacy of popular religious experience which was previously unheard of. Justification was to be *sola fide*, by faith alone. The Bible was translated from Latin into vernacular tongues as were the liturgies. All this was religiously and politically cataclysmic. These new Churches were self-controlling, save where they were subject to the authority of the State. This was particularly the case in England where they were required to observe common norms and be tolerant of each other. Anglicanism came to be in this way. Its origin is to be found in the so-called Elizabethan Settlement. This is the general term for Acts passed by Elizabeth the first. They covered issues such as religious toleration and the supremacy of the English crown over every '...foreign prince, person, prelate, state or potentate, spiritual or temporal'.[17] This was followed by an act which required uniformity of religious observance in the English churches.

By the eighteenth century the Anglican Church, in the eyes of many, had become complacent largely as a consequence of its socially privileged position in English society. Abuses were rife. Clergy were often absent from their livings and they often held many of them in plurality purely for financial gain. Nepotism, for this same reason, was commonplace. Privileges, such as education at Oxford and Cambridge, were reserved to the clergy. Thereby they became an elite ruling class alongside the Squirearchy. Lay people were considered to be spiritually and socially subordinate to them. Not all of the Church even at this time was so structured, but enough of it was to cause a vacuum into which religious change could sweep.

In 1848 two Anglican clergymen, themselves sons of a clergyman, met a Moravian Christian who emphasised the importance of the immediacy of religious experience for every individual believer. Those clergymen were, of course, John and Charles Wesley and the Moravian was Peter Bohler. What followed was nothing less than phenomenal. By the end of the century, Methodism had broken from its Anglican parent. It was ordaining its own ministers, first in America. It had established a remarkable network of lay organisations for the promotion and support of the faith. As a result, it became a people's movement on a scale not dissimilar to those then emerging in France and elsewhere. Methodism, it is even sometimes claimed, prevented Britain from social revolution by creating an outlet for proletarian articulation and hope. It became and remains a world-wide church. There are now some sixty million Methodists in a hundred countries world-wide. As it expanded, so it fragmented. It reunited in 1932. The World Methodist Council was created in 1951. Two attempts to reunite it with its parent Anglicanism failed to be accepted by the latter in 1969 and 1972. It is now being attempted again by the signing of covenants. These, however, are seldom anything other than devices for keeping things as they are, albeit wrapped in pious sentiment.

The Unitarian Church is the most demonstrably liberal of the free churches. It originated in Poland in the sixteenth century as part of the Protestant Reformation. After this it combined an emphasis on rationalism with its biblical theology. Its main doctrine is the unity of God. It, therefore, does not hold that Jesus is a semi-divine being. He is, rather, understood as an inspired and even supernatural one. Unitarians are welcoming of both free thinkers and members of other faiths. In all this they are to be commended. They frequently come into conflict with the Church of England. For example, in 2006 they were refused permission to hold an annual service in Chester Cathedral because of their views. On occasions like this they, rightly, see themselves as caught up in the wider conflict of liberalism an orthodoxy in the Church of England. Their view of Jesus is much in line with much modern scholarship and their reconciling work among the Christian denominations and beyond is to be admired.

In the UK other so-called Free Churches because of their independence from the State, came under the aegis of the Free Church Federal Council in 1896. These include Baptists, Congregationalists and Presbyterians. The latter two have now joined to become The United Reformed Church. In Scotland the Free Presbyterians separated from the Church of Scotland in 1843. Their several branches united in 1900, but some remained separate, these are the so-called 'Wee Frees'. The Christian church is, therefore, made up by numerous traditions and these are broadly related in the way we have described.

Each of these traditions have subdivided over the years. In recent years, the so-called *ecumenical* movement has attempted to bring them together. The word *ecumenical* is from the Greek word for house, *oikos*. The movement has produced a great deal of rhetoric and self-congratulation which is, in truth, often disproportionate to its actual achievements. Official inter-Church discussions have produced little, or only halting progress. All this is in marked contrast to the progress made by ordinary church members in all these denominations. They invariably share intercommunion and fellowship which is far beyond that envisaged, or officially permitted, by their Church authorities. At the informal level there is now much, if not for the most part complete, understanding, mutual respect and collaboration between the Christian denominations. At the formal level, however, there is comparatively little or no real progress in this. The Anglican Roman Catholic International Commission was founded by Archbishop Michael Ramsey and Pope John Paul VI in 1967. It has been sitting ever since and has come to the agreed conclusion that there are no unresolved theological differences between their churches. None of this has led, however, to any real institutional change. The Roman Catholic Church, for example, will still not admit non-Roman Catholics to its altars and it still, officially at least, disapproves of its members attending the altars of other Churches. Both of these things, however, often happen informally. This sort of ecumenical stalemate does religion little credibility in the eyes of the non-religious. The more so, because these churches have frequently veritably boasted about their official ecumenical progress! In some instances this has been true. Ecumenical witness in some divided communities has been effective at lessening tensions between them. However, the greater by far cause of the improved Protestant/Roman Catholic relationships in the UK, for example, is the fact that fewer members of both now attend either Churches at all. In their daily lives, they share other aims and activities which generate social cohesion: sport and consumerism to mention only two.

Other Churches have made better progress with their ecumenical re-organisations. Anglicans and Methodists have succeeded in their collaboration particularly well at local levels. Again at institutional levels, however, the story is has not been so successful. The Anglican Church has twice rejected union with Methodism, but the matter is now well up the agenda of both Churches again. Some other Protestant churches have done better. The United Reform Church was formed out of a union between Congregationalists and Presbyterians and Baptist churches have come closer together, though they still value their congregational independence.

Clearly, members of different churches at grassroots levels live their interdependent lives of faith more spontaneously that those who govern them officially are able to recognise. For them so many other considerations of power, influence and money come into consideration. For these reasons, a not unjustified cynicism sees such churches as more concerned to protect their own interests, than to serve the best interests of their members. This could well be just one reason for the seemingly inexorable decline in some of their membership.

The Bible remains central to all Christian thought and practice. It is, however, variously understood. Some take their interpretation of its face value to be its true meaning. The general term used to describe this view is Fundamentalism. Others stress the need to subject the Bible to minute scholarly analysis. This, biblical critical, view has its origins in the eighteenth century. It has much to show for its labour and is an ongoing field of scholarly enquiry. It increasingly helps us to understand both the nature and meaning of the Bible.

Academic Christian theology, as it is known today, arose with the Schoolmen whom we have already mentioned, in the Middle Ages. It is virtually co-terminus with the history of modern Universities. Its study was until at least the eighteenth century pre-eminent in them. Christianity has always been a formulaic religion in the sense that it has paid minute attention, as we have briefly seen, to the detail of its doctrines and orthodoxies. Knowledge of theology is a universal requirement in the training for the Christian ministries. Their erudition has set the standard of theological thinking. This has led to some confusion, to which attention has only recently been addressed. Theology, so understood, has been identified with hierarchical authority and control. In the late twentieth century different sorts of theologies began to appear in Latin America and elsewhere. These began by rejecting the hierarchical models and sought to do theology from the ground up. This was achieved in poor and disadvantaged communities as they addressed the causes and possible remedies for their plight. What they did soon became known generically as 'Liberation Theology'. This challenged the orthodoxies of traditional theology and was remarkably effective in doing so. It spawned many versions which are still influential. All this raises the question of the relationship of theology to ordinary grass roots human experience, from which much of it seemed remote. There has been an attempt to address this problem, particularly in the Scottish Churches and universities. They have distinguished theology from what they call 'practical theology'. This latter is literally the study of the practical and every-day application of theology 'proper'. I have challenged all this elsewhere and suggested a simple solution.[18] This is that we should see theology proper as the articulation of the life of faith as and where it is lived. It is what Christians do when they think about the practice of their faith. Like prose speaking, it is done without the conscious knowledge of doing it. It is part of the everyday life of believers. Academic theology is extracted *from* all this for study purposes. This is a proper academic discipline in its own right with, as we have seen, about a thousand years of pedigree in its modern form. When seen in this simple way there is no need to devise tortuous forms for its 'application'. The real thing is part of the living experience of faith. Academic theology which is derived from it, is as necessary an academic discipline as any other. It informs and clarifies the life of faith, but that faith is not *derived* from it. Such theology is, rather, derived from faith.

Some have sought to separate theology completely from the life of faith and created so-called 'Religious Studies' for this purpose. This phrase is used to describe a form of theology which is independent from and, indeed, objective about theology as understood studied and taught in the religious traditions. This distinction is now, however, increasingly breaking down. One the one side, this is because those traditions are ever becoming more objectively analytical of themselves. On the other, because the objective analysts of religion increasingly recognise the importance of the lived life of faith in any understanding of what religion and theology is about.

We have now briefly looked at the historic and world-wide phenomenon of religion. There is, of course, much more to it than we have been able to encompass. It is an infinitely rich and always surprising area of study. No understanding of what it has ever meant or now means to be human is complete without it. This is because it addresses the fundamentals of individual and social life alike. It is inconceivable that we will ever live in a world where religion plays no part in either. On the contrary, religion in one form or another is here to stay. This, as we began by pointing out, is the reason why we all need to be informed about it whether we profess it or not.

An important attempt to understand what the religions have in common has recently been made. It deserves our brief consideration before we continue.

After serving for years as a missionary, Wilfred Cantwell Smith became the Director of the Centre for the Study of World Religions at Harvard University. In 1962 he published *The Meaning and End of Religion*.[19] It is subtitled *A Revolutionary Approach to the Great Religious Traditions*. The main theme is this book has not received the attention it deserves from those traditions. Little wonder, we might reflect, given the industry they devote to defending their distinctiveness and, thereby, self-interest.

Smith writes: 'I have come to feel that, in some ways, it is probably easier to be religious without the concept that the notion of religion can become an enemy to piety'.[20] He then immediately muses that the rise of the concept of religion has been marked by a decline in its practice. He concludes that the word religion has been used in at least four different ways which still persist in common usage. These are, briefly: (a) to mean personal piety, (b) to refer to overt systems of belief, or whatever, (c) to designate empirical historical phenomena whereby the religion(s) become distinct from each other and (d) its use as a collective noun for all of them. Smith concludes from this that uses (b)–(d) of the word should be dropped.[21] It should only be used to refer to (a) personal piety. Even here it should be used with caution because of misleading connotations with its other uses. Better, Smith suggests, to 'rehabilitate the venerable term 'piety'.[22] By this he means personal faith. If this were done he adds that it would lead to 'for the devout a truer faith in God and a truer love of their neighbour; and for scholars, a clearer understanding of the religious phenomenon that they are studying'.[23] This is a perceptive attempt to understand what the religions have in common.

In the next two chapters we will consider some of what we will call the 'problems of religion' and focus on how they relate to Christianity. These will show why it is that Christianity and modernity are so often ill at ease with each other. Chapter Three will discuss the historical, political and social problems of Christianity and focus on the problem of its proximity to violence. Chapter Four will discuss theological, and philosophical problems. We will see why these difficulties have to be faced if we are to profess Christianity with integrity. In the course of this discussion we will consider the writings of some recent and much publicised critics of religion. None of these will be rejected out of hand. Indeed, the force of many of their criticisms will be respected.

From now on, for the reasons explained, the discussion will focus increasingly on Christianity.

CHAPTER THREE

Its Problems (1): History, Providence, War, the Environment, Society

In this chapter will consider some of the reasons why people reject Christianity. It will focus on its proximity to war and violence. In the next, we will consider more philosophical and abstract, though none the less important, reasons. In the course of these discussions the ways in which Christianity needs to be rethought if it is to have a right relationship with modernity will become clear.

The Human Place in History

Although we know more about the origin of the universe than human beings have ever known, it is still effectively obscure to us. Its secrets are yielding to the onslaught of scientific investigation, but the prospect of us knowing exactly when and how it came into existence remains as elusive as ever. We do know that it has an unimaginably long and obscure pre-history. This is a remarkably recent feature of human consciousness.

The earth is generally thought to be some 15,000 million years old. Biological life is, also, of almost unimaginable antiquity. The date of its origin is the subject of constant scholarly debate. Terrestrial biological life, when organic matter began to leave behind the earliest found fossil evidence, is thought to be some 3.5 billion years old. It might be unique to this planet, or not. Much of the debate about extra-terrestrial life remains in the field of imaginative speculation and science fiction. However, the probability of finding at least the conditions for it in some form elsewhere is now increasing rapidly. As we probe outer space it seems increasingly likely that there are other planetary systems such as ours some of which could sustain life in some form. It is therefore becoming difficult to make easy claims about the uniqueness of our planet or universe.

All the available fossil evidence points to the fact that human life as we know it began in Africa which is still the habitat of our closest relatives. These are gorillas and chimpanzees. Somewhere about seven million years ago species of ape, first the gorillas and then the chimpanzees, began to separate and develop independently. The humanoid derivatives of the latter appeared in upright form some four million years ago. *Homo erectus* was the result of all this. Stone tools took another million and a half or so years to appear. Some fifty thousand years ago the so-called 'Great Leap Forward' brought evidence of treasured artefacts. Also at this time, by now recognisable human beings began to migrate to Eurasia. Ten thousand years later, they began to appear as Cro-Magnons in Europe. From this time we can gather evidence of their partially settled existence which indicates the emergence of rudimentary social arrangements.

Two observations about all this need to be made for our purpose. The first, is that human beings are a very late development in the history of the now-known universe. The second, is that the origins of organised religion as we now also know them are comparatively even more recent. These date from only some four thousand years ago. The Christian revelation is, of course, only two millennia old and the Islamic one six centuries younger still. To point out the obvious; natural history and the history of organised religion operate on radically different timescales. That is not to say that human beings prior to the latter were not religious. We have already noted that they probably were. All we need to be clear about, for now, is that organised religion as we know it is historically a very recent phenomenon.

As well as recognising the almost unimaginable antiquity of the natural order, we also have to accept the fact that it will not last forever. This is because it will be unable to sustain its fragile equilibrium indefinitely. It will eventually self-destruct. Such 'balances' of nature that we might observe are only transitory. Physical and biological history is also redolent with massive upheavals. Two hundred and fifty million years ago the Permian Extinction wiped out all but some ten per cent of the earth's species. Only sixty-five thousand years ago practically all the dinosaurs met the same fate. It is often quoted that some 99.999 per cent of all species are already extinct. Some biologists predict that life as we know it is already half over. On the bright side that means that there is much to be done in the next three billion years or so! Done that is, whilst human beings are still around.

Against this background of the dramatic new understanding of our prehistory and fragility, the timescales of the religions are put in serious doubt. Although the once widely held biblical view that the world was no more than 4,000 years old was mistaken, it at least had the virtue of correlating world, human and religious history. They all fitted together. World, human and religious history was all on the same timescales. More to the point, it was possible to believe that God's purposes were evident in them all. Some Christians still even vehemently defend the truth of all this. These so-called Creationists insist on the abiding truth of their literal biblical interpretation and on it being taught in schools. The plain truths of it all, however, are that world, human and religious history is on radically different time-scales.

Whilst the Eastern religions do seem to have comprehension of longer time-scales, they, nevertheless, also believed them to be similarly comprehensible from the creation to the present. In these ways, the religions attempted, in their different ways, to account for the nature of creation and for their understanding of their own place and that of humankind within it. The fact now is that human beings can no longer rest assured that their place in the universe is comprehensible from the beginning, privileged in the present, or assured for the future. Nor can they assume that any such privilege affords them superiority over all other life-forms with which they share mortality.

The Judaic religions are clearly not a historically integral part of the actual history of the universe or of its provisions for human welfare. They are of much later dates. The reasons for them occurring when they did are not at all difficult to find. They have to do, not with us understanding the mind of God from the beginning of history (as if we could do that anyway), their stuff is of far more earthly origin.

The actual reason for the emergence of Judaism in the form it did, clearly has to do with Israel's emergent nationalism. From about the middle of the second millennium BCE the previously independent nomadic Semitic tribes of Sinai formed an 'amphictiony'. This was an organisation of the six and then the twelve tribes of Israel into a single Tribal League. All of these tribes claimed the ancestry of Jacob and shared the covenant which God made with Moses at Sinai. They did all this at about the time they began to settle in Canaan. These tribes were then bound together by the observance of religious obligations. One example was their regular pilgrimage to a central shrine. This was originally to Shechem, and later at Shilo. What this, in effect, did was to create an effective, if rudimentary, unitary social organisation. This, in turn, led to the increased sharing of customs and objectives. Above all, they shared the means of self-defence. They became militarised. This gave them a capacity which could be used for attack as well as for defence. The emergent cohesive social identity was, therefore, coterminous with a growing military presence. At the same time, a priestly Levitic caste emerged. This, in turn, provided the laws necessary for Israel's ever consolidating single identity. Some of these laws were borrowed from both Canaanite and Mesopotamian societies. Priests worked alongside another caste, the Judges, to rule Israel. The socio-political results of all this became increasingly apparent. Somewhere by about the end of the thirteenth century BCE Israel had conquered Canaan and settled in Palestine. By that time, other national influences in the area had already waned and Israel faced no other immediate foreign threat to its occupation of the land. It then soon called that land its own. More than that, even, it also claimed that its possession was a divine right.

The actual circumstances of Israel's origins are, of course, much more complex and debatable than these brief outlines suggest. However, they serve our purpose by showing in outline when and how Israel, as such, came into existence.

We have already discussed the formation of the monarchy in Israel. The recording of Israel's nomadic past based on its oral traditions is more or less coterminous with its establishment. These oral traditions are rich in information about Israel's past and modern methods of study have prised open their secrets as never before. We know, for example, that they contain much material which was borrowed from the surrounding nations and adapted for Israel's use. This point is vitally significant to our interpretation of the literature to which the traditions gave rise. In these records, Israel brought to completion a long process in which it gradually adapted world history and culture to suit its own needs and purposes. There is, of course, nothing particularly unique about this. Most emergent nations have done similar things. What was different in Israel is that it did this at a crux of history when the Middle Eastern emergent nationalisms were in growing conflict – and Israel won. It won not only in the military sense. Even more significant was the success of its literary achievement and the triumph this secured over surrounding national literatures. It created new narratives to undergird its new national order, ones that would serve its purposes more explicitly than the older oral tribal traditions were, by this time, able to do.

Put bluntly, it is impossible not to notice in all this that in the period from about the ninth to the sixth century BCE, Israel effectively re-wrote world history in its own interest. In doing so, it also effectively wrote all the other adjacent nations out of that history: the Egyptians, Babylonians, Mesopotamians, Hittites, Assyrians and the Medes, along with sundry others. Most of these nations already had long histories and immense cultural achievements to their credit. By comparison, those of Israel were hitherto relatively insignificant. Marginalising all this accomplishment of other nations was a remarkable (military and cultural) achievement in so short a time scale. Tracing how this was achieved in any more detail is beyond our present scope. We will add to it simply by looking at the creation narratives in the Book of Genesis. They are key part of the wider corpus of Israel's earliest literature.

There are two accounts of creation in the Book of Genesis, the first book of the Bible. The second account Genesis, 2.4b–25, is the so-called Yahwist's work because that is the name there used for God. (The first account dates from some three centuries later and reflects the more vested Priestly interests that had by then developed.) This second account is the great story of the Creation, Paradise and the fall from grace by Adam and Eve. It is a grand aetiology; an explanation of the way things are in the created order and of the place of humans within it. This is, above everything else, a grand narrative by and for a nation of people who are among the world's greatest story tellers. It compellingly interweaves the common motifs of oriental story telling. In a definitive commentary on the text Gerhard Von Rad writes, 'Genesis Chs. 2ff is a sublime representation of the original state, which uses some mythological ideas freely. Its simplicity, however, is not archaic, but rather the highest command of every artistic means'.[1] In this literary way, Israel established itself as the chosen people of God, the most privileged among the nations. Moreover, all creation was at its command. This oldest biblical account of creation was part of a wider Yahwist, literature which is of epic proportions. Its time-scale covered the whole period from the creation to the entry into Cana. It focusses on Yahweh's saving acts in the Exodus, the Wilderness, the Conquest and settlement. The cultic expression of the faith this inspired is to be found in Deuteronomy 26:5–10. Nothing is excluded, all the central institutions of Israel's ancient life are featured. In addition, the Yahwist drew heavily on the literatures of the surrounding nations. Chief among these is that of the Babylonian creation myth, *Eneuma Elish*. By this means, the Yahwist writer(s) created a narrative which gave plausibility to the political and geographical aspirations of the Jewish people. This then became a powerful propaganda tool in the war with the surrounding nations and their similar narratives. In all this, emergent nationalism and religious and literary genius became fused. By these means Israel became a religiously and politically dominant nation.

The point of all this for our purpose, is to notice that the manner in which Israel achieved its national identity has, in one way or another, influenced world history ever since. The traditional view taken of all this in the subsequent history of both Judaism and Christianity is that it is all of the will of God and quite literally true. The Jewish people *are* the chosen of God and they *were* given inalienable religious and territorial privileges.

The scientific controversies of the nineteenth century attenuated the historical interpretation of the creation story(s) for most Jews and Christians alike. However, it incredibly left the more literal interpretation of the truth of the rest of the narrative virtually intact. All Jews and probably nearly all Christians still believe that their religions are an integral, God given, part of the history of the universe and of its provisions for their welfare.

This is a major problem for both Judaism and Christianity. It is the reason why they have so often been in opposition to each other. It is also a cause of the horrendous anti-Semitism which has caused so much death, suffering and distress throughout history. That God should have chosen *one* nation on earth as his most dearly beloved is, frankly, inconceivable. That God should then have bestowed upon them the only then known strip of fertile land, simply beggars belief. The fact that it does not do this for the majority of Jews and Christians is simply because the vested interests of both of them are, equally, premised upon it being true. In spite of all the difficulties, they go on believing it. Christian and Muslim subsequent narratives are, therefore, based on the assumption that the Jewish interpretation of its own history is true. They are all mutually reinforcing. When they do ostensibly discuss their differences they are but mutually affirming this. They are alike therefore weakened thereby for the reasons we have discussed.

Massive national, economic and cultural self-interests were created by the Jewish people in this short time three millennia ago. (A mere blink, in fact, in the history of the earth and its peoples.) These interests have shaped Middle Eastern and Western world history ever since. Their force is as strong as ever. The reason for this is because so much wider political and economic vested interested is premised upon it. It is of the very fabric of Middle Eastern and Western culture in all its manifestations.

Given that world conflict is now as it manifestly is, Jews, Christians and Muslims must all be prepared to reconsider their understanding of the origins of their religions. Justifying them uncritically as being 'of the will of God', is not now acceptable. Full stop. This is a big ask. Too big, perhaps, to stand even a chance of being met. Followers of these religions have too much self interest invested in them for them to divest themselves so easily, if at all. This human self-interest has been evidently at work in the three religions from their beginnings. Facing this fact does not mean, as we will see, that the Bible is now irrelevant. Indeed, the Jewish and Christian Bible is one of the world's greatest compendiums of religious writings. It is still worthy of continued respect for its profound religious insights. For this reason alone, interpreting its history as we have done cannot possibly be construed as anti-Semitic. The Semite contribution to human understanding is far greater than that premised upon its narrow interpretation of its own history. It includes so much more which is of abiding worth to our understanding of the relationship of the human to the divine. We have touched upon some of this already and will continue to do so in what follows.

The Jewish people were driven from Jerusalem a second time (the first remember was in 586 BCE when they were driven out by the Babylonians) by the Romans in 70 CE when the Second Temple was destroyed. They did not return again as a nation until 1948. This, as we have seen, was part of the, in itself honourable, international post Second World War attempt to help redress the evil of the Holocaust. The extent of the displacement of the Palestinian people this settlement caused has been the problem ever since. Some extremist orthodox Jews now talk of building the Third Temple and they are invariably supported in this by some Christians who believe that it would be of the will of God. In this way the chilling logic of the centuries old narratives of self-interest continue.

The post 1948 displacement of such a large proportion of the Palestinian people and the subsequent history of the conflict arising from that to the present time, can only be understood as the legacy of Jewish (and Christian) history which reaches back three millennia. Unless this is recognised, finding a solution to the 'Palestinian problem' will remain as difficult and intractable as it presently is. Of course, it is unthinkable that such self-interests will ever become so enlightened (not even on reading this!). The plain fact is, however, that the present impasse is part of a legacy of darkness which Jews, Christians and Muslims have all cast over the Middle East and occasionally the rest of the world. The Jewish, Christian and Islamic religious texts with their embedded narratives of self-interest have always had and retain in part the capacity to cause bloodshed. They can kill people. No pious protestation otherwise on their behalf can ever gainsay this.

Jews, Christians and Muslims all need to be sensitive to these unacceptable implications of their shared interpretation of history. Unless they can achieve this, at least is some measure, their credibility in the wider world will be increasingly at stake. This is a seemingly incredible thing to expect. It would appear impossible were it not for the fact that there are some who actually achieve it and they deserve our respect. For this they often have to suffer the criticism of and alienation from their own communities, as well as from secularists who are nervous of the political and economic implications of their views. One such example of self-critical reflection is that of the Jewish dissident theologian Marc H. Ellis. He sees the present state of the militarisation of Israel as the betrayal of its history. He observes that the ever growing Israeli resort to military retaliation has brought about a situation in which Jewish life is transposed as it ceases to be oppressed and becomes the oppressor of Palestinians. His writings are redolent with pleas for the recognition of their rights.[2] He is transfixed by the implications for Judaism caused by Israeli helicopter gun-ships surrounding and menacing, as they are alleged to have done, defenceless Palestinian children. Things have come to this pass, in his view, because Israel has, like Christianity before it under Constantine, now assumed the mantle of the state. It has done this in a singularly focussed way which leads it to adopt extreme attitudes against Palestinians and resort to excessive uses of military force. Ellis points out how comparatively recent all this is and how, hitherto, Jews were markedly less militaristic. He is even more opposed to the excessive military means used by Israel to suppress subsequent Palestinian protest. He comes to the conclusion that Israel is destroying itself. He writes: 'For how much more can ethics be challenged than the wholesale dislocation of a people, aerial bombardments of defenceless cities, closures of towns and villages for weeks and months at a time, assassination squads and torture legitimated by the courts? How long before an ethical tradition is simply declared dead rather than argued for in compromise?'[3] He claims that this presents what he calls 'Jews of conscience' such as himself with the realisation that it could lead to the end of Judaism. The solution he proposes is one in which Israel seeks a 'revolutionary forgiveness' of the Palestinians in the hope that it can lead to new beginnings. Though Ellis would not claim it himself, he writes in a long tradition of Jewish internal dissent which was first epitomised by the Prophets of the Hebrew Bible. His stand is a personally courageous one which focusses on his befriending of Palestinians. His work is a moving attempt to redeem what he sees as an Israel which has lost its way from within. This is a modern fine example of how religions can go about redeeming their aberrant excesses. It deserves the respect and support of all Jews, Christians and Muslims who care, as

Ellis does passionately, for the integrity of their religions. There are many other such examples of religious believers who are prepared to be as revisionary and courageous a this.[4] In this endeavour they can and do support each other. Religious believers of whatever tradition who sympathise with them should lend their support as well. This shared collective integrity is already a massive force for peace. It has the potential to become an even greater one.

Religious integrity of his kind should receive the recognition it deserves in the peace processes. Pragmatists on all sides know that there must be workable alternatives to decades of killing and strife. For example, the United Nations Security Council persists in trying to get Israel to recognise the State of Palestine but to no avail. As a result, the conflict seems to worsen daily as both sides try to justify their actions to the wider world. Jewish, Christian and Muslim people are all embroiled in this, in Israel, Palestine and throughout the world. We stress again, they are of *three* (related) religions, fighting over *two* countries. They are also, *one* people, the 'children of Abraham'. Biologically they have all recently been identified as of one genetic stock.

The ultimate solution to the awesome problem of resolving their continued conflict must be a workable political one. However, the point we have been making here is that this will require more than political good will. That has been and still is tried by all sides. It leads to serial failure. Finding a solution will also require, among other things, nothing less than the sort of revisionary religious thinking we have briefly discussed. If that cannot be achieved, then the future of all those who suffer from this conflict is a bleak one. The hope must be that a shared deeper religious humility and wisdom will combine with political pragmatism to achieve a lasting peace in the very best interests of all.

Providence

Human existence has always been vulnerable as the plagues of old remind us. These can no longer be thought of as just being of the past. The HIV retro-virus is already affecting world demography, particularly in sub-Saharan Africa and its possibly equally devastating effect on Asia is only just becoming at all predictable. It must still be hoped that medical advances in the treatment of this awesome disease will continue to mitigate the untold human suffering it causes. Other such viruses not only could, but must be expected to appear. Annual scares about different sorts of influenza are but another recurrent example. Human existence is as fragile and as vulnerable as it ever was. Even if it avoids the frightening prospect of destroying itself with weapons of mass destruction, its destruction by viral conquest remains an equal possibility. Some life forms might survive. It is sometimes argued that worms or beetles will be the most enduring because they will be the first to push their noses above the surface after cataclysm. These are admittedly depressing thoughts. They are, however, unavoidable for any who want to understand the circumstances of modern life as they actually are.

The religious belief which is most directly challenged by all this is that of providence. This is the belief that the world was created and is sustained by a loving God according to God's purposes principally for the benefit of human beings and that, no matter what may befall, that benefit would always prevail. On this view, God's providence could be trusted against all evidence to the contrary. Indeed, such trust was even thought to be consummate when the evidence against it was at its strongest. Job's utterance of 'blessed be the name of the Lord' (Job 1:21) in the face of loss and dereliction is an ultimate expression of this. Given that we now know what we do about the universe, however, human beings are seemingly no more sacrosanct than any other biological creatures. The last century saw an illustration of this on a cataclysmic scale. Nowhere in the scope of the religions has the doctrine of providence been more firmly held that it was, and still tenuously is by some, in Judaism. The scale of the Holocaust belied this when some six million Jews were put to death in the Nazi concentration camps. Trusting God after personal misfortune like Job is one thing, but doing it after such awesome genocide is quite another. This is an example of the profound effect the loss of confidence in God's providence has had on just one great religious tradition. The problem of God's seeming lack of providential care for God's creatures is not now just a Jewish problem. It is a problem for Christian and Muslims, no less, since they share the doctrine of providence in their family of religions. The latter, however, compensates for this-worldly misfortune by affirming heavenly reward. This has became part of the chilling logic of some extreme Islamic terrorism.

When such recent misfortune is placed against the background of seemingly timeless natural history, it is clear that there is no self-evident historical correlation between the created order and God's providence as it is expressed by the three Judaic religions. For example, the too often and too easy naturalism of Christianity is directly challenged here. All is not always 'safely gathered in', grateful though it is proper for us to be whenever it seemingly is. Christian harvest festivals, for example, play an important role in the observation of the natural seasons, particularly in rural communities, but they often present a personalised and romanticised view of the relationship of human beings to the natural order. To the contrary, the spectre of world food shortage caused by climate change and population growth is looming ever larger. There is no room in the face of all this either for romantic naturalism, believing that God will do something about it if we do not, or for complacency. If we do not do something about it, no one else will.

Christianity is, to say the least, an optimistic religion. It sees the world as a drama which is taking place between its creation and its consummation in the Kingdom of God. In this drama, it claims, all things are actually being redeemed and those not yet obviously so eventually will be in the Kingdom. That redemption will bring with it a state of everlasting bliss and eternal life in the sight of God. All this is breathtaking, to say the least. Clearly, the belief that there is a correlation between the ceaseless activity of a loving God and the way things are in the world is central to this understanding. It presupposes that God created the world for a purpose and that God will see that purpose through, whatever the evidence may be from time to time to the contrary. Not surprisingly, such a breathtaking doctrine of God's continuing relationship to the created order has led to problems. One is the question about whether or not God's providence is universal. Will it, therefore, affect everything and everybody regardless of their circumstances? Another is the problem of human free will. If God's providence is universal, is free will always and everywhere overridden? If the answer to this is 'yes', then it is difficult to make sense of the notion of individual and collective free will and of moral responsibility. This notion is in so many other ways central to the Christian life. One way of reconciling this seeming contradiction is to believe that God's providence works through human agency rather than through nature independently of it. There is much to commend this view. Let a passing reflection illustrate this. Human beings, as we have seen, now possess the capacity to destroy themselves times over. They are also prey to threats to their well-being which are not directly a consequence of their own actions. If Christians were to believe, in all this, that they could be quiescent in the expectation that God would sort it all out, they would command scarce credibility. There is clearly a direct correlation between human responsibility and human welfare. It is, therefore, better to see human beings as co-creators with God with a particular responsibility for redeeming the here and now. Such a view ascribes immense responsibilities to human beings. An awareness of this alone can be seen as a good reason for approaching this responsibility with humility as well as resolve. Because humans are created in the image God they do not just possess the capacity to reflect God's love. They also possess a responsibility for the ever ongoing process of creation. This means that they cannot be quiescent about their own well-being, providence and survival. They have a shared God-given responsibility for it.

Belief in providence is so central to the Christian understanding that it has, of course, been secularised in the Western, at least, belief in inevitable progress of the human lot. A prominent example is the often so-called 'American Dream'. But is this view of the cosmic order really any longer sustainable? We have already touched throughout on two main reasons for thinking it not so. These are the unbearable scale of much human suffering, and the fragile and finite nature of creation. The awareness of both of these is now part of the human lot in a way which was not the case only, say, half a century ago. It really is that recent. Although this awareness can be dated back to the eighteenth century, modern television images have done more than anything else to bring home to the masses the realities of suffering and fragility of the planet. Media reporting after the Asian tsunami on Boxing Day 2005 was the most graphic example of this and the October 2005 earthquake in Pakistan is yet another. As is the Japan earthquake of 2011. Cheap optimism is not an acceptable response to all this. Religious people such as Christians must face the fact that disasters such as these count against the optimism of their theism. Why does an all-knowing and all powerful God allow such things to happen?

An obvious consequence of all this is that people increasingly live for the present. The phenomenally generous financial response to the Asian tsunami disaster was a welcome good example of this. People immediately wanted things to be better for the victims. Something immediate, therefore, had to be done. The sentiment that this '...ain't no dress rehearsal' is a common one. People generally are living longer than ever before and they want to live life to the full. The rewards have to be present, tangible and certainly not deferred. Is this because, in the knowledge that no one or nothing else will do it for us, we have to redeem life for ourselves? If this is the case, then it should be seen as a remarkable human achievement. The triumph, no less, of the human spirit over unbelievable misfortune. Much of this triumph is hard and deservedly wrought. All this might well, of course, be the predominant experience of the affluent and healthy world, but it is certainly not so for many others. The human lot for them is still nasty, brutish and short. Those not so affected should never forget this. All thoughts, therefore, about providence must be thoughts about the whole human race. Far too many people still have to live with the realisation that their lives are not provident, even in modest degree. For them, any belief in an after-life which will redeem their plight is an immense blessing. The moving cultural example of this is the faith and spirituality of African slaves two centuries ago. Whatever their present hardship might have been, there was always the hope of a redeemed after life '...across the river' and this is centrally celebrated in Negro spirituals and culture. This faith and hope is probably what made those people as traditionally accepting of their plight as they were. In many ways and for the infinitely better, this is now a lost world to us. This is why we want to do something about misfortune in the here and now.

There is, however, an even deeper question in all this. If the view of life which religion purports has to do with ultimate values such as love and peace, how can it be that life is often so full of misfortune, hatred and distress? There is a Christian doctrine which addresses this issue. It is that of the Kingdom of God. This Kingdom is frequently mentioned by Jesus either as a present condition which can be experienced, or as a future one. In either case it refers to conditions under which human and divine purposes are at one with each other. Even the possibility of this oneness ever occurring is a blessed thought which is not to be taken lightly. Daring to think that the human and the divine are capable of being at one is a central part of the understanding of most religions. It clearly mattered greatly to Jesus. As an aspiration, alone, it raises the human spirit to new levels. It does this, moreover, never more dramatically than when that spirit is dashed for whatever reason. None of this should be dismissed lightly. It deserves the respect of even those who are most sceptical about its possibility. It also shows how such scepticism need not be a bar to seeking the realisation of the Kingdom in earthly affairs. Indeed, Christianity requires that we do just that. Jesus' teaching is never more inspirational than when it shows us that the Kingdom is, so to speak, under our very noses. Lying, so to speak, in places where we are not accustomed to look for it. Even among the despised and the outcast. Those whom we often consider to be the epitome of sinfulness. The irony of all this in Jesus teaching is that he pointed out repeatedly that those who think themselves self-righteous, i.e. the religious establishment, are the least likely to find the Kingdom. Little wonder that he caused the religious establishment so much offence.

So, for all the obvious difficulties which attach to older notions of God's providential care for God's creatures, given that we now know to world to be as it is, there is yet real value in the notion. It derives from understanding human agency as an integral part of God's providence. This agency when used for the good, whatever that might mean in particular circumstances, can be understood as being co-creative with the divine will. In this way, human beings achieve a heightened awareness of their creative powers and of their obligation to use them for the good. Though the notion of God's providential care for God's creatures is problematic for the reasons we have considered, it yet remains, in this way, an important and insightful Christian doctrine.

War

As if all this were not problematic enough there is, of course, the related question about whether or not over the centuries religion has been at least *a* cause of war and conflict and perhaps often *the* major one. The honest answer must, of course, be yes, in some instances. One such was the twelfth century Crusades. They were officially authorised by the Papacy to subdue the Infidels and secure access to the Holy Land and Jerusalem. They were all a disaster in one way or another. Crusaders discovered to their surprise that the alleged Infidels were a civilised people whose cultural achievements often far eclipsed those of Western Christendom. These crusades were also logistically impossible to sustain over vast territory for extended periods. Throughout European history, at least, such often extended 'wars of religion' have been common. They have ceased for secular reasons rather than from religious changes of mind. In Northern Ireland in the last century it was as though these older European wars had been geographically marginalised to the very edge of the Atlantic Ocean. Here again, they are thankfully being circumscribed by secular forces for peace. Not the least among these is the desire for social stability and economic prosperity. Even here the battle against terrorist attacks motivated by the religious bigotry of a few is not, sadly, over.

The indictment against religions like Judaism, Christianity and Islam for being agents of war looks an extremely strong one. It is among the most fundamental of all of the problems of religion. It has been recently voiced by Richard Dawkins as a part of his much publicised wider criticism of religion. The reason why he thinks that religion causes violence is because it engenders certainty and because this, in turn, is used to justify extremes of violent action. His conclusion is not based on extensive analyses of numerous conflicts. It is, rather, derived from a general reaction to the manifestation of contemporary religious extremism and its proximity to violence. Whilst this might be criticised for being empirically unsubstantiated, it is a conclusion which many will also draw from the now seemingly constant portrayal of the role religious certainty plays in theatres of conflict. This ranges from blatant religious self-justification to the more sophisticated citation of religious reasons for political and other stances. It cannot be gainsaid that religion and, in particular, the use made of it in self-justification does play a prominent part in causing contemporary conflict and violence. It is, of course, not the only part, but it is a suspiciously common one. Given the long history of religious violence in Western culture it, clearly, is not just a modern phenomenon. It is more, rather, a contemporary manifestation of something which is seemingly perennial. A strength of Dawkins' analysis is that it does not single out *a* religion, as such, as the cause of violence. It is, rather, the certainty that religion engenders across the religions which on his view causes the problem. Of course, secular ideologies are as susceptible to this certainty as religious ones. Common examples are extremes of Nationalism, Communism and Nazism, tribal loyalties or whatever. There are many others. In the last century secular ideologies killed more people than, arguably, in all the previous centuries put together. These ideologies all embrace certainties which translate readily into self-justification. For all these reasons, Dawkins' identification of certainty as a necessary condition of violence cannot be lightly dismissed. It deserves, rather, to be treated with seriousness.

David Martin, an accomplished Christian sociologist, does this in *Does Christianity Cause War?*[5] This book was, in fact, prompted by his desire to reply to these views of Richard Dawkins as well as by his concerns about too easy Christian invocations of peace.[6] He points out that nations which have made war in the name of religion could often well have been expected to go to war anyway. Religion, therefore, often gets involved in war as a consequence of it being waged for other reasons. In discussing this view David Martin observes that one of its strengths is that it chimes with widespread public opinion.[7] Martin rightly comments that what Dawkins is, in fact, saying is that religion is clearly a major factor in an unacceptably large number of conflicts across the globe. He comments: 'The trouble is that ideas (such as this) are not necessarily influential by reason of actual scientific content but because they chime with an established narrative and are authoritatively promulgated under the auspices of scientific magisterium.'[8] He adds that those agreeing with the proposition that religion causes war are not likely to be over troubled by exactly what they might mean by the words 'religion' 'causes' and 'war'.⁹ Martin's important point here is that we need to be much more precise when conducting such an important debate. Religion, he reminds us, relates to society in many different ways. He distinguishes between its 'differentiated' and 'undifferentiated' ones. In the former it is distinguished from the state and in the latter it is not. When it is differentiated it is more likely to be critical of the state's warring tendencies and when it is not it is more likely to support them. It therefore becomes noticeably problematic when religion is geographically co-extensive with secular power.¹⁰ When this occurs, its belligerence predominates and its contrary impulses to peace become too readily subsumed. Even here, however, there is more to be said because even in these situations religion can still be a moderating force for peace. He also notes that the causes of war are invariably complex and that in different conflicts they always interact in different ways. Drawing on his ongoing work on the theory of secularisation, he observes that war entails social differentiation and that there are many 'markers' of this of which religion is only one.¹¹ These 'markers' interact dynamically. When this happens religion becomes part of the fabric of social differentiation. As a consequence, it subsumes what he calls the 'stigmata of power'.¹² This is precisely when it is most open to the charge that it causes war.

The issue is so historically complex that it is impossible to draw general conclusions from it. For this reason, simply asking whether or not religion has caused more war than peace in world history is the stuff of pub arguments, an unanswerable question (which is, of course, why the genre is so perennial). That religion always has been and still is prominent in world conflicts is undeniable. The causes of war are several, complex and invariably confused. We cannot exclude the fact that religious certainty has been and is so often one of them. Some wars are explicitly religious beyond dispute. Others more or less use religion to support innumerable other causes of conflict. Examples of all this are both too numerous in history and, sadly, too familiar in the present to quote. This support is often tantamount to a justification of this or that war, which in turn provides certainty in the rightness of its being waged. Wars fought in national interests are clear illustrations of this. Favourable changes in those interests are therefore often interpreted as evidence of divine intervention and approval. A famous example which is often quoted is that when a sudden change of wind, the 'Protestant wind', gave the Armada victory over the Spanish fleet. Closer to the truth is the fact that experienced West Country sailors like Francis Drake and Martin Frobisher knew the tidal eddies and gateways in the English Channel better than their Spanish counterparts and were therefore able to keep their fleets to windward of the Spaniards thereby gaining immense tactical advantage. Another factor counting against the Spanish fleet was the now proven inferior quality of its ordnance.[13] But, with God (let alone the likes of Drake, Frobisher and English gunsmiths) on our side who, indeed, can be against us? There is, simply, no justification more ultimate and self-justifying than divine justification. This is the nub of the problem. There is even more to it.

Religions are not always the pious and self-denying things their proponents claim them to be. We have already seen how they are embroiled with and even derive from blatant self-interest. They can be what has been memorably described as, '...a final battleground between God's and man's self-esteem'.[14] This occurs whenever the sin of mortal pride manifests itself in spiritual pride. This, in its turn, is nothing less than a potent cocktail of self-righteous certainty that can lead to the committing of extreme atrocities in the name of virtue. Religiously motivated acts of terrorism invariably contain this chilling logic. They are the more dangerous when those about to commit them are promised an abundance of whatever they most desire in the next life. One obvious reply to all this is to say that one's own religion is not like this at all. The problem is simply with other peoples' religions. Again, to more or less extent, this might be true in this or that instance. The real problem, however, is that *all* religions have the potential and are seemingly actually capable of doing this, Judaism, Christianity and Islam in particular. Why is this the case? The origins of Judaism which we discussed above clearly have at least something to do with this. It understood successful military conquest as divine justification for its actions. Christianity and Islam both inherited this view. It has been one of the causes of world conflict for three thousand years. In virtually every other respect than this, of course, the three religions are profound sources of peace. Jews live happily in liberal democracies throughout the world and make immense contributions to their welfare. Jewish people are, moreover, gifted with a religious genius which is a constant source of insight and inspiration to others. But all this can come, in part, at a terrible price. *The price, no less, of turning self-justifying privilege into a religious virtue.* Nowhere is this more prominent than it is in the disputes over Jerusalem. Jerusalem is not mentioned in the Koran (though it is recognised as the site of the two Temples). It was the place where the Prophet ascended into heaven, leaving his footprint in the Rock of the Dome. Early Muslim homage was paid to Jerusalem before it was transferred to Mecca, the place of the Prophet's birth. Its sacredness to Christians is because it was the place of the culmination of the ministry of Jesus in his crucifixion and resurrection and, according to the Gospels of Luke and John, the place of his post-resurrection appearances to his disciples. The sadness of it all is that a place, which is held to be so sacred by three religions, has become the focus of their conflicts with each other.

We have already touched on the possibility that views such as those here expressed could be interpreted as being anti-Semitic. The history of the last century and of centuries before of ill-treatment of Jewish people alone makes most of us want to retreat at this point and let the matter rest. No civilised person, let alone, as here one with immense respect for Jewish people and the abiding treasure of their religion, would want to be thought even remotely guilty of such a charge. The term was first used in Germany towards the end of the nineteenth century. It has since been used generically to describe a hostility to Jewish people which is as old as their history. The political triumph of Christianity over Judaism in the West led to Jewish castigation, and social marginalisation. This has been historically so sustained that the Jewish people have often been demonised in the worst possible of ways. All this came to a head in Germany from the end of the nineteenth century with such horrendous consequences for the twentieth. The scale of the pogroms of the Second World War is and will always remain, a deep hurt on the conscience of humankind. None of all this can, or should ever be gainsaid. What that must not do, however, is prevent us from critically examining the place of self-justifying religious privilege as a cause of war and conflict,

Such self-justification which leads to morally unacceptable excesses is not, of course, unique to Judaism. Christians are notorious for having persecuted each other down the centuries. This has occurred whenever this group or that have become dissident and believed themselves spiritually and morally superior to their former co-religionists. Both sides of the Protestant Reformation are redolent with ghastly examples of this. Their burnings of each other in public occurred long after an enlightened Europe was awakening to a new secular humanism, which was to have such a large influence on its future. Certainties and self-justification on all sides led to unbridled depravity. The result was a Europe which became religiously and politically divided throughout the centuries and this has left its mark on its modernity. We are still, in so many ways, living with the consequences of it all. The genuine and widespread desire for a united Europe is a moving response to all this. What that might actually mean politically and economically is, of course, still far from clear. What is, thankfully, clear is that there is a will for a better, mutually supporting and peaceful future.

The military excesses of Islam are no different. Notwithstanding its cultural triumphs which we have already noted, it too has believed that barbarisms are justified in the name of religious truth. Justified, because of the requirement for its adherents to be totally submissive to the perceived will of Allah. As we saw earlier, conquest and plunder were a central part of Islam's phenomenally rapid geographical expansion. The seemingly ready resort to arms is an all too familiar graphic image still associated with some Islamic sects.

This story of the ways in which Judaism, Christianity and Islam have arguably all either caused or at least been close to the causes of bloodshed down the centuries is, perhaps, the greatest of all indictments against their collective integrity. The same is, of course, true of other religions whenever they do the same thing. If there is reason enough for not being religious, this must assuredly be it. The problematic of religion does not come in any sharper focus.

All this is well charted territory, but it stands as an important reminder that statements about religion causing war need to be carefully analysed before conclusions are made about them. What Martin, effectively, claims is that religion is no more a cause of war than are number of other things such as ethnicity, race, territorial aggression, commodity acquisition or whatever. For this reason he concludes that the claim that it causes war is disproven.[15]

Martin's point about religion being one among many usual causes of war is well made. However, it remains to be asked whether or not religion is so frequently such an extremely potent force in war that we ought, nevertheless, to be singling it out for special attention. Nothing less than monumental historical analyses could ever settle this question. Even after that, the evidence would remain open to different interpretations and but little progress would be made.

As well as questioning what is meant by 'religion' in such debates, we also need to be careful about what is meant by 'cause'. Martin's point is that it is no more a cause than a number of other factors. This is well made, but the fact remains that it is a seemingly perennial and pervasive cause. Even if it is not always used to instigate war as such, it often soon gets also sucked into its justification. The reason for this might well be because it provides the sort of certainty to which Dawkins draws attention.[16] Religious believers who exemplify this are, invariably, to be found among those who take their religion fanatically. Although these are often in a minority among their co-religionists, they invariably receive inordinate publicity. Indeed, they also become adept at exploiting this. Fanaticism in the pursuit of violence is a real problem for religion. It remains so, even after the proper semantic cautions of David Martin are well heeded.

Keith Ward has also addressed the same question in *Is Religion Dangerous?*[17] He agrees with Martin that religion is most likely to be perceived as a case of war when it is blended with social institutions. He writes 'It is when religious institutions are blended with political institutions that religion can be enlisted in the use of force – and even then it is one "identity-marker" among others, varying in its importance from one context to another'.[18] He also observes that genuinely religious wars are few.[19] Like Martin, he does not discuss whether or not the religious component in the justification of war is different in kind from other such. Both writers simply observe that it one such among many. Again, it must be acknowledged that this point is well and importantly made. The suspicion must remain, however, that when religious elements are compounded with other causes of war they stand out among them. The charge of Dawkins remains because of the lingering suspicion that religions add the dangerous element of certainty to the lethal melting pot of war. Critics like Richard Dawkins are making an important point. They are able to exploit it against religious believers as successfully as they do because the latter so frequently fail to give it the critical attention it deserves. David Martin and Keith Ward have here been cited as writers who make important points in defence of religion against critics like Dawkins, but who also fail to deal adequately with the vexed problem of the role certainty plays in our understanding of the relationship between religious convictions conflict and war. This is why dogged critics, such as Dawkins, understandably remain at their heels.

Throughout this book it is being argued that certainty is a weakness of religion not its strength. It is what exposes it to exploitation particularly in the ways we have been considering. Those who want to find support for other certainties, be these political, economic, territorial or whatever, readily welcome into their company any such as those religious believers who can contribute compoundable certainties of their own. The notion that some land is 'God given' is precisely such a cocktail. Another is any religious belief which seeks world domination. Another is any religious belief which treats unbelievers as inferior beings. The list of variation on these certainties is endless as are the opportunities for their annexation in this conflict or that.

It is also a central argument of this book that excesses caused by certainty in religion can be avoided. This requires religious believers to take courage, step back from their own certainties and make common cause with other believers who are prepared to do the same. The cause which is here centrally important is the cause of seeking peace. So much else in the treasury of the religions enables them to do this. Once freed from their vulnerabilities and particularly from the vulnerability of their certainties, they have immense contributions to make to the betterment of the human condition. Christianity has, in fact, pursued this from its earliest beginnings. Let us now remind ourselves how it did this.

Christianity was born, recall, among a subjugated people living under Roman rule. This created an ambivalence to secular authority which is evident in the New Testament itself. For some, the Roman authorities were to be obeyed (Romans 13:1–7, 1 Peter 2:13–17.), for others they were thought to be or to have become idolatrous (Revelation 17). There is little reason to doubt that Jesus was a pacifist or that the Early Church was effectively the same. However, Roman soldiers were not apparently expected to give up their occupation on conversion to Christianity. For reasons such as this, it is now recognised that the emergent Christian Church was not as universally pacifist as it was once thought to be. It was simply not a prominent issue for a communities living as they were forced to do under unchallengeable rule. The Roman authorities were all powerful and that was that. This power was awesomely demonstrated when the Jewish Revolt was put down ruthlessly in 66 CE. The prevailing mood among the Christian communities was represented by St Paul who possessed citizenship of both Tarsus and Rome and who believed that the civil authorities were ministers of divine authority. Christians paid their taxes to Rome in the knowledge that Jesus approved this (Mark 12:17). Things were, however, to change dramatically as Christianity spread geographically. That mainly came with conversion of the Emperor Constantine in 312 CE. Christianity then became the religion of the State. Constantine established a new capital of the empire at Byzantium, which then became Constantinople. The question of the moral acceptability, or otherwise, from a Christian point of view of the controlled use of force by the state could no longer go unanswered. Citizens had to be defended from constant external threats such as that which was soon enough to bring Rome down at the hands of the Goths in 412 CE. Two contemporary Christian thinkers addressed this problem. They were Ambrose of Milan and, influentially, St Augustine in whose conversion to Christianity Ambrose played a major role. Ambrose became Bishop of Milan by popular acclamation in 374 CE having previously been a civil governor. He established a principle which still retains its influence in the understanding of Church/state relationships. This was that Churches were independent of or, more controversially, above state rule and that the actions of states were subject to their stricture. The lasting effect of that was the establishment of the fact that states could no longer exercise war beyond the purview of Christian morality. However, by the fourth century some Christians had come to accept the, however regrettable, necessity of some wars. What they now had to do was to find ways of distinguishing between those which were just and those not. Both Ambrose and Augustine set out to achieve this by seeking to reconcile Old Testament understandings of war as an instrument of divine justice with approaches to war in classical antiquity, both Roman and Greek. In this way, Christians joined the by then already centuries old debate about the justice of war.[20] This still continues, as it must, given that the world is as it is. It is motivated by the recognition that (a) there are some states of affairs that are worse than war and (b) that limited warfare can be used to achieve peace.

In this way, the fifth century marked the formal break of mainstream Christianity from its pacifist past. Not all Christians even then agreed with this and the pacifist tradition continued as it does to the present. Some still hold with conviction that their Christian faith requires them to eschew all violence. Two Christian churches make this the centre of their spirituality. They are the Quakers and the Mennonites. They are the so-called historic Peace Churches. Christian pacifists have often distinguished themselves by serving in battlefields in non-combat roles such as the medical corps. Many Quakers also remain prominent in contemporary debates about war and peace. In these ways they bring an important aspect of Christianity to bear on conflict and the ongoing debate about it. Without them the Christian pursuit of peace would be immeasurably impoverished. Other Christians who reject their views, need to do so with respect for them. This is, simply, because to be a non-pacifist Christian is a very serious undertaking. This is why Christians have long been involved in wider debate about the morality of war. It is called Just War theory and is in two parts. First those concerning the morality and manner of its engagement, the *Jus ad bellum*, and second those concerning its conduct once it is engaged, the *Jus in bello*. The development of the theory has spanned the centuries as the available means of warfare changed, as did the circumstances in which it was used. Wars, it generally holds: must only be fought in a just cause, by legally constituted authorities, as a matter of last resort, after a formal declaration, and with a reasonable hope of success. The means used in them must be proportionate to desired ends and they must also be directed towards military and not civilian targets. The discussion of all this in the Christian tradition is as lively as it has ever been. In the last century it made major contributions to the formulation of international rules of warfare.[21] It then also made major contributions to thinking about the morality or otherwise of deploying nuclear weapons as deterrents to war. The modern Christian literature on this is literally vast.

The debate about Christianity and war is a lively as it ever was. A central issue now is whether or not the Just War tradition can be developed so that pre-emptive military intervention against aggressors could be considered to be just. I have recently argued elsewhere that the traditional two parts of the Just war theory, the *jus ad bellum* and the *jus in bello* now need to be extended to include two more. The first of these is the *jus post bello*, which requires as a matter of moral obligation that before war is engaged provision for its cessation by negotiation has to be in place. The second is the *jus in pace* which requires that plans for the restoration of civil society also have to be in place before engagement.[22]

This passing mention of the Christian just war tradition and of the extent of its application to questions of modern war fighting has been necessary for our purpose. It shows that the engagement of a religion like Christianity with war is at least ambivalent. Whereas it can sometimes be seen to be a cause of war, it can equally be seen to be a sustained restraint on it. For those who accept the regrettable necessity of some wars, i.e. those who are not pacifists, the Christian tradition is as good and probably a better position than most others from which to think these issues through. Christian Churches and individual Christian writers are constantly engaged with these and similar issues. Were it not for all this, it is at least possible that the world would long have been in a more sorry state than it now is.

These are great matters. Human beings, as never before, need to live together in peace. They are their own greatest impediment to that ever happening. The greatest, that is, threat to their own survival. To be fully human in the face of all this is to want to do something effectively about it. Religion in general and Christianity in the ways we have considered clearly enable us to do that.

The Environment

Judaism and Christianity traditionally share similar views about the environment. Accordingly, they hold that it was created by God to serve God's own good purposes and that it is self-sustaining to that end. They are now having to reconsider this view because it is abundantly self-evident that the natural environment is an extremely vulnerable one.

Awareness of the extreme vulnerability of the natural order did not come to prominence until the last half of the last century. It is now so widespread that it is sometimes difficult to remember how recent all this actually is. Some identify its origin in the reactions to the dramatic photographs of the earth from outer space which were relayed by manned space flight. For the first time the earth could be seen as a tiny oasis in infinity. These perceptions of its very uniqueness and miniscule size brought the realisation of its vulnerability to mass attention. Acute global environmental concern is, therefore, a modern phenomenon. Public awareness of this has never been greater and for this reason environmentalism has become newsworthy and politicised.

It is widely assumed that the main threat to environmental sustainability comes from the pollution caused by human life-styles. The extent to which this is actually the case, however, remains open to lively and important scientific debate. The evidence is sometimes equivocal. Is the ozone layer really depleting? Are the oceans really warming up? Is modern global climatic change really beyond the scale of anything that has happened before? These and other such questions dominate our daily environmental preoccupations. This is compounded with issues about economic growth and the manner of its control in developed and undeveloped nations alike. Can or should economies afford the huge costs of emission controls now being contemplated. Even allowing for all this, however, it remains incontrovertible that climate change is an issue of our time. This change is also on a vast scale. It is also seemingly uncontrollable. International efforts such as the Kyoto Protocols do try to do something about it, but they run into repeated difficulties.

If it is true that we now live in ways which are counterproductive of our well-being and probably long-term survival, what has made us do this? Why have we become so stupid? Some reply to these questions by pointing to the Industrial Revolution of the eighteenth century. This clearly has something and possibly a lot to do with it. New methods of mass production required the consumption of fossil fuel on a scale never seen before. Coal had to be transported in vast quantities. The canal system in the UK initially came into being to enable this. In 1760 the Duke of Bridgewater created an underground canal link between his mines in Worsley and the centre of Manchester where it was consumed in vast quantities. Industry was never to be the same again. Vast carbon and mineral extraction is now practised world-wide. Need for energy is now largely met by market forces. Its unlimited supply came to be and still largely is, taken for granted. Energy conservation is in its infancy and shows little sign of being taken seriously on an international scale. A few worthy individuals leading pioneering lifestyles in Earth Centres and suchlike are light years away from attracting little more than curious tourist attention. Finding alternative forms of energy to fossil energy is also not being taken seriously on the scale necessary for it to make a difference. Fissile nuclear energy has the capacity at least to be exceedingly dangerous. The extreme vulnerability of some of the reactors in the Japanese earthquake is already causing a rethink about the design of future reactors as well as, some say, about the advisability of building any more anywhere at all. The problem of what to do with nuclear waste from reactors refuses to go away. It remains unresolved as stockpiles of waste such as plutonium increase. In spite of all this, fissile nuclear energy, when it works properly, is not so atmospherically polluting as are carbon alternatives. The safer fusion alternative is as scientifically elusive as ever. It does not create significant nuclear waste. But, as yet, it can only be generated in miniscule quantities The world is facing an escalating energy crisis.

Why have we come to disregard the vulnerability our relationship to the natural order as we have done? Why are we so seemingly incapable of changing our ways? Is there something deeply flawed in our natures which causes all this? Some would say yes, there is. It began, they add, with the Judaeo/Christian tradition and has had such widespread effect because of the influence of that tradition on Western culture. Here as elsewhere, in ways we have been noticing throughout, the stories of this tradition have made us in the West largely what we are, whether we think of ourselves as being religious or not. These great stories live on in their own right in secular guise. All this, it is argued, is what has happened to our attitude towards the natural order.

Recall, that there are two creation stories in the Book of Genesis. The earliest of these, by some three centuries, is Genesis 2:4b. It tells the story, not only of creation but also of the fate of the first humans Adam and Eve. Of how and why they fell from living in a state of blissful grace in the Garden of Eden to the often wretchedness of a lot which has been recognised and experienced by human beings ever since. This is an incredible drama which explains not only creation but also why the human condition is as it now is. Its later corollary Genesis 1:1–2:4a, is less ambitious. It only tells the story of creation! Humans, male and female, are created in the image of God as the pinnacle of the created order (Genesis 1:26). They are then immediately given 'dominion over the fish of the sea, and over the birds of the air and over the cattle, and over all the earth, and over every creeping thing that creeps upon the earth'. In short, over everything. In the second Genesis account of creation 'man' is created first, then the rest of the created order. God brought all created beings to the man for him to name them, and therefore have dominion over them. Only after that was woman created out of the rib of the male. 'And the man and the woman were both naked and were not ashamed' (Genesis 2:25). There are fascinating reasons for the differences and similarities of these two accounts of creation. For our purpose, we only need notice that in both accounts human beings are equally emphatically given dominion over the natural order.

The underlying effect of all this has been an understanding which separates human nature from nature in the Judaeo/Christian tradition and, more widely, in Western culture. This understanding, alone, has been enough for some to conclude that it is the reason why humans have considered their personal well-being to be independent of that of the natural order. The reason, that is, why the Judaeo/Christian religion lies behind the abandon with which Western culture has exploited nature. As one would expect of such a serious charge this has been rebutted.[23] It is pointed out that although they were given dominion over nature, humans were also given strict responsibility for it as its stewards. They were therefore to care for it as well as use it for their own interests.

Whatever view we take, there remains at least a strong possibility that the Judaeo/Christian tradition has unhelpfully had something to do with the separation of our understanding of nature and human nature in Western culture. It certainly looks as though this culture has failed to exercise the necessary care for the natural order in the face of its incessant exploitation. It is, of course, extremely unlikely that the Judaeo/Christian bifurcating view of nature and human nature is the only source of environmental problems in Western culture. However, it needs to address the extent to which, to some extent or other, it has been and still is one of them.

Society

Religion is, clearly, a common source of social cohesion, but it is also a common one of social division. In some instances it often looks like its sole cause and in others it seems all too ready to identify with causes of such division which come from elsewhere. This is increasingly problematic for the simple reason that multicultural societies are becoming the norm in the world's democracies. People of different religions and none are increasingly required to live alongside each other in peace and to each others' mutual benefit. Multicultural societies are now so common that 'multiculturalism' has for decades been promoted as an intrinsic virtue. It is treated as such, for example, in educational programmes for the young as well as in many national and local political initiatives. Multicultural societies have much to commend them. Their members invariably get on well with each other even across marked ethnic and religious divisions. Many individuals and groups dedicate themselves to achieving this. Their successes are often lost sight of when problems occur. Little wonder that multiculturalism has become something of a mantra in liberal democracies. However, for all its apparent wisdom and success, it is bedevilled by a serious flaw. It often encourages the too ready recognition of difference between ethnic and religious groups. Moreover, it invariably does this in ways which create the impression that such difference-recognition is, in turn, intrinsically virtuous. This constant recognition and celebration of difference can be dangerous. It takes difference so much for granted that it seems to encourage it, often without further reflection. Its repeated emphases on the differences between people, is often made to the neglect of noticing the equally important and greater, similarities between them. This creates an ambience in which social and religious division can be perpetuated in the name of virtue. This is why many now think that we need to rethink popular assumptions about multiculturalism. In its place we need a focus on the far greater extent to which human beings are fundamentally alike whatever and this is the point, their religious and other differences may be. Alike, that is in their basic needs and aspirations. However, religions, in general, will not find this mono-culturalism as conducive as multiculturalism for the simple reason that they have invariably found it convenient to allow cultural difference-recognition to act as a cloak for perpetuating their unexamined deeper religious differences.

All this impinges, for example, upon debates about education. The German Chancellor, Angela Merkel, claims that denominational education has failed in modern Germany because it has discouraged the recognition of levels of common identity which are essential to nation building. Debates about segregated primary and secondary education invariably make the same point. Denominational primary and secondary schooling, in the UK for example, is invariably so successful according to secular criteria that there is a demand-driven need for its increased provision. This has been acknowledged by the government. However, many people now feel that it is inappropriate to segregate the young into religious and denominational schools regardless of how successful those schools might be. The call for them to be abolished in Northern Ireland in the interest of social cohesion is a poignant example of this. Non-denominational schools play a crucial role in the inculcation of ethnic and religious toleration and respect in communities which are otherwise segregated. In some inner city areas such schools are the only significant place where children can come together unhindered by difference recognition in the rest of their lives. They often live, for example, in streets which are effectively separate ghettos. Such schools therefore play a vital role in creating social cohesion. In general, it may be observed that denominational schools work well enough in secular communities where religious and cultural toleration is already well and widely established. Where it is not, unless they are skilfully managed they can but serve to exacerbate that toleration.

In this chapter we have looked briefly at some of the historical, political, environmental, and social problems of religion. In each case we have found religion wanting to some degree. Where it has wanted most, is where it most parades as the justification of group self interest. This is where it needs most revision. It is the continuing nub of the Arab/Israeli conflict just as it was and regrettably still among some dissident minorities in Northern Ireland. Religions like Judaism, Christianity and Islam make their most constructive contributions to healing social divisions whenever they re-mine their own traditions to bring to the fore their capacities for repentance and forgiveness rather than those leading to separation and self-justification. Unless they do this so much of what they stand for will remain unacceptable in the eyes of many, including many of their own faithful.

To the extent in which the religions and denominations are complicit in perpetuating social divisions they have much to answer for which is not to their credit. Unless they amend this, the wider contributions they can and must make to the common good will be frustrated and even lost. Before we explore these more fully, we need to consider other ways in which Christianity, in particular, needs to adjust to modernity. By comparison with those we have considered in this chapter, they will appear somewhat abstract. They are, however, no less important for that reason.

CHAPTER FOUR

The Problems of Religion (2): God, God Incarnate, Christian Uniqueness, Evil

In the last chapter we discussed problems which were actual rather than abstract. They all had to do with issues which affect our understanding of history, providence, war, the environment and society. In this chapter we will discuss more abstract, but no less important, problems; God, God incarnate and Christian Uniqueness. We will also discuss the problem of evil and this will also require some abstract reflections. All these topics are central to a religion like Christianity. If we live by them they can be among the most important things which affect our lives. They are often what we take for granted. They motivate and control our wider thoughts, both consciously and unconsciously. Indeed, when they are unconscious they are invariably the more influential. This is because, in this mode, their immense influence is unchecked. In general, orderly life would be impossible without some such central ideas. We all need some of them to live by whether we are religious or not. The subject of philosophy is so interesting because, amongst other things, it is the discipline of identifying and analysing such ideas. It is the oldest of all the academic disciplines. Its most formative early period in Western culture coincided with the Greek empires. The names of Socrates, Plato and Aristotle are, of course, central. It has often been speculated that individually we are all instinctively either Platonists or Aristotelians. This is because we either think with Plato that the world beyond our perceptions is the most important one, or with Aristotle, that what we immediately perceive is the most important.

These opening remarks will, of course, have been unnecessary for any at all familiar with philosophy and its history. Those of us who are, however, always need to be aware that there are many otherwise educated and intelligent people to whom this does not apply. For one reason or another, they simply have not had the opportunity of even minimal formal philosophical education and never seen the need for it. This does not mean that they cannot think philosophically, or that they cannot do so with considerable success, some of them noticeably so. Most people have innate philosophical abilities which they exercise all the time often without realising it.

God

The concept of and belief in a being who is responsible in some way for the existence of all that there is and for the manner of that existence, is common to Judaeo, Christian and Islamic religion. Everything that exists is dependent on this being. In sharp contrast to finite existence, such a being is thought to be infinite, all knowing and all powerful.

This immediately gives rise to a central question in theism: namely, how can creatures who are finite have *any knowledge at all* of a creator who is not? Some claim that the very essence of religion focusses on knowing God as God is, fully and completely. Others, who find this an impossible notion (how can finite creatures ever know what an infinite one is like) often claim that it is, however, possible, by whatever means, to have a partial knowledge of God. Those who claim the former have often been incensed by this more limited claim. The issue in the UK, for example, in the mid-nineteenth century which filled most pages of popular print was not between Darwinists and others, it was precisely between two groups of believers who were divided on this very issue.[1] It remains central to our understanding of religious belief and often lies behind differences which are seemingly about other things such as morality.

The God of the Jewish Bible is an awesome figure. This God of the earliest biblical writers and of Moses created all that there is, chose Israel as God's favoured people and steered their destiny through the vagaries of history. This God chastised when necessary, engaged in battles and, in the law, provided all the life-style guidance Israel ever needed. The belief that this was and still is the case is central to Jewish thinking.

Christians inherited much of this. They too were preoccupied with wanting to fulfil God's will in every aspect of their lives. Jesus was repeatedly asked about his attitude to the law and famously replied by giving what came to be known as his Great Commandment. '...you shall love the Lord your God with all your heart and with all your soul and with all your mind and with all your strength' (Mark 12:28, Matthew 22:34–40). St Paul addressed this issue as one of the main themes in his rapidly emerging new Christian theology. Justification, he insisted, was no longer by the law. It was now to be by faith alone. This made possible living the Christian life as a 'New Being' (Galatians 6:15). This was now sufficient for all the practical purposes of daily living in place of the law.

Jesus was called, among many other things, the 'son' of God. This phrase had been used in the Hebrew Bible, but usually to refer to the whole people of Israel. Whilst Jesus did not seem to favour this designation of himself, it was used of him by others. In this they were probably influenced by the concept in the Hebrew Bible as well as later by the use of the term in Greek religion. In addition, of course, Jesus spoke of God as his 'Father'. In so doing he created the possibility of an immediacy and an intimacy in the relationship with God which was in contrast to that found in the Hebrew Bible. The earliest Christians also had a concept of the Spirit of God and they used this centrally to explain the phenomenon of the incredible growth of Christianity after Pentecost. These three conceptions of God, Father Son and Spirit, were not thought about relationally in the earliest Christian writings. The later doctrine of the Trinity, of God as Father Son and Holy Spirit, is only found in one place in the Christian Bible (Matt. 28:19). If it was as important in the earliest Christian thinking, as we have seen, then more frequent such mention would have been expected. In fact, even the Matthew reference might well be a later interpolation. The idea that these three persons were separate but related manifestations of one Godhead worked itself out as we have seen in the developing creedal formulations of early Christianity.

The later Christian doctrine of God was, however, as derived from Greek philosophy as it was from the Jewish Bible and from the earliest Christian experiences. This came to the fore in Christian tradition towards the end of the second century as the Roman Empire was declining. At this time, the works of Christian teachers who were cognizant of Greek philosophy were becoming increasingly influential. These were writers such as Irenaeus, Philo of Alexandria, Clement of Alexandria, magisterially St Augustine and others. In their several ways they brought together the conceptions of God in the biblical traditions with the philosophies of Plato, Aristotle and others. The subsequent Christian conception of God is therefore, the result of a breathtaking synthesis of ideas. This does not, of course, necessarily count against it. On the contrary, it shows the remarkable ability in Christian history and thought to assimilate all that is best from wherever it comes. In the so-called centuries of Christendom (however they are counted) there was broad agreement between the Christian and the secular philosophical understanding of God. Everyone seemingly knew that God was: one, eternal, unchanging, perfect and good. Classical philosophical arguments to defend all this and more about God, elicited near universal agreement. They divided roughly into those which claimed that God existed of necessity and those which, largely after Aristotle, saw God as the Prime Mover, or first cause of all that exists. St Anselm of Canterbury championed the former with the famous so-called, 'Ontological Argument' for God's existence. This, from the Greek word for *ontos*, 'being', claimed that God could not not exist. The double negative is central to the argument. As the most perfect being God had to exist because if an even more perfect being existed that being would be God. And so on. St Thomas Aquinas famously formulated this view into the last two of his seminal five arguments for the existence of God. The first three were all versions of Aristotle's view mentioned above.[2]

All his meant that theism was the predominant religious idea in Western culture for some fifteen hundred years. Christian thinkers played the main part in achieving this. Their stupendous success is an immense credit to their creativity. As we have seen, this focussed mainly on their ability to fuse all that was biblical with all that was of other, particularly Greek, origin. This was the bedrock of everything that was thought and

The Problems of Religion (2)

written about God. That it effectively remained unchallenged for so long is something almost incomprehensible to modern people who are used to and even thrive on the constant analysis of our central intellectual ideas. The first major challenge to it came at the end of the eighteenth century from the pens of the Scottish empiricist philosopher David Hume and, after him, from the German Idealist philosopher Immanuel Kant. This challenge was and remains so seminal that latter-day theists can broadly be divided into those who think that the Humean/Kantian challenges were unsuccessful and that the classical tradition therefore survives and those who think that they did succeed and that theism, therefore, has to be either reconstructed or abandoned.

David Hume (1711–1776) was a historian and radical empiricist philosopher. That is to say, that he focussed his attention only on those truths which could be verified in sense experience. In this he was taking the work of previous empiricist philosophers such as Locke and Berkeley and pushing it to more radical conclusions. His *Treatise on Human Nature* of 1739 discusses the understanding, the passions and morality. His *Natural History of Religion* (1757) approached religion anthropologically. His *Dialogues Concerning Natural Religion* were published, at his request, posthumously in 1779.

Hume's philosophy is in part an attack on the fact that, in his view, philosophy had for too long been accepting of metaphysical assumptions which were based only on custom and habit. These assumptions, he held, do not exist in themselves of necessity. Such necessity, he repeatedly insisted, exits only in the mind. In his understanding of the latter, he made a distinction between 'impressions' and 'ideas'. Impressions create ideas which faintly resemble them. Ideas are simple. They can be verified in sense experience. When ideas become complex they fuel the imagination. This, in its turn, creates ideas which have no basis in impressions, or sense experience at all. These complex ideas, such as that of causation, are nothing but figments of our imagination. They serve no purpose other than to mislead us. Another such misleading idea is the idea of God. Hume also applied this radically empirical philosophy to the notion of the 'self'. His conclusion was that, like causation, we can have no actual knowledge of it. Of the self we have only fleeting impressions which do not correspond to simple ideas which can be verified in actual sense experience. Therefore, the 'self' does not actually exist. Hume said the ideas of 'causation' and 'self' only exist in the mind. From the impressions of contiguity and succession we cannot construct the idea of either. If we do we are turning such ideas into something complex and, again, imaginary.

Two reactions are usually made to all this. One sees it as the absurd reduction of empiricism to nonsense. Of course we know that we exist as 'selves' and of course we know that it is part of the nature of things that A 'causes' B. The other reaction, however reluctantly, respects the fact that Hume's scepticism is making an important point. It is the point that whilst we can in reality never totally prevent ourselves from making assumptions and exercising them as beliefs, we should, nevertheless, do everything we can to limit them when we are in the pursuit of true knowledge. Since so many areas of life and thought were dominated by such assumptions there was plenty of scope for the application of this new method. One such area was that of religion. Hume, as we have seen, began to do this himself.

He wrote his famous *Essay on Miracles* when a young man, but it was not published until 1757 as part of the first of his philosophical *Enquiries*. At the time it was commonly held that the existence of miracles alone validated the other claims of Christianity. This view, of course, continues to be held by many Christians. Hume simply pointed out that a wise man should proportion his belief to the evidence. Miracles are a purported violation of the laws of nature. We have such detailed evidence of the operation of those laws that it must always preponderate over claims that they have been violated. He wrote: 'no testimony is sufficient to establish a miracle, unless the testimony be of such a kind that its falsehood would be more miraculous than the fact which it endeavours to establish.'[3] The real point being made here is not about whether or not miracles happen. It is about the prior fact that we should not too readily accept that they do on spurious grounds.

The main force of Hume's criticism of religion, however, came with the publication of his *Dialogues*. These conclude that whilst there is seeming evidence of design in the universe which is analogous to designs produced by human intelligence, it is not sufficiently unambiguous for us to conclude that the universe was designed by a being of supreme intelligence. One of the main reasons for this is because of the abundance of our observations that force us to conclude that much of the universe is dysfunctional. Tennyson famously made the point in his *In Memoriam* in 1850 when he observed that nature was 'red in tooth and claw'.[4]

We might well want to draw back from the extremes of Hume's scepticism. Indeed, he might well have wanted to do so himself. It, nevertheless, serves to remind us, at the very least, that we cannot base our ideas about something as important as religion on sloppy thinking.

Immanuel Kant (1724–1804) said in his *Critique of Pure Reason* (1794), the first of his three such works, that David Hume had awoken him from his 'dogmatic slumbers'.[5] As a result, Kant wrote his most important works, the critical ones, towards the end of his life. Their influence on subsequent philosophy has been and still is immense. He claimed that there was need for a 'Copernican revolution' in philosophy. In this we should not as hitherto, try to make our minds conform to the 'objects' of our knowledge. By doing this, he reminds us, we did not make any real progress anyway. We should, rather, make such objects conform to our minds. In other words, philosophy and knowledge should begin with the knower rather than with what is known. After Hume, Kant claimed that this should not transgress the categories of what can be known through sense experience. The admonition of Hume is here strictly acknowledged. Kant concluded that such metaphysical speculation, 'is a completely isolated speculative science of reason which soars far above the teachings of experience'.[6] We cannot, therefore, have any real knowledge of 'things-in-themselves'. The noumenal world of things-in-themselves cannot be accessed from the phenomenal one of sense experience. In this first *Critique*, Kant famously criticises the classical Five Arguments for God's existence. He began by pointing out that 'existence' is not a predicate. It is derived from the subjects it is predicated upon. Rather like saying that a ball is 'round'. It adds nothing to our perception on the ball. He then claimed that God's existence cannot be said to be necessary, because we cannot infer that God is a first cause from our observations of causation.

The three *Critiques* are based on Kant's extremely popular lectures at the University of Konisberg. One reason for this popularity is undoubtedly because they contain a great deal of irony and humour. He mused, for example, that we could no more make God exist by believing than we could add to our real wealth by adding noughts to our bank accounts. Kant was, however, far from being anti-religious. He did as much to set out good arguments for religion as he did to destroy the bad ones.

This brief discursus into the impact on traditional forms of theism and other religious beliefs by the philosophies of David Hume and Immanuel Kant has been necessary because they both still have an important impact on the way religion can be thought of in the modern word.

The existence of God is now for many, to say the least, no longer thought to be rationally self-evident in the way it was thought to have been for about a millennium and a half. The problem is that such a belief in God's existence is still often presented as the central test of whether one is a religious believer or not. Bishops have even been known to sack clergy unless they state categorically (that is to the Bishops' liking) that they do believe in God's existence. When this happens the fact that the notions of 'belief in' and 'existence' are hugely problematic in themselves hardly gets a look in. The plain facts, that some people believe in God but are not particularly religious and the corollary, that some people are religious but do not explicitly believe in God, at least to the satisfaction of some Bishops, further complicates the issue.

There is more to religion that 'believing' in God's 'existence' or not. This can be discovered by thinking much more creatively about the role 'God' plays in understanding and practising the religious life. That life is perfectly compatible with an open mindedness, to say the least, about the exact manner of the existence of such of a God. Ever since Thomas H. Huxley coined the term in 1869 this view has been described as 'agnosticism'.[7] This does not deny or affirm God's existence as such, it simply concludes a healthy 'don't know'. The grounds for disbelief, on this view, are no better than those for belief.

There are, of course, those who disagree with this and who still maintain that the arguments for God's existence are as rationally self-evident as they ever were. Several modern attempts have been made to understand God in such rational ways. For example, Charles Hartshorne, following the philosopher A.N. Whitehead, developed a belief in God as a process and this gave its name to a whole theology. Others such as Alvin Plantinga

The Problems of Religion (2)

have argued that belief in God is a 'basic belief' which does not require rational justification as such. He based this argument on the argument that belief in God is as rational as belief in other minds.[8] There are many other such attempts. In complete contrast, some American theologians in the 1960s even celebrated the 'death of God' as a religious triumph. Only in this way, they argued, can the immanence of religious truths be discovered 'an immanence dissolving even the memory or the shadow of transcendence'.[9] All this shocked many traditional religious believers, particularly ecclesiastics. One American Methodist Bishop, Gerald Kennedy, said that theologians who believe this should not take money for their work from Christian churches. The death of God movement did not last. (Perhaps it did run out of money!) It was, however symptomatic, at least, of a wider excitement about understanding religion in new ways. Much of this was inspired by Dietrich Bonhoeffer's theology with its concept of 'religion less Christianity'.[10] The then Bishop of Woolwich, John Robinson, caused a considerable stir in 1963 when he published a small book entitled *Honest to God*.[11] This might have been yet another largely unnoticed book about religion were it not for the fact that a newspaper article carried a piece on it entitled 'Our Image of God Must Go'. The book then became an instant bestseller. It opened up the possibility of serious religious belief to a whole new generation in the 1960s. Here, in brief, was an approach to religion which did not require intellectual suicide. It both understood and took seriously genuine concerns people had about the intellectual integrity of Christianity. In responding to them, Robinson showed that religious orthodoxy was not always sacrosanct and that it often needs to be redefined. The redefinitions he offered were widely appreciated and were central to the book's popularity. It is salutary to note that all this put him somewhat at odds with the establishment of the Church of England. He never received further Episcopal preferment. Some informally note that this might have caused him subsequent discomfort. When the ecclesiastical history of this period is more fully understood, this might be interpreted as yet another sign of the progressive abandonment of intellectual integrity the by Church of England establishment.

The debate about God never, of course, stops. What it does, as we have seen, is change over the years. Versions of theism come and go according to prevailing intellectual outlooks. There is one, however, which has came out of the post-Kantian criticism of traditional rational theism in the nineteenth century and which still powerfully survives. This calls attention away from the 'being' or 'existence' or whatever of God, to the way in which the knowledge of God functions in human life. We will look at it in detail and favourably as we proceed.

Being religious, or not, is clearly not synonymous with believing in God or not. Unless that is, you might be an unfortunate clergyman on the mat in an unfavourable Bishop's study. There are ways of avoiding that. The mat that is! Being religious is quite compatible with joining this debate with an open and even a sceptical mind. In fact, doing just that can itself be a liberating religious experience. Just, as we have seen, *Honest to God* so refreshingly demonstrated at its time.

God Incarnate

In different ways the New Testament claims that God is 'revealed' in the life, teaching, death and resurrection of Jesus. Most explicitly, it claims that this is because Jesus is described as the 'Son of God' (e.g. John 3:17). This is nothing less than the claim that the God whom we cannot see became incarnate in the human one that we can, or at least the first Christians did. Different New Testament writers put this in their own ways. The Gospel of John is most explicit. 'No one has ever seen God; the only Son, who is in the bosom of the Father, he has made him known' (John1:18). Throughout the same Gospel this theme is reworked. Jesus is explicitly quoted as having said that, '...no one comes to that Father except by me' (John 14:6). This Gospel is generally not thought to portray the historical Jesus as closely as the other three, but it has an immense influence on mainstream Christian belief. It does much to sustain the belief that Jesus reveals God in a unique way. So understood, Jesus is believed to be totally different from all other religious figures because he achieved something, or something more fully, than any of them have ever been able to do. This is because on this view

God became incarnate in his person as in no other. There can be little doubt that this is precisely what the vast majority of Christians believe. So many of them, when pressed, really do believe that *their* knowledge of God in Christ is different from and more complete than *any* other knowledge of God whatsoever. Anyone in the Christian tradition with the temerity to even question this, particularly a Clergyman, risks re-acquaintance with the afore mentioned mat!

The implications of the belief that Jesus was a semi-divine being gradually emerged in the early centuries of the life of the Church. It created an obvious problem. Was Jesus primarily man or primarily God? If he was primarily man, then in what sense was he also God? And if he was primarily God then in what sense was he man? This was a serious problem. The Church gave it an immense amount of attention. The truth is that it never solved it. In the end it settled for a political solution. The view of the majority prevailed. Belief in the equal humanity and divinity of Jesus became Christian orthodoxy. This was established at the great Council at Chalcedon in 451CE. It affirmed the view of earlier Councils which were held at Nicea and Constantinople. This was, in short, that the human and divine natures in Christ were indivisibly united. It also insisted that, for this reason, Mary must be referred to as the mother of God. The Council did not state exactly how these natures were united. It just affirmed that they were. In doing this it hoped that disagreement and dissention in the matter would cease. Of course, it did not, has not and will never do so.

The breathtaking claim that Jesus was the 'son of God', in whom two natures fully existed, gives Christianity nothing less than a colossal spiritual arrogance. It is based on a construct of his person which is far removed from much of what can be read about him in the New Testament. There was an implicit reason why the Church made this claim. It was the basis for its rivalry with Judaism. Jesus, the Messiah had fulfilled and eclipsed Jewish expectation. With this claim the makeover of the historical Jesus was complete. The extent of our historical knowledge of Jesus has long been debated and was the subject of much controversy in the second half of the last century. Some scholars, such as Rudolph Bultmann, then claimed that we could learn hardly anything about the historical Jesus from the New Testament because everything we read there is about the Christ in whom people believed.[12] This provoked a huge debate In reaction, one of his pupils retorted with the reply that 'the Christ of faith is brim full of history'.[13]

This debate continues. In 1991 the American biblical scholar John D. Crossan concluded that Jesus was a 'Peasant Jewish Cynic'.[14] This view is based on New Testament scholarship which draws attention to the fact that the four Gospels are interpretations of the ministry of Jesus from different points of view. They are not dispassionate historical records. Whilst they overlap in much of their content, their writers pursue their own interests and purposes. They do this, moreover, without always feeling bound by each other. This recent Jesus scholarship has endeavoured to push back through these records to see what we can learn about what Jesus was actually like. He was, most assuredly, not like the famous nineteenth century portrait of him by Holman Hunt. This painting, entitled *The Light of the World*, shows him as a strikingly composed figure in a white gown with an immaculate beard holding a lantern. Though a striking piece of romantic art, it is but a figment of the pious imagination. In stark contrast, the historical Jesus was a very strange figure. He did not conform to the conventions of his age and upset numerous groups of people as a result, particularly groups of religious people. In calling him a Peasant Cynic, Crossan is calling attention to the fact that Jesus delivered his message in simple everyday language and in open spaces. He did this among ordinary people with whom he often ate and carried out healing in the manner of the time. He also preached a radically economic and cultural egalitarianism which was an affront to the established religious and other authorities. Even more controversially, he pointed to sinners and outcasts as often being exemplars of God's kingdom. His message was about the immediate availability of a relationship to God amid the circumstances of everyday life. The words 'cynic' and 'egalitarian' are, therefore, extremely appropriate. This is certainly not what one would expect a semi-divine being to be like. The earthiness of it all is of its essence. The later Christian orthodox picture of Jesus is therefore very different. Perhaps it is also even unrecognisable. It came about, as we have stressed, simply because the Christian Church in its earliest centuries was preoccupied with the construction of a power narrative about Jesus which would match and trump the older Jewish claims to a knowledge of God. This was an understandable thing for them to do under the circumstances. As we have seen, however, it created problems of its own. The wider Christian Church has still not solved them and, regrettably, often ignores the very scholarship which addresses it.

The Christian claim to have a *unique* relationship to God in Jesus as a semi-divine being is, therefore, not supported by recent Jesus scholarship. The claim is unacceptable because it is based on an elaborate construct of the person of Jesus. It is just as unacceptable as the older Jewish claim about *their* unique relationship to God. Most Christians, sadly, choose to ignore modern scholarship and retain their traditional beliefs in spite of it. But, as we have seen, they are based on nothing but a centuries old political consensus of the Church's own making. In a world which is as divided by inter-religious debate and rivalry as it ever was this will not do. Anyone who hears the familiar words from St John's Gospel '...nobody comes to the father except by me' without feeling uncomfortable is either religiously blind or politically profoundly insensitive.

This was importantly discussed in *The Myth of God Incarnate*.[15] In its introduction, Maurice Wiles wrote: '...it is at least worth asking as an alternative possibility whether some concept other than incarnation might better express the divine significance of Jesus that is intended'.[16] In different ways, the essayists show that the view that Jesus was literally God incarnate cannot plausibly be attributed to him. Once, that is, we remember that the fourth Gospel is not a source of historical information about what Jesus actually said and did. Many Christians who want to reject these criticisms, of course, choose not to accept that. In the same volume the Patristic scholar, Frances Young, came to the conclusion that. '...there are strong reasons... for seeing the patristic development and interpretation of incarnational belief, not as a gradual dawning of truth inspired by the Holy Spirit, but as a historically determined development which led to the blind alleys of paradox, logicality and docestism'.[17] (This last word is the name for the view that Jesus really was God and only appeared to be man.) Two important points are being forcefully made here. The first is that, as we have seen, the divinisation of the person of Jesus was an invention of Christian Church in the earliest centuries of its existence. The second is that this is not borne out, as we have also seen, by what we can learn about Jesus from careful study of the New Testament. The language the Church came to use in the early centuries about Jesus was, in fact, mythical and poetic. Its intention was to understand and communicate the person of Jesus in the language and through-forms available to it at the time. It centred, as we have seen, on understanding Jesus as a semi-divine being. This is still presented by the majority of Christians as the only way to understand Jesus. Accepting it is, in effect, often by them made a criterion of Christian orthodoxy. If you do not accept it you cannot, on their view, be a Christian. The myth of God incarnate debate has seriously challenged both the intelligibility and necessity of doing this. It is far from iconoclastic. It still points to the person of Jesus as someone who revealed God in a profound way with lasting significance. Some might find it more helpful than the Church's traditional way of understanding him. Others, might well want to continue to use that understanding but only as mythic and poetic expressions about Jesus. On this view, these need not be taken literally to be helpful. If we do this, however, we will do well always to remember that they are what they are, mythic, and nothing else. They help to *interpret* Jesus' significance for us. They do not depict his earthly person. Indeed, the more we come to know about this the more we might even come to find that very earthiness to be more revealing of God than the later elaborate interpretations.

The scholarly case for these conclusions was well made in *The Myth of God Incarnate*. It has still not been seriously challenged in academic debate. Of course, there have been plenty of protestations in the name of Christian orthodoxy. These, however, have not produced quality replies to the careful argument of *The Myth of God Incarnate*. None, that is, which justify a reconsideration of its conclusions. Moreover, the book has largely been ignored by the wider Church. One recent commentator cites 1977 when *The Myth of God Incarnate* was published as the date from when the Church, in the UK at least, became detached from academic theology.[18] If this judgement is borne out it will prove to be an extremely significant one. Hitherto the Christian Church had invariably been noted for generating theologies which commanded intellectual respect if not, of course, always agreement. Its modern intellectual marginalisation is injurious to its well-being. However, the strictures of *The Myth of God Incarnate* and other such writings can be heeded and we can still call ourselves Christians. This, however, requires that we seriously rethink our understanding of the person of Jesus.

Christian Uniqueness

The Christian orthodox belief that Jesus was a semi-divine being led to another belief that we now do well also to question. It is that of Christian uniqueness. Christians have long believed and the majority of them probably still do, that their knowledge of God in Christ is unique. By this they mean that it is qualitatively different from and superior that knowledge found in other religions. We have come across this belief several times in our discussion already. The reason for that is simply because it is so all pervading in Christian thinking.

The Myth of Christian Uniqueness was published in 1987.[19] It addressed the issue as a corollary to the earlier volume we have just discussed. John Hick Edited that and Co-Edited this later work. He acknowledges that the belief that Christianity contains a unique revelation of God needs to be reconsidered because of 'the discovery of God's saving activity in other streams of human life. The resulting perception is that Christianity is not the one and only way of salvation, but one among several'.[20] He, therefore, acknowledges that the name of God refers 'to the ultimate reality to which, as I conceive, the great religious traditions constitute different religious responses'.[21]

In the same volume Wilfred Cantwell Smith, again and in line with his earlier important work which we have already discussed, goes so far as to describe the Christian belief about its own uniqueness as nothing less than idolatry.[22] By this he means that the belief can now seen to be a fetish. Whereas it might once have been held sincerely and for seemingly good reasons, it now has to be recognised as the spiritual arrogance that it always was. It generated, among other things, patronising attitudes to other religions which can have no place in the modern world. He writes: 'Each "religion" is an "idol" in the best sense of the word, if one were going to use these words at all. Exclusive claims for one's own is idolatry in the pejorative sense'.[23]

It is imperative that Christians acknowledge the veracity these strictures. Once they do they can begin to hold their beliefs with integrity. It will also enable them to have a better understanding of other religions.

All this means that fundamental Christian beliefs about the uniqueness of Christ and the superiority of the Christian religion above all others now have to be rethought. This means, of course, that there is now a discrepancy between what the Church popularly preaches and teaches and what at least some theologians think. One reason for this is because in recent years many of the Christian Churches have become increasingly conservative and reactionary in their outlook. (Some Universities and other places of theological study are following this trend.) Of course, these Churches often have noticeable growth in their membership. There are seemingly plenty of people for whom the certainties they proffer are attractive. In reality, of course, the greater majority of people proverbially vote with their feet. There are, however, a not insignificant number of Churches where more liberal and scholarly views under-gird what is taught and preached.

The notions of God's existence and of the manner of God's supposed self revelation in Jesus are clearly exceedingly problematic. However, there are yet ways of holding to Christian belief and having faith without, and this is the point, committing the sort of intellectual suicide which so much popular Christianity seems to require us to do. The debates about 'God' and about the 'son of God' will not go away. They are both important and deserving of attention by all who seek the reconciliation of religious belief and practice with intellectual integrity.

Evil

Manifestations of evil are as tragically abundant as they ever were. News and pictures of wide-scale human suffering are a daily occurrence.

Evil is, perhaps, whatever causes the deepest suffering and affront to our natural sensibilities. It is what we can scarce bear. It comes from two sources. *Natural* evil clearly originates in the way things are in the created order. Things happen which cause us to suffer and they are not only beyond our control, we also scarce have the ability to predict them. It is just a fact of life which cannot be ignored and has to be faced. It might be logically possible to imagine a utopian world without it, but for all practical purposes it has to be accepted that the world is as it is and that is that. *Moral* evil is another matter. It is committed by human beings who are also capable of doing good. Why do they so often choose otherwise? This is, arguably, the most profound of all questions we can ask of the human condition. An explanation of it would help to save so much human misery and suffering. One has never been produced and shows no sign of ever being so. Explanations of evil, such as theistic ones, are also invariably counterproductive of what they set out to prove. It is inconceivable that God could either allow evil to occur or prevent it from happening. Secular philosophy and Christianity have both wrestled with the problem. We will now see why the first cannot help us and the second can.

Throughout its history, Western secular philosophy has tried to understand evil. Socrates did this by claiming that it was a privation of the good and that no-one ever committed it knowingly. This view holds that goodness could not exist without evil, that each necessitates the other. This was later championed by Plato in *The Republic*. He stressed that evil could, however, be mitigated, if not entirely avoided, by education. This was why, as is there argued, kings should also be philosophers so that they could reign wisely in the pursuit of good and the avoidance of evil.[24] No king, or other such educated person, he believed, would ever knowingly choose to do anything other than good. This is an attractive explanation of evil, but it also seriously flawed for two reasons. First, it presupposes that there is a moral order of goodness which exists metaphysically, somehow, somewhere 'out there' and that human beings can educate themselves about it, by dint of their own efforts. The obvious problem with this is that even if that order exists human knowledge of it is always tainted by the human ignorance which made it necessary in the first place. Therefore, humans can have no knowledge of good as it is in-itself. It follows from this that they can never know if what they are doing is entirely good. Second, this view does not explain why evil is so frequently committed by educated people who clearly should know enough about the good to do it. Evil is so often committed by people who clearly know exactly what they are doing. Whilst this view is right in locating moral evil in human beings, it is wrong in supposing that the problem they have is one of ignorance. The subsequent history of education has, therefore, not unsurprisingly shown that it has done effectively nothing to solve the problem of moral evil, mitigate it though it might. The problem of evil requires another explanation.

Most attempts to explain evil in Western philosophy have also understood it as a privation of good, as Socrates and Plato argued. Some have gone further and claimed that it is an illusion. Spinoza did this.[25] The obvious problem here is that evil could only possibly be even thought to be illusory to observers who do not suffer from it! The thought of explaining to those afflicted by evil that they are suffering from nothing but an illusion is an intellectual pomposity as well as a gross insensitivity. Some other philosophers have tried to avoid this by stressing, again, that evil is a necessity in the sense that without it we could not recognise the good for what it is. Leibniz is famous for putting forward a similar view, claiming that it was 'well-nigh nothing'.[26] The obvious problem here is, however, that it is at least possible to imagine a world where this need not be the case. Good in such a world could simply be what it is, period. Or again, on this view, how much evil needs to exist for the good to be recognised in contrast with it? Surely levels of evil which are far lower than those which exist would equally serve such a purpose. All these philosophical attempts to account for evil; that it is a privation, an illusion or a necessity, fail to explain the reason for it.

More recently, after the horrors of the Second World War, philosophers and others had to address the problem of radical evil. Many of them clearly thought that things had been as bad as they were in the Second World War because individuals had failed to impose their virtue on collectives. The famous Nuremberg trials made a similar assumption by insisting that following the orders of others was no defence against accusations of committing evil acts. The basic problem with this view is, of course, that individuals are as prominent in the cause of evil as are collectives.

Western secular philosophy, for all its labours over the centuries, has not, therefore, even come close to producing an understanding of evil which can be of any practical use. We are left to ask whether or not the Christian religion can do this.

The Problems of Religion (2)

Christianity stridently claims that evil was vanquished in the triumph of Christ on the cross. This victory, it adds, was complete and would last for all time until the future coming of the Kingdom of God. The first difficulty with this view is, of course, that only Christians can know this. Christians, that is, for whom the belief in the triumph over evil by Christ on the cross is central. There were other so-called Gnostic Christians from the second century CE who did not believe in the finality of this triumph. They held, rather, that good and evil still existed in a dualistic tension. Whilst this view had the obvious advantage of explaining the continued presence of evil, Gnostic teaching did not prevail. This was largely because it was widely claimed that it embraced too many teachings from pagan religions. Today, however, few thinking people are easily convinced by the orthodox Christian claim that evil does not exist solely because of the triumph against it by Christ on the cross. There is simply too much evidence to the contrary for this to be credible. (It is tantamount to the denial of its existence by some secular philosophers.) Christian thinking about evil is, therefore, equivocal. At its best, it claims that complete though Christ's triumph was, it will not be self-evidently so until the future coming of God's kingdom. In the meantime, apparent tensions between good and evil remain. This view should not be lightly dismissed. It contains a very real profundity. It counsels against despair in the face of evil and nurtures hope for the human condition.[27]

Evil is a problem for a monotheistic religion like Christianity because of its belief in the righteousness of God. This is the so-called problem of *theodicy*, of God's righteousness. How can a righteous and all powerful God either permit evil in the first place and or then allow it to prevail? Classically, in Christian tradition there have been two responses to this. The first, championed by St Augustine, claims that God did originally create a natural order which was uncorrupted by evil, but which was then corrupted by human disobedience. This is the classic story of Adam and Eve and of their fall from grace in the Garden of Eden. The second, championed by St Irenaeus in the second century, claims that there never was a time of un-corruption and that evil has been part of the God-given natural order from the beginning. The reason for this is because in living with evil, human beings pass through a constant process of 'recapitulation' in which they grow in grace and righteousness. Neither of these mainstream Christian approaches to the problem succeeds in *explaining* evil. The first, because it makes God look impotent in the face of evil and the second, because it makes God look less than righteous. Both, however, contain important insights. The Augustinian, clearly points to the fact that evil has something centrally to do with human corruptibility and the Irenaean to the fact that living with it has to do with human perfectibility. Both of these insights, as we shall see, remain important even though they fail to satisfy as complete explanations of evil. A religion like Christianity cannot, therefore, explain evil any more than secular philosophy can. Other religions cannot do this either. What Christianity can do, however, is to provide the means of confronting evil and coping with it.

Evil is to be endured and lived-with in the most responsible ways we can discover. It is not to be understood. The first step in achieving that is perhaps the most difficult for us of all. It is accepting that it has no explanation. It is just an awesome fact of life. An inextricable part of the human lot. Period. Reconciling ourselves to this is not a form of despair. It is an important realisation. This point is powerfully made in the novel *The Plague* by Albert Camus.[28] It centres on Oran, a small town which is horrifically plagued by rats. The occupants are driven to physical and intellectual distraction. Fr. Paneloux, the priest, preaches two sermons. In the first he explains the plague with seeming confidence. After this things get even worse in the town and he is required to preach again. This time he summons the courage to admit that he has no explanation of the evil. 'My brothers', – the preachers tone showed that he was nearing the conclusion of his sermon, – 'the love of God is a hard love. It demands total self-surrender, disdain of our human personality. And yet it alone can reconcile us to suffering and the deaths of children, it alone can justify them, since we cannot understand it, and we can only make God's will ours. That is the hard lesson I would share with you today'.[29] Movingly, in this powerful story, the priest then dies of the plague, clutching a crucifix and refusing medication. Christians, the sceptical observer in the story observes, are better than they seem. Eventually, the people of the town begin to recover their freedom and dignity and survive. Camus' story still resonates with those who are oppressed. No recovery of the peoples' ability to cope with their plight could even begin until the person most expected to explain why it was all happening, Fr. Paneloux, eventually had the integrity and the courage to admit that he did not know. This eloquent literary insight is as relevant, if not more so, to our situation in the twenty-first century as it was when it was penned in the middle of the last one.

Camus' point was not, of course, a new one. It is prefigured in the Jewish Bible, in the book of Job. Its literary form there is that of a dialogue and its setting in the life of one person, Job, is an analogy of the evils that had best Israel. It addresses the perennial question: why *do* the genuinely righteous suffer? The story forensically exposes the sheer human vanity of those who would try to explain Job's suffering to him. This vanity, note, is not in one whit mitigated by their good intentions. They were sincerely trying help. This was something he could desperately do without. His sufferings were problem enough, without having to cope, in addition, with spurious explanations for them. However, Job's faith in Yahweh remained unflinching. 'Behold, he will slay me; I have no hope; yet I will defend my ways to his face' (Job 13:15). Things could have been otherwise, but they are not and that is that. This is the stuff of tragedy. We only even being to recover our sense of human worth and dignity when we face the tragic for what it awesomely is – a protean fact of life. We have to summon the courage and humility to say that we do not know why this is so. Once we do this, like Fr. Paneloux, we learn not only how to live with evil, but also what we must do about it in this situation or that. This is the secret that Job knew. He trusted God in the face of unbearable losses and knew how he had to continue his life. Any who have suffered such profound personal tragedy, or who have had the privilege of being close to those who have done so, will know the power of this realisation. It is nothing less than the beginning of a hope and the promise of creating a new life.

One recent discussion of the nature of evil which has made this point is D.Z. Phillips's *The Problem of Evil and the Problem of God*.[30] He recognises, as we have done, that Christianity does not put forward an acceptable explanation of evil. What it does do is to offer an understanding of religion as sacrifice, not as a means to a greater end but as an end in itself expressed in the worship of God. In this way evil is not redeemed (whatever that might mean). It is, rather, lived with for what it is: an inexplicable part of the human lot. Phillips claims that, in the Christian tradition, this focusses on the passion of Christ. Of this he writes: 'this shows us what the love of God is, and it is in terms of it that the experiences of those crushed by suffering are to be understood from the perspective of eternity'.[31] In this way, Christianity provides a practical means of coping with suffering, short of explaining it. It joins the suffering of God with human suffering and provides, by the enabling grace of God, the means of enduring it. Any at all familiar with the way in which religious people cope with suffering cannot have escaped to notice this. It is something far more than an explanation of suffering. It is nothing less than a means of grace at the heart of human affairs when and where it is most needed. Moreover, it can be attained through religious beliefs and practices which do not require intellectual incredulity as a precondition of their effectiveness.

All this is a religion like Christianity at its most profound. It is pragmatism at its very best. As we saw at the beginning of Chapter Two, it is primarily what helps us to cope. Cope, first of all with ourselves and then with the world around us in all its complexity. Everything else, all joy and happiness can follows from this. Religion is the area of total human understanding and aspiration which addresses this truth most profoundly of all. Far from being, as many suppose, something at the fringes of understanding what it means to be human, Christianity is at the very heart of it. This is nothing less than a super realism about the human condition, its fulfilment and future. Christianity understands this as nothing less than a cause for thanksgiving and celebration.

So, we now conclude that religion is as profound a source of human wisdom as it ever was. It has its problems, as we have seen. These have to and can be faced in some such ways as we have suggested. What it has always done it still does. It enables us to cope with being human in the face of the most extreme difficulties. It does this with equal profundity at the social as well as at the personal levels of human experience. The need for it is as great as it ever was. Given, moreover, that the fundamentals of human life remain remarkably constant through time and amid different cultures, it is likely to remain ever so. Being religious is nothing less than the pursuit of being fully human in the most profound way available to us.

The Problems of Religion (2)

We have now understood what a central role religion plays in helping us to understand and cope with our humanity. We have also seen that it can be understood from the human to the divine. Seen why, also, it is primarily human stuff. More importantly we have also seen why we can avail ourselves of it whilst at the same time maintaining a healthy agnosticism about the ultimate questions which religion can throw at us.

We have also now addressed some of the main criticisms of and problems with religion in general and Christianity in particular. Some of the possible replies to these have already begun to emerge. In the remaining chapters we will examine some of these replies in more detail. In general, they will show how Christianity can be understood 'from below' and how this in no way compromises its relevance to modernity as we have understood it. To the contrary, we will now begin to see why it can still be practised with intellectual integrity.

CHRISTIANITY

CHAPTER FIVE

With Modern Integrity

In the previous two chapters we have discussed some of the most prominent contemporary problems with religion in general and Christianity in particular. In doing so we have seen partly why, if it is to continue to play the central role in human understanding that it has played for centuries, it needs reconstruction. This is mainly for two reasons. First, it is because it can no longer be used to justify group self interest in any way. This includes its being appropriated in the name of violence. Second, because it can no longer cling to long outmoded world-views. By this latter we mean views which pre-date Post-enlightenment modernity as we have defined it. Ones, that is, which now even embrace downright superstition and incredulity. In other words, as we now turn our attention to understanding reasons why, in spite of all this, Christianity need still not be beyond belief we will see why, alongside other religions in their different ways, it is still a powerful source of wisdom in the modern world.

We have referred often in passing to the need to understand religion, so to speak, 'from below'. The simple reason for this is because that is the way we have to understand everything else. We have to begin from where we are. There is simply nowhere else to begin from. Most people instinctively know this. This is, of course, why they are also equally no longer religious. They might well want to be religious in order to fulfil deep spiritual longings, but they simply cannot accept the paraphernalia of belief which religious believers invariably insist on inflicting upon them. The undoubted underlying reason for this is because we have been imbuing modernity for centuries in one form or another. Although we have touched on this in the foregoing, we now need to understand more precisely why this is the case. In doing so we will see why modernity did not come suddenly into existence. It has been centuries in the making.

If we have any intellectual integrity, we cannot deny our modernity. It is how we see the world and is part of what we are. Some people, religious believers often included, do not try to reconcile their beliefs with modernity at all. They simply do a double think. They hold their modernity with one integrity and their religious beliefs with another. Christians who are professional scientists can often be found to be doing this and their scientific credibility even seems to give them licence for it. Such double thinking should be avoided. If we do it we are but kidding ourselves. We are modern people. Our modernity is centrally defined by how we think and understand the world. If we are to be religious we need to be so with *the same* integrity that we bring to everything else in our lives. It is the argument of this book, as it will now unfold, that we can do just this. To understand why we need first to go back to the Middle Ages.

The philosopher of this time who can best help us is William of Ockham (c. 1290–1349). He was also known as Occam.[1] He stands out as a philosopher of the later middle ages who tentatively begun to pave the way for modernity. In doing so, he laid the foundations on which others still build.

These foundations were disarmingly simple. Just, in fact, as philosophy invariably is at its very best. Medieval philosophy and popular thought was comprised of innumerable assumptions. These were thought to be axiomatic in the literal sense that they needed no further explanations for the simple reason that their truth was thought to be universally self-evident. They were, in fact, called just that: 'universals'. They were taught in the great medieval philosophical schools. Differ though these might in this detail or that, the schools all agreed that there were such universals and that they were axiomatic. A 'universal' in this sense was understood as a 'subsistent form'. Something, that is, which constituted the essence of this observed phenomena or that. For example, all observed horses would have one thing in common: they were manifestations of the universal subsistence of horsiness. The origin of this view, of course, is to be found in Platonic philosophy. Plato called these universals 'forms'. These were the distinguishing essences, or whatever, which inhered in all the differing objects of our observation and, in so doing made them what they are. In the early medieval schools of philosophy Platonism was both dominant and unquestioned. It was so intellectually established and unquestioned that it dominated thought in philosophy and religion. Each complemented and confirmed the truth of the other. This achievement must have looked both impregnable and permanent. It was not.

William of Ockham, was one of the many thinkers of this period to take up these issues on behalf of the modernisers. In his magisterial study of the period Dom David Knowles says of Ockham that many '...have seen in him one of the great creators, one of that group of contemporaries in whose writings Cartesian philosophy, anti-papal reform, modern science and the secular state can be seen in embryonic form'.[2] Ockham, a Franciscan, paid little attention to these wider implications of his work, nor could he have been expected to have been aware of them. He saw himself as a logician. This is famously epitomised in his so-called 'razor'. This holds that in the explanation of anything, 'entities should not be multiplied beyond necessity'. This simple device at once laid the axe to the metaphysics which were so beloved by the medieval schoolmen. It caused Ockham to question the authority of Papal annunciations and for this reason he was excommunicated for life. In all this, the modern way of thinking was born. It spawned many different philosophies and, of course, it continues to so. The general name for them is 'Nominalist'. This means that what we perceive is what there is. We can *only* know anything by this method. This simple view then prevailed over the centuries. Other factors were, of course, at work but this powerful change in philosophy influenced the Italian Renaissance, the Protestant Reformation, the eighteenth century Enlightenment and the rise of science. It influenced most anything, in fact, that we identify with modernity. It stands among other things as a powerful reminder that we ignore philosophical ideas, even simple and centuries old ones, at our peril.

Seeing things from where we are, then, is the touchstone of modernity. We have already seen how in the eighteenth century the Scottish philosopher David Hume took this a stage further by pushing our understanding of empirics, the way things are, to its limits. We have also seen how that affected Immanuel Kant and how he brought about a 'Copernican revolution' in which the task of philosophy was to make 'objects' conform to thought and not the other way around. The effect of all this was to complete the process of the separation of modern philosophy from traditional religion which was begun those centuries earlier by Ockham and others.

There are, as we have already noted, Christians who still believe that this is not the case. They argue that this eighteenth century onslaught was ineffective. That the old rational arguments for God's existence are still valid and that many of the truths of religion are as capable of rational self-evidence as they have ever have been. In other words, they cling to understanding religion in ways which the majority of us have long found to be impossible. More than that, they invariably argue that unless we return to these older ways of seeing things we will never be able to be religious at all. Even more than that, they often claim that this is the famed 'stumbling block of faith' which the rest of us are not able to take. They, of course, think that they have taken it and have access to religious truth in all its profundity. What this anti-modern understanding of religion, in effect, does it to render it an irrelevance to the modern mind. But this, in turn, leaves a gaping hole in modern consciousness. A consciousness which is ever seeking a deeper source of wisdom to combat things like radical evil, but which is left bereft of it, simply because it is not prepared to compromise the integrity of its modernity. Nor should it do so. If a religion like Christianity can only be presented in pre-modern ways, it deserves to be seen as the marginalised irrelevance it now so often appears to be. People's minds dictate that they vote with their feet and stay away from the churches. They might, of course, return from time to time according to personal need or seasonal pleasure. Even then they will often hear nothing either to their comfort or inspiration. Just, in fact, the same claims and beliefs which caused them their problems with religion in the first place.

The rest of this book will now show that there is a positive alternative to all this. This is an understanding of the Christian religion which is both compatible with modernity as we have discussed it and which is also capable of enabling us to face a future which is as uncertain as it has ever been. We will see that this is not a new understanding of religion as such. This is for the simple reason that it is one which continues to draw on ancient wisdom and insight, on the Bible and particularly the teaching of Jesus and on Christian tradition. In its modern form it has already been over two centuries in the making and is still developing in exciting ways. It begins with the humility to see things as modernity sees them: from below. We will see in the last chapter why worship and prayer enable us not, so to speak, to end below. Both these activities, rather, enable those who practise them to aspire to more ultimate realities. For now, however, we will continue to confine ourselves only to what we know.

The German theologian Friedrich Schleiermacher (1768–1834) brought together two important influences in the creation of a theology which has rightly earned him, ever since, the title of the 'father of modern theology'. The first of these was the pietist influence of his Brethren upbringing. This convinced him that religion was essentially a matter of feeling, something to be experienced and lived. The second was his training in both classical and contemporary philosophy. He was steeped in Aristotle and Kant and knew, as Kant also knew, that the understanding of religion which had served Christian tradition for centuries had to be reconstructed. His first important published work was *On Religion: Speeches to its Cultured Despisers*.[3] In this he agreed with the so-called Despisers in their criticisms of prevailing religious orthodoxy. In particular, he accepted that the Deism of the eighteenth century was an arid rational abstraction of what religion actually is. (This was the view that the central truths of religion were rationally self-evident.) He also accepted that most of the disputes between Church people over doctrine were an internecine irrelevance. His claim that religion is essentially a matter of feeling and experience was, again, a reply to all this. He claimed that 'piety...is a state in which Knowing, Feeling, and Doing are combined'.[4] He is famous for identifying the main characteristic of piety as *a feeling of dependence* as well as for saying that in religious experience it combines with *a feeling of freedom*. The dependence is on God as 'the other' who is the source of the freedom which piety bestows. The sense of dependence and the experience of freedom are as one.[5] This, for Schleiermacher, is the key to true religion. It engenders, at the same time, a sense of the infinite and an awareness of its presence in religious experience. The other influence on Schleiermacher which is clear at this point is that of the Romantic movement which was active in Berlin at the time just as it was in England and elsewhere. It stressed that sense experiences are such an important aspect of what it means to be human that their place has to understood in all that we do. In Christianity those experiences were those of Christ and the prophets.[6]

Here we can observe the genius of a thinker who was widely read and well informed yet, at one and the same time, was capable of being both simple and profound. Little wonder that Schleiermacher's influence has been and remains as great as it does. It demonstrated how religion can be approached as we have been describing it, from below. Its shows how we can be fully religious without having, *as a precondition*, to accept questionable answers to speculative metaphysical questions. Even more pointedly, it shows that such answers are even a hindrance to true piety. *The Christian Faith* ends its magisterial survey of the resources of Christian faith by saying that explore the faith though we can and must, 'we are unable to go beyond these indications in such a way as to complete the whole task'.[7] The practice of the Christian faith is, therefore, on this view compatible with a respectful humility and an acceptance of intellectual limitations.

This latter point was taken up in mid-nineteenth century English theology. Much of it centred around a colossal disagreement between two of its main proponents, F.D. Maurice the Dean of King's College London and Henry Mansel the then Dean of St Paul's. Maurice claimed that the knowledge of God in Christ was complete knowledge in the sense that we could know God as God knows Godself. Mansel argued that this was an impossibility because of the finitude of our human knowledge. For him our knowledge of God was limited, but it was, nevertheless, sufficient for our salvation. Mansel's Bampton Lectures for 1858 set his views out under the title *The Limits of Religious Thought Examined*.[8] His conclusion is akin to that of Schleiermacher: that though we can know much about God in the life of faith, how much we can know is circumscribed by the limitations of our humanity and intellect. This disagreement, alone, shows that any who claim, as we are here doing, that religion can be understood 'from below' and that it is compatible with at least certain levels of agnosticism, must expect opposition to their views from traditional schools of religious thought. (Nothing changes!) These, for the most part, still continue as though the great criticisms of religion which we have been exploring have no real point! We, bluntly, are replying to this by saying that those criticisms have an integrity which is so bound up with our modernity that they cannot, therefore, be ignored. This recognises that just as our human knowledge of all other areas of life and thought is incomplete and subject to constant revision, so too is our knowledge and understanding of God and religion.

However much we might use this religious insight or that for inspiration and joy, we must always remember that it is always subject to our human interpretation. Heavenly things can come in none other than earthly vessels. This does not mean that those things are reduced to those vessels. The conviction that there is more to religion than them is an important one. That is what lifts the human spirit and human vision beyond itself.

Again many Christian believers will object to this. Some of them want what they curiously call a 'realist' metaphysic. This insists that entities which lie beyond our sense experience exist in the same way as those which lie within it. By this they literally mean that religion requires a belief in the 'existence' of religious entities which is equal to, or the same as, belief in the entities we encounter in everyday life. Accordingly, the central entity, God, must be thought of as existing in the same way as any other object of sense experience. That is, exist literally, not just analogously, in both space and time. They invariably apply the same conditions to other religious entities such as heaven and the after-life. One has no real objection to this. If that is what some religious believers think that religion requires, so be it and very good luck to them. But that, of course, is not just what most of them think. They also claim that the manner in which *they* hold their beliefs is a pre-condition of religious orthodoxy, anything less than that does not count as being religious at all. On their view, metaphysical beliefs are as real as any other. Unless, moreover, they add, these beliefs are held in this literal way they cannot function as religious beliefs at all. Before we challenge this view we need to recognise that it is making an important point which we have already touched upon. It is the point that unless religion lifts us beyond ourselves it is failing in one of its most central functions. That point is importantly made and can be well taken. What cannot be so easily accepted is that such a realist metaphysic is either (a) the *only* way to express that reality or (b) that it can be made *the* non-negotiable pre-condition of religious belief. This, as we are seeing repeatedly, is just the point where the modern mind shies away. It might once have been perfectly possible for people to hold metaphysical beliefs in this way. It is not easily so for us. Our belief capacities are circumscribed by our modernity which, as we have seen, requires us to begin from where we are, as well as not to stray further from that point than is strictly necessary. As we remember with Ockham.

Frankly, for religious believers who profess a realist metaphysic to insist that this is the only valid or true form of religious belief, displays something which can only be described as, at best, a colossal vanity and, at worst, an even more colossal arrogance. One has only to call to mind the spectacle of a Bishop dismissing a priest because the priest does not believe in God's existence in the same way as the Bishop does to see the horror of this. This is nothing less than the shadow of the Inquisition in which people were tortured and burned to death for not conforming to official beliefs. Moreover, the stronger the modernising forces of religion become, the conservative ones seemingly become even stronger in reaction. So-called 'Broad Churches' are better than all this and are tolerant of divergent views (perhaps even those here being expressed). Those, such as the metaphysical 'realists', who doggedly maintain the pre-modernist stances must, however, take a large part of the responsibility for alienating genuine enquirers after religion. Note that we have stressed that it is no part of those who seek, as we here do, other ways of understanding religion to reciprocate in kind. We do not say that religious believers who are metaphysical realists as we have defined them cannot be religious. What they can and should realise, however, is that what we might call 'realist metaphysical religious imperialism' does harm to the cause of religion by causing people who would otherwise be religious to reject it for good reasons.

Christianity is in steep decline in the Western world. Orthodox Christians would do well to look to themselves in the ways we have been indicating and at least to consider the possibility that the mistaken manner of their beliefs is one of the main reasons for this. It is curious, is it not, that religious believers who locate the essence of religion in believing what the Queen in *Alice Through the Looking Glass* calls 'impossible things,'[9] should call themselves 'realists'. That epithet should surely be more properly claimed by those who seek understandings of religion which begin with and, as far as possible, content themselves with what there realistically is. Just, in fact, as we are doing here.

Before we return to our ongoing discussion of exploring what it means in the modern world to understand religion 'from below' it is important that we are clear about an important distinction in the use of religious language. It is that between 'belief' and 'faith'. These terms are often used inconsistently. It is important to our main discussion that we avoid that.

Religious belief systems are many and complex even in a single religion like Christianity. This is true of these systems at any one time, it is the more so over the two millennia of Christian history. These systems all have one important thing in common: they are human constructs. Christian believers often like, at least, to create the impression that their beliefs are revealed in the sense that they come directly from God or whatever, but this is plainly not the case. Beliefs have human fingerprints all over them. These are, in fact, often so obvious that it takes no great feat of detection to identify precisely when, where and even who has been responsible for them. They bear most obviously the hallmarks of their age, its prevailing philosophy and its political circumstances. Indeed, the dramas of human history have often been punctuated by disagreements over the nicety of this belief or that. Christian belief in the doctrine of the Trinity, that God is three in one: Father Son and Holy Spirit, is, as we have already seen, the classical example of this.[10] The human imprint on its formulation is self-evident. It works well enough as an analogy and it is no less important for that. Claiming more for it, is to impute meaning into the Bible (so-called *eisegesis*) rather than derive meaning from it (*exegesis*).

Towards the end of the third century the Church had to resist heresies which claimed that the Son was not divine in the sense that the Father was. The most famous of these is known as Arianism. Arius was a priest and theologian who held the view that claiming that Jesus was God in the same sense as the Father, compromised the utter transcendence and purity of the Godhead. This view was firmly trounced at the first great Council of the whole Church which was held at Nicea in 325 CE. Its Creed established orthodoxy against Arius. (In fact, Arian strains have been held in fringes of Christianity ever since. They are firmly held in Unitarianism and feature in much modern scholarship about Jesus, not the least that being recommended herein.) The co-equality in Godhead of the Father and the Son is universally accepted in orthodox creedal Christianity. The status of the Holy Spirit, however, has always been and remains a problem, as we have seen.[11]

The central beliefs of the Creeds serve as the defining boundaries of Christian orthodoxy. This is why they are recited so regularly in Christian worship. They sound impressive. Reciting them is an important liturgical experience. In reality, however, individual Christians hold their beliefs much more dynamically. They ebb and flow through the liturgies often in beautiful ways, particularly in the celebration of the great festivals of the Church. What they actually mean and how important they are at any one time, is subject among other things to interpretation, fashion and above all the prevailing view of the majority. You cannot make yourself more or less spiritual by believing this or that more or less firmly. The question is often asked: what do I have to believe to be a Christian? It is a red herring. We cannot become religious simply by believing. Beliefs might help or, indeed, hinder us in the religious life. They certainly do not wholly constitute it. What they do is to help to sustain and inspire the religious life in dynamic ways. They are important for that reason and are not at all detracted from by the fact that they often unclear, disputed and even downright problematic.

Whereas religious beliefs, as we have seen, have human fingerprints all over them, 'faith' in the Christian tradition is best understood as a gift of God. Its manifestation in human life is through a committed disposition which is shared with others. This is essentially an acceptance to receive God's grace and interpret the world religiously. In Christian tradition, its main emphases are found in the writings of St Paul and, much later, in those of the Protestant Reformers. Paul knew through his Rabbinic training that the religious life could not be held without some form of justification. How, then, could Christians find some justification other than, by the Law? The answer Paul gave to this question was central to his emergent theology and it subsequently became integral to Christian orthodoxy. We are '...justified by faith alone' (Romans 4:5, 9:30). This faith is the free and undeserved gift of God to humankind. It demands an obedience (Rom. 1:5), which renounces all previous self-understanding and direction of the will. It cannot be justified by works, not even religious ones. Nor can it be humanly created. It comes only from God as an unconditional gift. Its reception is the only thing required for it to become the means of salvation. Paul listed faith as one of the three Christian virtues, along with hope and love (1 Corinthians 13.13). Faith has to be confessed and practised for it to be sustained. Only in this way can its distortion or loss be prevented. If that happens it cannot be recovered by human action or self righteousness. Not even and most certainly by religious self righteousness. According to the Christian view self-righteousness is the ultimate manifestation of the sin of pride – religious pride. Jesus, recall, was repeatedly vehement in its denunciation (e.g. Matthew 23:15).

If we are to be consistent in our actions day in day out, we have to see the world in some way or other. To do this in the Christian tradition is what it means to live the Christian life. Of course, what that might or might not require amid diversity is another thing. This always has to be worked at and is seldom easy. The exercise of such a faith is, therefore, no cop out. It is the point at which human endeavour meets the enabling grace of God. Much of what follows will be a discussion of the implications of understanding faith in this way.

Note that on this view that faith cannot be justified by belief. Faith alone what puts us right with God, which is what righteousness literally means. We cannot make ourselves righteous by believing things. It comes to us only by the acceptance of faith. We can believe this or that, or not, or doubt this or that, or not, it makes no actual difference to the living reality of faith. Christians do not, of course, always behave as though this were the case. They are beloved of defining their communities by including those who believe this or that and excluding those who do not. Would that such communities were defined, rather, by what they did, by how they exercised their common faith. Christian orthodoxy should be defined by volition, by what we do rather than by what we believe. This does not mean, as we keep stressing, to say that beliefs are irrelevant. They are important in the ways we noted above. They inform and help us to sustain the life of faith, but they do not and cannot do anything more than that. They certainly cannot be held, as we have seen, in some pedantically metaphysical way. Most of them, frankly, are not worth it.

The profundity of Schleiermacher's response to the intellectual bankruptcy of the Christianity of his age (and ours), is at one which understanding Christian faith in this way. Dependence is also a disposition. It is something human beings can feel, come to terms and discover how to live with. None of this requires the remotest intellectual suicide. Those who commit that invariably hinder rather than help the causes of true religion. All it requires intellectually, at this stage, is that we accept the life of faith, so understood, as a starting point. For many religious believers this is a simple and beautiful thing. It enables them to lead their lives to the full, both in adversity and happiness. Anyone who has ever had the privilege of exercising the Christian ministry to such people will know this better than most. Their example is invariably both humbling and inspirational. They know that faith is essentially trust and they know this best when all the evidence is contrary to it. This is a trust which exists between human experience and God, simple as that. It is a trust which is better left as uncomplicated as possible. All we need ask of it is: what does it require of us?

Henry Mansel, whom we briefly mentioned earlier, claimed that we can begin to understand this by only seeking a knowledge of God which was sufficient for our practical purposes. There are the purposes of 'regulating' our daily living. He took this use of the word 'regulative' from Kant and distinguished the knowledge it designated from knowledge which is 'speculative'.[12] Mansel referred to the knowledge of God we have in Christ, as revealed knowledge. Religion begins with the human act of knowing. What is so known is, above all, practical, regulative, knowledge. Its truth is verified in its use. It cannot be verified by either speculative reason or dogmatism. The most important thing about it is what we *do* with it. He writes:

> There is one point from which all religious systems must start, and to which all must finally return; and which may therefore furnish a common ground on which to examine the principles and pretension of all. *The primary and proper object of criticism is not Religion, natural or revealed, but the human mind in relation to it.*[13]

Mansel had imbibed Kant and broadly endorsed his views. He also did much to introduce them to his Oxford audience. (He was something of a wit and satirically wrote elsewhere of German philosophers, 'With a bug, bug, bug and a hum, hum, hum, thither the true philosophers come. From the land that produced one Kant with a K and may cants with a C'.[14] Though it was attacked at the time, Mansel's theology has remained important. It begun to receive renewed attention from the 1960s in the writings of Don Cupitt.[15] He has since done much to popularise Manselian theology in a continuing series of books and articles. These have given rise to a movement called, after a phrase in Matthew Arnold's poem 'Dover Beach', 'The Sea of Faith'.[16] It is mostly supported by English clergy who see themselves and are seen, as being at odds with the prevailing ecclesiastical/religious establishment. They are, however, an inspiration to any who seek the understanding of religion favoured here.

However, some aspects of Mansel's theology would provide us with difficulty today. His emphasis on the fact that our knowledge of God is revealed by Christ, for example, caused him to write extensively on the miracles as 'evidences' of revelation. Much of this has not survived the scrutiny of biblical scholarship. What, however, has forcefully survived is his claim that the most important thing about religious belief is what we *do* with it. Its thrust lies not in rationally self-evident, dogmatically held, or other such 'truth'. It lies in the fact that it enables us to live in a certain way by 'regulating' our life and thought. Religious truth is, explicitly 'regulative' truth. It cannot be truth of any other kind and, it does not need to be.

Regulative truths are those which are unrealisable in themselves, but which have practical applications. Kant, as we have seen, is their originator in modern philosophy. He called them 'rules postulating what we ought to do' and which we can follow for our practical benefit.[17] They operate only in the world of our experience, what he called the 'sensible' world. They, cannot extend our knowledge beyond it. They straddle, so to speak, the vast unknown on the one hand and, on the other, the immediacy of our tasks at hand. Tasks which, we instinctively know, cannot be carried out without such a broader reference. An example is a task which embraces 'scientific truth'. These truths come and go, but whilst they remain they serve the useful purpose of enabling scientific enquiry and furthering the application of science to human benefit. In fact, they usually go when they no longer help us to achieve all that and when we discover that some other formulation of such truth does so more effectively. Thomas Kuhn famously described this process as one which proceeds by 'paradigm shifts'. These do not always enable us to delve ever more deeply into objective truth, as the traditional understanding of the history of science might have us believe. In fact, they do not even enable us to access objective truth at all. What they do is to enable us to solve puzzles which could not be solved by previous paradigms and, thereby, stand as more plausible representations of reality.[18] We know only that, in time, their limitations will be similarly exposed and that they too will give way to new ways of thinking. Kuhn's theory is much debated, but it stands as an illustration of how regulative thinking can be seen to apply in just one area of human enquiry and activity which was, supremely, thought to have to do with relentlessly knowing ever more accurately how things 'actually' are. It shows, that is, just how we can make progress in this area of enquiry, or that, without establishing the sort of truths which we are incapable of establishing by dint of the limitations of our human knowledge. Kuhn showed both the eloquence and the sufficiency of understanding scientific truths in this way.

The point we are making is that religion can be understood in the same way. It is what Kant called 'regulative knowledge' or the 'regulative ideal'. It is what Henry Mansel made central to his philosophical theology. In an important modern study of this form of knowing the philosopher Dorothy Emmet accepted that regulative knowledge does not give us knowledge which is beyond our sense experience. She does show, however, much after the manner of Kant, what an important role it plays in the business of practical living. In a moment, we will quote the elegant conclusion of her book on the subject at some length. To understand it fully we first need to know why she steers a middle course between 'absolutism' 'I know that God exists and that is that' and relativism 'I know that God does not exist'. Neither of these alternatives do justice either to the human condition, or to the notion of the existence of God. The first claims more that can be claimed and the second can be a counsel of despair. We need, rather, something which touches our inmost spiritual longings and needs, but which does not do this by compromising our judgement. Something, moreover, which does this in a way which enables us to live the religious life that so many of us naturally and rightly crave. This is how Dorothy Emmet eloquently speaks of it:

> Rather than speaking of God, I can now more readily speak of signs of the divine. I believe that there can be one such sign where inner power meets a transcendent ideal, and a spark is struck which can kindle creative judgement and creative action. It will not take us out of life the limitations which are part of the human condition. We still live with the unrealisable. Nevertheless, living with the unrealisable frees us from self-destructive guilt about what we cannot achieve and from self-satisfied complacency about what we do achieve. Nor will we be tempted to swing from an over-simple absolutism to an over-simple relativism. We learn to live with problems which have no final solutions, and this is as well, since much of life is like this. Yet there are ways of going forward and ways of learning from failures. So 'we are perplexed, but not in despair'. St Paul's own words...have a cadence and a metaphor... our way is difficult, but we are not at a dead end.[19]

In this way we can know God as a 'regulative ideal' and in so doing live the religious life. The important thing about this knowing is that it does not and need not, claim more for itself than it does. What it does emphatically claim is that human life is brought to its fullness, or as religious believers often prefer to say, is redeemed in this way. In plain other words, *here is an understanding of the religious life which does not require intellectual suicide as its pre-condition.*

Understanding Christianity in this way focusses our attention on questions about what we have to *do*. Do, that is, about our humanity and, in particular about our relationship to others. This was addressed by John Macmurray in his Gifford Lectures for 1953 and 1954.[20] He pointed out that, that because all human beings are created by the single action of God they are profoundly defined in this way, by an action. Recognising this, he claimed, was a clue to understanding what he argued was a crisis in understanding the personal. Macmurray, a philosopher, argued that philosophers has long misunderstood the personal because they had, since Descartes, identified individual thinking as the key to the personal. Against this, Macmurray asserted '...the primacy of the practical.'[21] By this he meant that '...we should think from the standpoint of action.'[22] Thought is primarily an action. What we think is its abstraction. What defines us is what we do and the essence of action is choice.[23] In doing anything we are choosing, at the same time, not to do something else. This does not lead to obsessive egocentricity. What we do when we act is to contribute to a nexus of cumulative human action which cannot be undone. We always act in relation to others. This was the point of Macmurray's Gifford Lectures of 1956. We do this, not be interacting with some abstract notion of 'society'. We do it, rather, by living in communities. These originate in families and extend into religions. They have four characteristics: they are universal, they have no analogue, they are the matrix which crystallise culture and they are inclusive in their realm.[24] In the concluding section of his lectures he writes:

> There is, then, only one way in which we can think our relation to the world, and that is to think it as a personal relation, through the form of the personal. We must think that the world is one action... To conceive the world thus is to conceive it as the act of God, the Creator of the world and ourselves as created agents, with a limited

and dependent freedom to determine the future, which can be realised only on the condition that our intentions are in harmony with His intention, and which must frustrate itself if they are not.[25]

Macmurray's vision of religion is centred on the powerful idea that it both unites individuals and co-ordinates their actions for the total good. This is a vision which raises our sights from the boundaries of this (our) religion or that to see its potential for helping to create total human well-being. Seen in this way, religion provides a consistent way of dealing with life's collective, as well as individual, practicalities. Indeed, Macmurray's vision of selves-in-relation-to-others-and-to-God is a profound analysis of human potential and responsibility.

Religion therefore has a huge potential for achieving personal, social and world-wide human well-being. For it to become the force for good that it clearly is, those of us who are religious will need to see beyond the purview of our own religions to understand where they fit into the wider understanding of what it means to be human and live together responsibly. Whenever aspects of our own religions prevent that, we will have to have the courage to judge them seriously wanting. We discussed how Christianity needs to begin this task in Chapters Three and Four. It is admittedly painful to have to revise some of ones most cherished and hitherto perhaps unexamined religious assumptions. That is the price which has to be paid. Short of this, religious people will go on only shouting at each other when, for reasons we have seen, they should be shouting *together* for the total human and environmental well-being.

In the next chapter we will address two immediate questions which arise from understanding the potential of religion in this way. Is it Gospel and is it true?

CHAPTER SIX

Its Gospel and Truth

We have now understood the reasons why Christianity is best approached 'from below'. We have seen that in its modern form this approach has been some two centuries in the making and seen also that its philosophical origins reach back to the late medieval beginnings of modernity. We also reflected on the potential of all this which could be realised if the world's religious people understood each other better than, for the most part, they do.

One common sceptical reaction to understanding Christianity in this way is: is it Gospel? This is an important question because the Christian message has always been understood as 'good news': Gospel. The word is found occasionally in the preaching of Jesus, e.g. the Sermon on the Mount of Olives (Matt. 24:14, 26:13, and Mark 10:29). In both it refers mainly to the coming of the kingdom of God. It is used slightly more frequently when Gospel writers refer to the preaching of Jesus. Here it still contains Jesus' emphasis on the Kingdom, but its meaning is widened also to include reference to the preaching and ministry of Jesus. Its main use, of course, is to describe the four main accounts of Jesus in the New Testament. They clearly understand that there is but one Gospel and that their writings are separate, though as we know related in complex ways, accounts of it. St Paul describes his own message as Gospel (e.g. Romans 1:16). Initially it was a message for the Jews, but in the Gentile Mission it soon became applicable to the whole world. This is the sense it has retained in Christian doctrine and liturgy where the reading of the Gospel with the congregation standing is an important focus.

But, what exactly is the 'Good News' of the Gospel? This question has been the subject of much scholarly debate. Some understand it as being: authored by God through Jesus who has died, is risen and sits at God's right hand. It announces that God is love and forgives sins. In this way, it creates a transforming new relationship between God and the people of God who thereby experience a new righteousness. So understood, the Gospel is something authored only by God and revealed in the ministry of Jesus. By definition, therefore, it was not and could never be of human origin. It is nothing less than what God reveals about God's self. All this is never more emotively expressed than it is in the Christmas liturgies with their focus on the baby in an ox's stall who is visited by the Magi. Here it is presented as nothing less than the essence of belief and faith. It is, in fact, virtually impossible not to be moved by this story, as is evidenced by the large numbers of people who attend Christian Churches, many of them only at this season.

One much commented upon and obvious difficulty with understanding Gospel in this traditional way is that if one literally stands in the street and announces its formulae, as lonely souls of course often do, nothing is elicited except incredulity. It does not connect with the modern consciousness as it apparently did for those in the early Christian Church. Another difficulty is that, apart from when it refers to Jesus, its content is slim and not entirely new. God had previously been understood as love in Jewish piety and God's redeeming work was encountered in the Law.

In the Christian Gospel that newness is understood to refer to what is unique about Jesus as the one who reveals God as an only son. This literally causes some Christians to believe that their faith is unique among all the other faiths of the world. We have already critically reflected on this. When challenged, such Christians often reply by saying things like 'I really do believe that my faith is different'. These, note, moreover are often Christians who are well and even professionally educated in Christian theology. Little wonder that Christians invariably find it difficult to relate equally and in humility to people of other faiths! At its crudest, this understanding of Gospel as a unique Christian privilege is a none too subtle form of superior self-justification. Of course, there are seemingly no shortage of souls out there who want to receive this sort of exclusive spiritual self-understanding, or come to that no shortage of Christian evangelical preachers who will offer it to them. This, however, is not the end of the story of the Gospel. Rather, it begins here. The power of the Gospel is in what it does. This was emphasised by St Paul. He makes it clear that the dry recitation of formulae is not enough. We have to think about what we are saying and doing when we communicate the Gospel. He did this in two main ways. First, he worked out what it meant to preach the Gospel to Gentiles. This required nothing less than a new language. Second, he also considered what form the Gospel should take when it is addressed to Christians in specific situations. In all this he was ever probing the Good News, finding fresh expression for it and then ways of showing his readers and listeners how it applied to the actual circumstances of their lives. This is the dynamic of the Gospel in action and it is what, at its best, the Christian Church has done ever since. Gospel is, therefore, better understood as a dynamic activity than as dry formulae. It is, moreover, ongoing. This was stressed by the New Testament scholar Rudolph Bultmann. He pointed out that it is both 'grace' and 'event' and that the first essential message of the Church was not primarily about Jesus but about the proclamation of the imminence of the coming of the Kingdom of God.[1] As the arrival of this was delayed, so the message changed as we have seen that it does throughout the pages of the New Testament. It has gone on changing ever since and will have to do so until the final coming of the Kingdom. In the meantime we, again, have to think it out for ourselves in the light of our knowledge of Jesus and the Church. More than this, even, is now required of us. We have to think out its meaning, as we have been arguing throughout, in the light of our wider knowledge of the religious experiences of those of other faiths. This is just a little of the challenge which faces us when we understand the Gospel from below. It does not eschew the Gospel from above. It wants only to put that in the wider context of human understanding and action. This, of course, will be an anathema to unreconstructed Christian believers. Since, however, they are clearly in a decreasing minority we need not perhaps be too overly concerned about that. Beyond, that is, sincerely wanting to keep and value their spiritual companionship and friendship in prayer, worship and the Christian life.

Hearing and responding to the Christian Gospel is a momentous human experience as is the responsibility of preaching it to others. It requires of us the recognition that the power of God's love is available in our confused and complex world. In coming to this recognition we cannot take refuge in formulae or slogans. It requires, rather, our personal commitment including our intellectual commitment. The Gospel always requires us to think things out for ourselves. It is not just about what God's love does for us, it is equally about what we have to achieve, by the grace of God, in finding out what it can do for others and for the whole of creation.

Understanding religion 'from below' as we are doing engenders a sense of Gospel in arguably a more forceful way than understanding it 'from above'. We have to work out how it enables what is transcendent and beyond our understanding to relate to whatever it is that impedes human flourishing. Making even a little progress with this here or there is nothing less than a sign of God's grace in a fallen world. Nothing less than a cause for rejoicing and thanksgiving. Understanding Christianity and religion more generally as we are doing cannot, therefore, be dismissed on the ground that it is not Gospel. To the contrary, for the reasons we have now briefly discussed, it opens up ever new ways of appreciating what the Gospel is and how it relates to the world in which we live. It is an ongoing and interactive process. Let a metaphor illustrate this. It is one in which each separate light throws even more light on other lights as through a prism, in which the separate lights can be clearly recognised, but never actually separated from each other. Their luminosity is, rather, enhanced by their interaction. To be captivated by the beauty of this is directly analogous to being captivated by wonder of seeing even a little of how the love of God redeems a fallen world. Seeing, as through a glass darkly, is more than enough for us to be going on with (1 Corinthians 13:12). The eloquence of John Henry Newman can be well recalled here. In his great hymn 'Lead Kindly Light' he famously penned the lines 'I do not ask to see the distant scene, one step enough for me'. One step at a time should be enough for all of us.

So, there is every reason why the approach to Christianity we are taking leaves plenty of scope for understanding it as Gospel, but what about the perennial question of its truth. 'And is it true and is it true, this most tremendous tale of all, a baby in an ox's stall. The maker of the stars and sea become a child on earth for me?'[2] These words from the poem 'Christmas' by John Betjeman along with recall of Pilate's timeless question 'What is truth?' (John 18:38), more than set for us the awesomeness of the task of answering this question. It is one, however, than cannot be sidestepped. It will now become clear that we have been keeping it in mind throughout the foregoing, as the important and central question that it is. As frail human beings we instinctively crave to know whether or not the things we cherish are true. When we even think that they are we importantly enjoy both psychological reassurance and renewed self confidence. Little wonder, then, that we want to know that our religion, the ultimate source of or self-understanding, is true. But what, exactly, can we possibly mean when we say that a religion is true or false?

Even to begin to answer this we need first to do a little very simple, for that is all that it is, linguistic philosophy. This is not at all to suggest, of course, that every religious believer has to do this. Far from it. Many of them can merrily go on believing their religion to be true to great personal benefit and example to us all. Those who want more than this, however, will make no progress unless they reflect first on how it can be philosophically discussed.

Truth and its antinomy falsity, are both expressed in what are grammatically called *propositions*. These are sentences which purport that something or other is the case. That something is their *meaning*. It is this which we subject to the test of truth or falsity. Not all sentences have meaning, of course. (As you, dear reader, may know all too well). These cannot be either true or false for the simple reason that meaningless sentences do not purport anything which we can subject to truth testing. For this reason *truth* and *meaning* are closely related concepts in linguistic philosophy. Theories of truth embrace theories of meaning and *vice versa*. There can be no such thing as a theory of one which does not entail a theory of the other. First, we need to grasp another simple philosophical phrase: 'states-of-affairs'. These are what we perceive to be the case at some time and in some instance or other. They are descriptions of what is the case. The whole of our knowledge of the world is made up of our knowledge of states-of-affairs. We are fully aware that they are 'out' there whether at any particular time or circumstance we know about them or not.

Even this brief excursus into linguistic philosophy is already more than enough for us to define truth. *Propositions are true if and only if they accurately describe the state of affairs which their meaning purports.* This definition is so simple that it needs no illustration. When we check out propositions in this way we are, as philosophers say, setting out to *verify* them. Happily for our sanity, we do this for the most part instinctively. As we go about our daily lives, we verify the truth of the propositions we make and hear without thinking. Unless we could do this, in fact, we would go mad. Indeed, some clinically diagnosed conditions of madness help us to identify why it is that some poor souls either find this difficult or impossible. Thankfully for most of us, this is not the case and our everyday lives are lived in the midst of a process of verification of which we are largely, necessarily and blissfully unaware. This, of course, is not necessarily always the case and we have to spend not a little of our time and energy consciously establishing whether this or that is the case or not in particular instances. Much professional life embraces this in large measure. It comes under the general umbrella of the 'empirical sciences'. Our knowledge of these has much to its credit, but it is still, effectively, in its infancy. We are beset by ignorance in area after area of our lives as we try to come to grips with, for example, the biological, genetic, environmental and so many other branches of science. In spite of all our many and great scientific achievements, we are still exploring the fundamental natural order of things. The recent successful hunt for the Higgs Boson at the new Hadron Collider is a graphic illustration of this. In all this we endeavour to find out if our propositions can be verified by our observation of the way things actually are. This is the interactive process of empirical truth seeking.

This, the so-called 'verificationist' theory of meaning and truth, became the *leitmotif* of an extremely influential twentieth century philosophy. It is called 'logical positivism', and was made popular by A.J. Ayer's *Language Truth and Logic* in 1936.[3] The book became one of the fastest selling philosophical works ever, despite the fact that the then Master of Balliol College, A.D. Lindsay, was so incensed when he read it that, in a moment of prescience, he famously threw it through the window! Ayer claimed that he was a follower of Bertrand Russell who had expressed similar ideas, though not in such a relatively accessible form. Ludwig Wittgenstein had done the same in his *Tractatus Logico Philosophicus*.[4]

Ayer claimed that the meaning of statements could only be verified in two ways. First, if they had intrinsic, or what he called 'analytic' meaning and second if they could be extrinsically 'verified' by factual reference. An example of the former is the statement that '$2 + 2 = 4$'. The meaning of this is self-defining and therefore evident. No appeal to anything external to such a statement is necessary. Empirically verifiable statements on the other hand could only be verified through an appeal to the senses. Examples are the statements which make up the natural sciences, or those of history. Such 'verificationism' became the touchstone of popular philosophy in the 1930s and 40s. This, in its turn, had its influence on many other areas of life and thought. The propositions of religious belief, for example, were held to be neither self-evident or verifiable and were therefore purported to be meaningless. This so-called Logical Positivist challenge to religious belief then dominated debate in the philosophy of religion in the English speaking world. This would have continued were it not for two remarkable turns of event. Logical Positivism was renounced, though in different ways, by both Wittgenstein and Ayer alike! That of the former was in his *Philosophical Investigations* of 1953[5] and the latter in his *The Central Questions of Philosophy* in 1973.[6] Ayer previously tried to defend the verification principle by distinguishing between 'strong' and 'weak' versions of it the second edition of *Language Truth and Logic*. This was because it had been pointed out that the principle could not possibly be used to verify *all* statements for the simple reason that many of the statements made in science and law could not be verified in this way. These latter, he replied, were verified, but only in a 'weak' sense. He later had to admit however, that this 'weak' sense could be used to verify metaphysical statements. It was originally devised, recall, to show that these were meaninglessness! The verification principle was never, therefore, satisfactorily formulated. Either it was put plainly and led to unsatisfactory results, or it was qualified and meant effectively nothing. Once it was admitted that the principle had to be supported by detailed, even metaphysical, arguments its initial brash appeal had already vanished.

The theory of truth implied in all this is called, simply, the 'correspondence theory of truth'. It holds that any statement, or proposition, is true if and only if it is verifiable in sense experience. As we have seen, it came to be recognised that whilst this could well be an acceptable theory of truth for some scientific statements, it could not be so of all others. In fact, it applies to a comparatively few of the propositions we live by in ordinary life, religious ones included but not exceptionally so.

For all this, however, 'verificationism' is used popularly as shorthand for 'common sense'. As a result, the claims of religious belief, are often popularly dismissed as meaningless. 'Popular' here means something like 'what ordinary people without philosophical training instinctively mean'. It is, is it not, rather curious that alongside all this seemingly plain common sense we so often observe an equal craving for knowledge that is fed by the lurid imagination in, for example, literature and the cinema? It is as though we live in one 'common sense' world, but are ever eager take our refuge in another. The deeper truth, of course, is that our robust common sense is useful to us, as we have already seen, but we also know that its use is limited. How then do we understand truths which are as important to our well-being as are those of common sense, but which we cannot verify in the same way? There are, amazingly perhaps, only two ways in which we can do this. We will discuss them in turn. As we do so we will notice that acceptance of the second has already begun to emerge in the foregoing.

The second theory of truth discussed by philosophers is the so-called 'coherence' theory. This holds not that a statement is true if and only if it refers to some sense experience as we saw above. It holds, rather, that it can be true if it coheres (*sic*) with other similar statements. Truth on this view is a relation not between statements and states-of-affairs, or whatever. It is, rather, a relation between statements themselves. It does not, however, require only that such statements do not contradict each other. They have to do much more than that; they have to support each other. An example is, if a number of independent witnesses to an event such as a crime gave testimonies which corroborated each other they could be used to construct a truth or truths about that crime. These testimonies could be apparently quite separate. One saw 'x', another 'y' and another 'z'. Each might not know the wider significance of what they saw or know its relation to the other two. An investigator such as a trained detective, however, could well spot this and establish the truth between the statements accordingly. This would be a truth, moreover, which could be made to stand in a prosecution regardless, and this is the point, of that fact that it could not be verified in sense experience. This is why, for example, the truth of a murder can often be established legally without anyone finding a body. All that has to happen is for a significant (whatever that is) amount of corroborative evidence to be established. Clearly, such a theory of truth has its important uses, particularly where corroborative empirical evidence is not available. Could then, religious truth be understood in this way? Could, that is, religious truth be established if the propositions of religion cohered with each other to some satisfactory degree, even if they were not empirically verifiable? Some influential religious believers have certainly thought so and they should not be easily dismissed. Though, as we shall see, their position is also not without its difficulties, which is why we will conclude this chapter by expressing preference for the third way of understanding truth and its relevance to religion.

The view that religious language is coherent and true specifically to religious believers has been popular throughout the history of Christian thought. It is called Fideism. This literally means that faith precedes reason. In the words of St Augustine of Canterbury faith *seeks* reason and understanding. Such understanding then confirms faith. Faith, so understood, is a stance or orientation towards the world which brings its own understanding. Although this can easily be dismissed by simply pointing out that nothing can be made true simply by believing it (though many religious believers invariably create the impression that it can be), it deserves more consideration. One reason for this is because it can be well argued that much of our lives is, in fact, made up of such assumptions. We all share with others, views about things which are expressed in common languages which we would be hard pressed to find further justification for. Indeed it could be argued, again, that life is so complex that we would be generally disoriented were we not able to do this. Groups of like-minded people do use their own languages for practical purposes and to great benefit. In the Christian tradition this has been consistently demonstrated and defended. Being well aware that the gospel was rejected by some Greeks because it was intellectually offensive, St Paul calls such offence 'foolishness' and contrasts it not with 'true' wisdom but with the wisdom and the power of God. The wisdom of man for St Paul is unable to understand God simply because it is human wisdom. The wisdom of the Greeks is of human construction. For this reason the 'wisdom of God is wiser than men' (1 Corinthians 1:25). Humans can only acquire that wisdom by faith. St Paul might have come to this view during an unfortunate debate with 'the men of Athens'.

They certainly treated him with scorn 'when they heard of the resurrection of the dead, some mocked, but others said "we will hear you again about this"' (Acts 17:32). Tertullian's famous remark 'What has Athens to do with Jerusalem?'[7] expresses the same view as that of St Paul. For him, Christian belief comprised of revealed doctrines. The wisdom of Athens was inimical to this. When that was embraced by Christian believers it was the source of division among them. (Other early Church thinkers of course took a much more positive attitude to the synthesis of Christian and Greek thought and their influence on subsequent tradition has been by far the greater, and for the good it must be said.) Fideism of this kind has persisted in Christianity and it became popular as a response to the challenge of logical positivism we discussed above.

It drew heavily on the amazingly influential philosophy of what is referred to as '...the later Wittgenstein'. (Wittgenstein was, recall, the author of the *Tractatus Logico Philosophicus* which so influenced A.J. Ayer.) Wittgenstein later underwent a huge change of mind which caused him to refute all that he had written before including everything in the previously influential *Tractatus*. That, he later wrote, contained 'grave mistakes'.[8] He still believed that the central key to meaning and truth had to do with the use of language, but found it difficult to formulate his later thoughts. He published them in what he called 'an album' in 1953. This was his famous *Philosophical Investigations*. It immediately became the most influential philosophical work of the second half of the twentieth century. That influence is to be found in innumerable branches of philosophy and applied philosophy such as education. It clearly filled a philosophical vacuum which had been created by the collapse of Logical Positivism and the previously imperious claims it made for its referential theory of meaning. More than that, its 'album' style proved widely captivating as any who have been privileged to study and debate it professionally will know well. Wittgenstein's new philosophy was prompted by the following passage from St Augustine's *Confessions*: ...as I heard words repeatedly used in their proper places in various sentences, I gradually learnt to understand what objects they signified; and after I had trained my mouth to form these signs, I used them to express my own desires.[9]

In response to this Wittgenstein wrote 'Uttering a word is like striking a note on the keyboard of the imagination'.[10] To this he famously added, 'I shall also call the whole, consisting of language and the actions into which it is woven, the "language game".[11] To speak a language is to enter into '...an activity or a form of life'. To this Wittgenstein added '...the meaning of a word is its use in the language'.[12] By understanding words in this way we bring them back from their '...metaphysical to their everyday use'.[13] There are innumerable ways in which words can be used in different language games. Their meaning is not what they, the words, have in common but how precisely they are used in the different language games. This later philosophy of Wittgenstein received so much attention that it soon became widely accepted as philosophical orthodoxy. It gave philosophers of religion who had been beleaguered for decades by the onslaughts of logical positivists a new opportunity for understanding religious language. Something called 'Wittgensteinian fideism' soon flourished.[14] This claimed that words used in religious language did not mean the same as they meant in other languages. This, quite simply, then made way for an alternative meaning to be offered. Take, for example, the central word in the concept of religious language 'God'. Religious believers could now and did aplenty, claim that non believers could not gainsay or question the meaning of the word because only religious believers knew what they were meaning when they used it. Meaningful disagreement between religious believers and non-believers was, therefore, impossible. Note that it was not even necessary to include the notion of faith in such an explanation as the older fideism was obliged to do. Simply claiming that the use of a word was unique was enough to establish a meaning of it which could not be understood by anyone not on the inside. In all this there was no such thing as common speech from which words derived their meaning. There were, rather, as many meanings as there were uses which could be found, religious ones as legitimately included as any other.

However critical we might now be of this view it has a perennial attraction. Language usage must be to some degree as mercurial as this. Particular words clearly have different meanings in different usages. This goes some way to explain the dynamic of human language. This is what makes it capable of so many different things from its use in scientific formulae to metaphysical poetry. In the midst of all this, differing common uses in which particular words accrue different meanings flourishes. One such common use is obviously the religious use. Indeed, religions like Christianity invariably encourage the repetition of such uses in creedal and other formulae, thereby maintaining their particular meanings. None of this can be denied. But the view goes further than this. It entails the belief that there is no commonality of meaning at all among these different uses. None, that is, which could possibly provide the basis for disagreement between them. Is this going too far? Is the price we have to pay for maintaining the legitimacy of any one such use of language the price of solipsism? Of living, that is, in circles of meaning which are immune to any encroachment, even by words from elsewhere that look the same? Could we, therefore, at any time we wish, simply go off and invent a new language game to our own liking for any purpose we desired? And, is this in fact what people have always done as new language games have come into existence? This is one thing. Claiming that all such games have discrete and immune meaning systems is quite another.

Fideists presuppose that we either understand words or we do not. We are either, so to speak, in the game or out of it. Surely this cannot be the case. Our everyday experience of language shows us that 'understanding' is susceptible of 'levels'. We seldom understand many things immediately. What happens is that we engage in processes of understanding and misunderstanding. The comic muse is beloved by the idea. This means that our awareness of meanings is always growing and, even, changing. This is what happens in the melee of common speech. Fideists, at least implicitly, deny that there is such a thing as common speech. However, as new language games come into existence words are taken into them from common speech. These carry with them the meanings they previously had which made their choice so eligible in the first place. Religious believers, for example, speak of God as 'loving' or 'acting' because these verbs are common parlance. It is this that makes such belief commonly intelligible. If this were not the case, then religious belief would be unintelligible. It would be as well to speak in unintelligible tongues and claim meaning for them. (Some religious believers, of course, do just this!) To ignore the way words carry meanings across areas of discourse in this way, even into religious beliefs, is to ignore the importance and place of metaphor in common speech. Wittgenstein called this 'language going on holiday'.[15] He tried to cope with the sheer nonsense of this by claiming that words have 'primary' and 'secondary' meanings, but this is tortuous in the extreme. It is, frankly, a cop out. Why are some uses 'primary' and others not? What about the 999th use etc.? Words, thankfully, cannot be pinned down in this way. They are far too mercurial, not to mention fun, for that. Language ebbs and flows in a never ceasing dynamic which makes possible ever new understandings and insights. The art of poetry is an expression of all this. It invariably relishes in the metaphorical ambiguity of language and in so doing also surprises us by its seemingly inexhaustible revelatory power. The cadences of Wordsworth, Hopkins or Eliot, for example, serve to bring joyous entertainment, but they also bear precious insight. This is also of the essence of the use of religious language at its best, particularly in liturgies. The reason for this is, plainly, that our understanding, by dint of common reason, can literally swim through different areas of discourse with their attendant meanings and at the same time, this is the point, maintain a continuity of flow. Metaphors bear much of the grace and beauty of language and facilitate the ever fascinating interaction of its components.

Before we leave this criticism of the modern fideist account of religious language there is one other problem with it we need briefly to note. This is the problem of the relationship between reason and commitment. Strictly according to the fideist view, reasons for commitment could never be given because prior to commitment they could not be understood. The reasons could, therefore, only be understood after commitment. This clearly makes initial commitment a-rational and even irrational. Is this really how we live or would even wish to do so if we could? Would we want to go about the business of living by committing ourselves, *without reason*, to this cause or that. Would the world be a better place if we did? Surely not. Shared understanding and rational explanations are the very stuff of civilisation. They facilitate inter-cultural understanding and toleration. All this is to be infinitely preferred to world in which individuals and groups go about their doings without any explanation to others. Where this is done by, for example, extremist or fundamentalist groups of one kind or another, the wider social consequences can be devastating, as we know only too well in the modern world.

The coherence theory of meaning and truth, including religious truth, is not, therefore, without some insight, but its failings are all too obvious for the reasons we have briefly considered. Like the correspondence theory we considered before it, it cannot deliver what we require. Require, that is, an account of the truth of religion which is both philosophically coherent and religiously appropriate.

There is fortunately, however, one such which achieves both of these things. Its explanation is here based on the writings William James (1842–1910), the brother of the novelist Henry James. After a career in medicine he was successively Professor of philosophy, psychology and, again, philosophy at Harvard University. It is, of course, the 'pragmatic' theory of truth. This is the view, simply, that we can call things true if they 'work' and false if they do not. We will now explore this more fully and see why it is a view of truth which is both philosophically defensible and religiously appropriate.

What exactly we do when we assert that something 'is true' has always been a central topic of philosophical debate and it doubtless will always remain so. What, then, can we possibly mean by it if the 'correspondence' and 'coherence' theories are not philosophically defensible? By this we mean, as we have seen, that they are philosophically defensible only in the sense that they have limited applications which relate to the theories of meaning of which they are part. In what other way, then, can we explain what we mean by saying that something is true? The issue can be clearly stated. If we assert (a) 'p' and further assert that (b) 'p is true', what are we saying in (b) that is not said in (a)? If we are doing something more in (b) than reassert (a), what is it? It must, so to speak, be *something*. But what can this something possibly be? We will now see why the so-called 'pragmatist' answer to this question is philosophically defensible as well as religiously appropriate.

In his *Essays in Experimental Logic*, the American philosopher John Dewey equates the true with what he calls 'the evident' and writes: 'If a scientific man be asked, what is truth, he will reply, – if he frame his reply in terms of his practice and not of some convention – that which is accepted upon adequate evidence'.[16] What is so 'evident' is whatever end it is that any particular enquiry has in view. Dewey held that this view required a '...whole new logic of enquiry'. Unlike previous, e.g. Aristotelian, logics of enquiry, this new one would not make any metaphysical presuppositions. It would, so to speak, be metaphysically 'baggage free'. That is to say that it would not require, as a pre-condition of being understood, the acceptance of any assumptions *other than those it proffered*. It requires only that we establish what exactly any particular truth claim can be seen to be *doing*. It could, of course, do many different things, but it has to do *something*. Something, that is, which confirms, corroborates, or whatever the truth or otherwise of the proposition in question. This is known as the 'Instrumentalist' theory of truth. What it requires is an analysis of action.[17] (William James far more prosaically called this 'what works'!) Accordingly, there is no distinction between theory and practice. True knowledge is successful practice. This, moreover, has to be publically observable and rationally demonstrable. This insistence was an important development to the theory. Its ends cannot be exclusively personal. They might well bring personal benefit, but even the reasons for that have to be publicly demonstrable. Truth on this view has to have a practical outcome and be a shared reality. Dewey illustrates this with a story of a man lost in the woods. He claims that it is typical of a reflective situation in which both a successful outcome has to be achieved and reasons for it given. The man's quest is for a '...practical idea or plan of action which will lead to success, or the realisation of the purpose to get home'.[18] The immediate solution will come from the extent of the woods in which he finds himself. He will have to recall his previous footsteps and visual markers from memory. Above all, he will have to act on the evidence he finds. If it gets him home it will not only have become true, it will also be capable of explanation to others because it will bear relation to observable reality. In the sense, that is, that dreams would not since they do not partake of reality. Actions in space and time do. They can be seen to be true actions if the reasons given for them being thought so are publicly observable. They can be very different sorts of reason relating to equally different sorts of circumstance. None of this matters when examining their truth. The only thing that matters is that the reasons lead to observable actions which secure desired and equally observable outcomes.

So understood, the pragmatist theory of truth is universally applicable to the human condition. There is no area of human thought and activity to which it cannot be applied. All that is required is that the disarmingly simple rules we have briefly considered are observed. This is truth laid bare and reduced to a conceptual minimum. Compared with alternative theories which require some knowledge of metaphysics or linguistic philosophy (or both in large measure), this theory of truth does not require a philosophical training as a precondition of it being understood. It is both disarmingly simple and uncomplicated. This is because, to use the term we used above, it is 'baggage free' in the sense that it does not carry any luggage which has be unpacked before whatever it is that is being claimed as being true makes sense. No luggage, no unpacking, nothing except Dewey's simple instrumentalist theory which was made even more simple by James's immortal phrase 'truth is what works'.

William James applied the pragmatism of John Dewey and that of Charles Pierce to religion. James was a prolific, popular and witty writer. Re-reading him is always a pleasure. His work does not fit latter day subject classifications. Rather, it straddles what we know as the subjects of psychology, philosophy and theology. James was a philosophical pragmatist, after the manner of Dewey and Charles Pierce. In his famous book on the subject James defined it as, 'a new name for some old ways of thinking'.[19] In its definition he famously wrote:

> The pragmatic method is primarily a method of settling metaphysical disputes that otherwise might be interminable. Is the world one or many? – fated or free? – material or spiritual? – here are notions either of which may or may not hold good of the world; and disputes over such notions are unending. The pragmatic method in such cases is to try to interpret each notion by tracing its respective practical consequences. What difference would it practically make to any one if this notion rather than that notion were true? If no practical difference whatever can be traced, then the alternatives mean practically the same thing, and all dispute is idle. Whenever a dispute is serious, we ought to be able to show some practical difference that must follow from one side or the other's being right.[20]

Again, famously, James called this the 'cash value' of ideas. True ones are those which can be 'cashed in' by experiment. It is 'The attitude of...looking towards last things, fruits, consequences, facts'.[21] Such truth is not a '...stagnant property'. He writes:

> It is astonishing to see how many philosophical disputes collapse into insignificance the moment you subject them to this simple test of tracing concrete consequences. There can be no difference anywhere that doesn't *make* a difference elsewhere – no difference in abstract truth that doesn't express itself in a difference in concrete fact and in the conduct consequent on that fact.[22]

All this follows Pierce closely. He called pragmatism '...primarily a method of settling metaphysical disputes that otherwise might be interminable.'[23] In this way disputes about meaning are simply settled by looking at doing. The only abstract beliefs which could be entertained at all were those which informed our actions in ways which made tangible differences. By 'beliefs' Pierce meant literally any such that informed action, including all scientific principles and formulae. For him this has the discipline of a principle of logic which could be tested by experiment. Only in this way could this belief system or that, this formulae or that, be tested in experience. Unless knowledge informed action and unless it did so by making observable differences to it, it was meaningless. This is what James meant when he more graphically referred to beliefs having to have 'cash value'. With such turn of phrase, it is little wonder that William James became the first populariser of Pierce's philosophy. In a letter to his brother Henry, William referred to Pierce as a man of 'sententious manner and (of) paradoxical and obscure statements.'[24] But he also recognised Pierce's genius and the relevance of that to his own work as an analytical and descriptive psychologist. It is important to understand James as the latter for the simple reason that he wrote before the rise of the fashion for experiment in psychology, something which we instinctively now associate with the subject. He first trained in medicine and taught physiology and anatomy at Harvard. However, he soon moved from these subjects to philosophy and psychology. He did so in the belief that they provided the greater possibility of attaining insight into human life and into understanding important questions about the manner of its fulfilment. It was here that he was to achieve his fame as Professor of Philosophy in the same University. Possibly for these autobiographical reasons, James has never received the wider recognition he deserves as a philosopher in his own right. He was clearly untrammelled by the orthodoxies of a philosophical training. He therefore brought to his eventually chosen subject a freshness which was complemented by his gift for literary eloquence. The often commented upon outgoing warm nature of his personality and humour were other obvious reasons for his popularity. He wrote, in his best-known book *The Varieties of Religious Experience, a Study in Human Nature*, 'Good humour is a philosophic state of mind; it seems to say to nature that we take her no more seriously that she takes us. I maintain that one should always talk of philosophy with a smile.'[25] This was published in 1904 and was based on his Gifford Lectures given in Edinburgh in 1901–1902. With the exception of *The Will to Believe* (1896), his explicitly philosophical works followed the *Varieties* and stand as commentary on it. In 1904 he published an article entitled 'Does Consciousness Exist?'.[26] In this he challenged the hallowed philosophical assumptions of Cartesian dualism, namely: that minds and bodies are discrete entities. There is, James argues, no evidence for thinking that the act of knowing is comprised of the knower and the known. Consciousness, he believed, was a fiction which should be discarded.[27] He was interested not in consciousness itself, but pragmatically in what was done with it. In the *Varieties*, James set himself a daunting task of interpreting religion as a psychologist by looking at '...the immediate content of the religious consciousness'.[28] By looking at what he called '...personal religion pure and simple', as it is manifest in the lives of believers. James saw this as the defining characteristic of the religious life, 'an element or quality we can meet nowhere else'.[29] He called this quality 'saintliness'. He writes:

> The collective name for ripe fruits of religion in a character is Saintliness. The saintly character is the character for which spiritual emotions are the habitual centre of the personal energy; an there is a certain composite photograph of universal saintliness, the same in all religions, of which the features can easily be traced.[30]

Saintliness inculcates 'a wider vision of life than that of its selfish little interests'.[31] It also creates a friendly continuity of the power in our lives, an elation of freedom and a general disposition to be lovingly affirmative. It also heightens aesthetic awareness, creates fortitude, inculcates purity and increases charity. None of this proves the existence of God. James quotes Leuba, approvingly when he says that 'God *is not known, he is not understood, he is used* – sometimes as a meat purveyor, sometimes as a moral support, sometimes as a friend, sometimes as the object of love. If he proves himself useful the religious consciousness asks for no more than that.'[32]

Therefore, James continued, we must be ready to judge the religious life *exclusively by its results*. That is not to say, crudely, that it works demonstrably in this or that specific instance. It is to say that one believes that a religious view of life accounts most adequately for its known and anticipated complexities. He calls this 'a faith based on desire'.[33] It affirms that the best things are eternal things. Accepting this is a 'momentous option, a trust'.[34] It establishes the criteria for a moral view of life in which good overcomes evil. For the most part, people overcome evil by pursuing the distractions of happiness and this should not be despised. It brings immense relief to people under duress which is all of us at some time or other. This is normal human 'healthy-mindedness'. It 'is inadequate as a philosophical doctrine, because the evil facts which it refuses positively to account for are a genuine portion of reality; and they may after all be the best key to life's significance, and possibly the only openers of our eyes to the deepest levels of truth'.[35] To aspire to this we have to embrace the optimism of religion in trust and faith. This, of course, is a central Christian view which, interestingly, James did not necessarily share. He acknowledged that being religious was for him personally difficult. This might have been because he could not embrace Christian optimism about the triumph of good over evil. (Was James a pessimist at heart or a realist?) He recognised that 'The normal processes of life contains moments as bad as any of those in which insane melancholy is filled with, moments in which radical evil gets its innings and takes its solid turn'.[36] Evil, for him, represented what he called 'the totality of things' and he reluctantly concluded that not even religious reconciliation with it is possible.[37] This, to him, was not a cheerful subject. The only religions which should be contemplated are those which face the totality of evil. 'Buddhism of course and Christianity', he wrote, 'are the best known to us of these'.[38] This is because they are both religions of deliverance. James implicitly approved the advance of liberalism in Christianity on the grounds that it moved attention away from an unhealthy individual preoccupation with personal salvation and drew it to the dignified possibilities of human life.[39]

The pragmatism of James and others has remained a potent force in Western philosophy and has many contemporary advocates. Its freshness, even brashness, is as engaging as it ever was. In North America, at least, it has been all-pervasive across a range of subjects including religion, politics, sociology, psychology, law and order, economics, labour theory and civil rights. In all this, it epitomises the practical doggedness and optimism of contemporary American culture, no understanding of which is explicable without consideration of its influence. All this is so self-evident that it belies the popular misunderstanding that philosophy deals only with what is esoteric and removed from everyday life. This has never been entirely true of any philosophy, but it is plainly not so of later nineteenth century American pragmatism. It makes prominent, as we have seen, the task in hand and pursues only questions about what has to be done. Done, that is, for reasons which are observable to all and which are acceptable or not for demonstrably practical reasons.

It is central to the argument of this book that this pragmatic philosophy enables us to understand the profound sense in which a religion like Christianity can be said to be true. However, whilst he believed that William James, as we saw, drew back from accepting that religion enables us to overcome evil. He is not alone in this. For many people this claim is just too much. Evil, for them in an intractable, given and inexplicable part of the human lot. Not even religions like Christianity and Buddhism which address it as directly as they do can serve to dent its reality. There is, of course, an admirable Stoic resignation about this view which deserves respect, even if we do not share it. In its way it effectively is a triumph over evil. This is rather in the manner of captives who know that there is no escape from their captivity and have the courage to face it for what it is. Instances of such are the stuff of the heroic spirit. Things are as they are and we have to accept that and make the best of it. Would that we could change them, but we cannot.

In the following two chapters we will see why the truth of religion understood in this way is not just rhetoric. See how, that is, it translates itself into the practicalities of everyday life. How it engages with this issue or that, as we make the inescapable and innumerable moral decisions with which we are daily beset. Here it will become immediately apparent that the essence of Christian morality is far from the irrelevant thing it is commonly and mistakenly by many supposed to be. Many of those who both profess and reject it invariably suppose that its main strength is that it is a source of certainty in the face of so many uncertainties. These certainties are located by them either in either the Bible or the Church. Either or both are thought to bring all debate and confusion to an end as they reveal God's word in this situation or that. The greater truth, however, is that neither the Bible nor the Church are capable of achieving this level of certainty. To believe that they can is to treat them idolatrously and to fall victim of dangerous illusions. The Bible and the Church do great things, but delivering unquestionable certainty is not one of them. They both, for example, provide great insight and sustenance. This is much more profound and relevant to the human condition, as we have been exploring it, than can ever be provided by certainties. This is an uncomfortable truth for many biblical pundits and ecclesiastical prelates. When confronted with uncertainty they invariably dig themselves deeper into the holes of their own making and shout loudest when their arguments are at their weakest. Even a casual awareness of their doings in public affairs well illustrates all this. Anti-this or that, pro-this or the other in ways which seldom bear on the issues at stake with a credibility that commands any wider respect. Little wonder that so much Christian moral witness in our ever more complex and demanding world is marginalised. It marginalises itself. Spiritual pride on this scale is a major cause of the rejection of faith by thinking people. As a result, they seek other sources of wisdom. That for the reasons we have seen in our discussions about radical evil is nothing less than a tragedy. There is more, much more, to Christianity and to the profundity of its relevance to our human lot. In the next chapter we will now see how this is true of life in general of the moral life in particular.

CHAPTER SEVEN

And Morality

In the foregoing we have shown that Christianity enables us to live with evil in spite of that fact that it does not provide us with an explanation of it. We have also seen that there is a philosophically defensible sense in which it can be said to be 'true'. We will now widen this discussion to look at ways in which the Christian faith engages with our moral decision making. Again, we will see that it has widespread practical applications. This is because it facilitates a particular style of engagement with moral problems. On the on hand, it draws on the Bible and Christian history. On the other, it is hard-headed in the sense that it requires moral problems to be thoroughly understood, however complicated they might seem. For this reason, it invariably seeks the help of appropriate technical expertise. This enables a detailed engagement with the world and its problems which, again, belies the popular misconception that Christianity is otherworldly. It does not set out with all the answers. In many instances, all it can realistically do is to identify tentative steps forward. These need not be shunned. Rather, they might be understood as steps of grace which can and must be taken in the name of moral seriousness and responsibility.

Christianity inherited from Judaism an understanding of morality which made it an intrinsic part of faith. They are as two sides of a coin. This is because of the so-called 'ethical monotheism' which emerged in the writings of the Hebrew Prophets. Prominent among these was Amos. He made it explicitly clear that righteousness was a divine requirement which exceeded that of the ritual with which Israel had become preoccupied. In a memorable phrase he demand that it '...run down like rivers in an ever flowing stream' (Amos 5:24). Such prophetic thinking left an indelible mark on the Jewish understanding of God. This is why it is so centrally reflected in the teaching of Jesus. For him too faith and morality were inseparable.[1]

In his teaching, human fulfilment is closely bound up with being morally responsible. It is a condition of faith and of social responsibility. The same is still true for us. We share moral responsibility for one another. We all have to form opinions about and contribute to the collective well-being. The agenda here is awesome. The list of issues we need to form opinions about is seemingly never ending. It is, moreover, one which is now exacerbated by the ceaseless technical and other innovations of modernity.

A modern consequence all this is the general uncertainty which attaches to most of our moral decision making. We encounter this in two ways. First, we are often uncertain about whether or not the moral precedents and values of the past are always a sure guide in the present. Second, we are beset with so much uncertainty about the possible consequences of our actions in the present. Ever since the eighteenth century, when Jeremy Bentham published his magisterial *Principles of Morals and Legislation* (1724), we have come to recognise that to some degree at least the morality of our actions has something to do with the desirability or otherwise we attach to their consequences.[2] For this reason, Bentham's book really is one of the founding texts of modern culture. It effectively still defines the way most people commonly think about morality. This view of morality was famously also championed, though qualified, by his disciple John Stuart Mill in the nineteenth century.[3] It is not without its problems, as Mill was aware, but it has survived in the popular mind as a central account of the nature of morality. We now scarce approach any moral problem without recognising that we have to evaluate the consequences which will follow from any chosen courses of action. Indeed, we will invariably find ourselves deciding between actions by evaluating those consequences alone. Recurring harrowing cases of what to do about Siamese twins more than illustrate this. Not long ago we could do nothing but let nature take its course. Though many of the twins survived for years with love and tender care, their life-expectancy was comparatively short and when it ended for one, both would die. With the rapid advance of medical science all this, of course, has now changed dramatically. Even with twins who have but weeks to live it is now possible to contemplate the separation of one who can be reasonably expected to live a quality life of perhaps normal duration. Not all agree, of course, and older 'let nature take its course' views still persist. But we do not let nature take its course in other areas of medical ethics. If we did, child mortality would still be at the unacceptable levels it used to be and the ever improving human life-span would be less than half of what it now is. If we can improve on nature we are obliged to do so in the name of common humanity. Most people, therefore, instinctively feel that if the life of one of such twins who are both expected to die can be saved by separation from the other then it should be done. Here we are now well-served by a reasonably assured expectation of the outcome of our actions. That this invariably sways the debate shows just how important understanding the morality of our actions in this consequential way has become. Unless we are students of moral philosophy, we no longer much argue about whether or not we should evaluate the desirability or otherwise of the consequences of our actions when we seek the right thing to do. That argument, as we have seen, has long been won. What we do argue about is what those consequences might be and whether they are acceptable or not. This is why thinking about the acceptability or otherwise of our contemplated moral actions is now a major cause of modern moral uncertainty. Here we are constantly frustrated by the sheer limitations of our knowledge. Debates about the use we ought or ought not to make of the rapidly emerging bio-sciences are a good example of this. What about the use of stem-cells in medicine? What about genetically modified crops? The only honest answer is that we do not always know. Know, that is, whether or not enhancing crop yields and preventing their disease is preferable given the possible long-term and irreversible dangers of doing so We are now less than human unless we face all this. We have to cope with it and exercise our moral responsibilities in ways which bequeath benefits and not burdens to ourselves and to future generations.

All this uncertainty is now clearly caused by the fact that we live constantly at the limits of our ever expanding technical capabilities. We can, therefore, be sure that our present list of uncertainties will be added to inexorably. The next generation will experience the same and so on. When all this happens on a number of fronts simultaneously it is little wonder that we experience such widespread uncertainty. This experience alone can, in fact, enervate us as moral agents. This is extremely dangerous. It paves the way for others to impose their will on us and that, in turn, erodes democracy and freedom. Such uncertainty now pervades so many of our everyday concerns that it makes us individually and socially extremely vulnerable.

All this is why any who are morally serious must seek the very best a available technical advice. There is no substitute for this. It can only be obtained by listening to and working with specialists in the many disciplines which relate to our moral confusions. This is not always an easy thing to do. Moral philosophers and theologians cannot, for the most part, become specialists in the disciplines they enquire into. What they, therefore, have to do is to try and discern exactly what it is in any area of enquiry that bears most precisely on the moral issue at stake. What this might or might not be is not always self-evident. It can only be discovered by diligent and careful analysis in which moral philosophers, scientists and others work patiently together. Fortunately, this is often not too difficult to arrange. Scientists, for example, who are well aware of their moral responsibilities to wider society are invariably only too willing to engage in the sort of dialogue which is required. This is also invariably true of politicians and others involved. All it requires is good will and self-discipline all round for the work to begin in earnest. This latter requirement is an important one. Proper enquiry can be frustrated if any taking part suppose, too readily, that they have the answer to the problem. They seldom do. Those who want to contribute to the debate must be prepared to make it with more humility. When this happens, progress can thankfully be made. This is marked whenever even tentative agreements can be reached about a way forward with any particular issue. Given that the world is now as complicated as it is, moral seriousness requires nothing less.

Yet another reason for such widespread uncertainty in moral debate is that we now have a far greater knowledge of life-styles and belief systems other than our own than our predecessors have ever had. This alone causes us to engender respect for others even when their moral choices are very different from our own. This learning process is now world-wide. It is well established in the comparatively new science of social anthropology and serviced by the modern revolution in communications technology. We all know more about each other than we have ever done. This is a wholly good thing. Providing, that is, we gladly expose ourselves to the incessant learning

And Morality

curves it imposes upon us. And providing, moreover, that we do not shirk these by retreating into our pre-defined insularities. But, all this is unsettling. So many of the answers to moral perplexity which might have served us well in the past now frequently seem to do so no longer. Knowing as much as we now do about alternatives to such answers is clearly one cause of this.

The usual Christian response to all this invariably comes in three forms. The first is based on the Bible and the second on the Church. The third is a version of the second which stresses the importance of the believing community. We will discuss each of them in turn. In each we will find that they can be unhelpful. It will be shown that this is because they are widely misunderstood by Christians themselves. Alternative understandings will then be explained and these will show why both the Bible and the Church are both still crucially important in our quest for moral responsibility.

The first way in which Christians try to counter moral uncertainty is by confronting it with what they believe to be the moral certainty in the Bible. Those who proffer this invariably also claim that the Bible is the revealed word of God which is applicable in all life's circumstances present and future. Let the example of understanding human sexuality illustrate the point. We no longer take our understandings of it as for granted as we even recently did. It now embraces among other things, female emancipation, birth control, and the proliferation of alternative sorts of family arrangements including same sex relationships. In recent Western culture, at least, it used to be held widely that there is only one of these which is morally acceptable, the heterosexual. However, many people now believe that this is not the case. They recognise that for many individuals a homosexual orientation is equally as natural and that it is not always a choice for those who experience it. It is, rather, for them a part of the givenness of their nature.

Most of the mainstream Christian Churches have produced Reports on the topic in recent years. These have combined compassion with scholarship and a concern to reconcile the deep divisions among their membership which the debate causes. Some of these Reports have urged more Christian toleration of homosexuality than has previously been the case. For example, a seminal report by the House of Bishops of the Church of England in 1991 was called *Issues in Human Sexuality*.[4] It stressed that the Church should be welcoming of all people whatever their sexual orientation and practice. It also called for a time of patient reflection on the issues. For these reasons, the Report was rightly seen as an encouragement to people who felt estranged from the Church as a consequence of their sexual orientation. It provoked an, at times, bitter debate which still continues.

As the case for the greater toleration of homosexuality grows some Christians object on the grounds that it is prohibited in the Bible. They do this by quoting isolated texts. All this is much discussed elsewhere and need not detain here in any more detail.[5] What we do need to note is that the belief that the Bible can be used in this way to settle moral problems is profoundly mistaken. The Bible is a complex collection of writings which span well over a thousand years and these refer to many events which occurred nearly another thousand years before that. Naturally, these writings all reflect the cultures and times out of which they came. Little wonder that they are not always, even seldom, coherent, or that they contain conflicting views on ranges of topics. Furthermore, many of the books of the Bible have been arbitrarily and even controversially included. Their very selection, in fact, tells us as much of the times in which it was made as it does about the texts themselves. The Bible, in brief, is not God's final word on all matters for all time. It is a living and vibrant witness to how that word has been understood at different times and in different places by different people with different preoccupations and anxieties. Seen in this way, it is a source of huge and ongoing inspiration, providing only that it is understood properly for what it is and not for what it is manifestly not. Those who claim that the Bible, or that particular biblical texts, can be cited to settle for all time our contemporary uncertainties about human sexuality, or whatever, are so seriously off the plot as not to be taken seriously. They turn the text into an idol, abase themselves before it and thereby abrogate any responsibility for thinking the issue through for themselves. None of this would even be worth mentioning, were it not or the fact that people who think like this are invariably politically well organised and vociferous. This enables them to punch far above their intellectual weight in ongoing debate. What they, in fact, invariably do is to provoke an understandable reaction among people who conclude that religion is an irrelevance in the pursuit of the serious moral life. People who use the biblical text in this way are idolators, pure and simple. That is what they are, although they draw seemingly large numbers to themselves in what look like flourishing churches. They are, however, thankfully but a minority on the wider Christian contemporary scene. In fact, they often appear to have more in common with extremists of one sort or another in other religions than they do with their co-religionists who, as here, are of more liberal outlook.

This is an admittedly harsh judgment on the way some Christians use the Bible. It does, however, need to be made with a caution. There are many Christians who make similarly incredible claims for the Bible, but who actually use it with discretion when forming their moral judgements. For this, they are to be respected. It enables them to engage with others in serious debate and to do so responsibly and constructively.[6]

Until about fifty years ago it was generally believed that the Bible could yield consistent views on most matters of morality because it was the word of God. Books which included the phrase 'the biblical view of' were common. They served to reinforce the assumption that moral problems could be approached by using phrases such as 'the Bible teaches'. The Bible is still understood in this way by some commentators.[7] As we will see, the Bible certainly does have a teaching role, but this is not the way in which it can now helpfully be understood. The reason for this is simple. The Bible, as we have acknowledged throughout, is a compilation of many different sorts of writing from many different cultures over a long period of time. Their authors wrote to serve many different purposes, often in quite specific situations. There is no evidence at all in the variety of these texts that they are or can be welded into one as if they were all equally and coherently the single word of God on different issues. If the Bible is the word of God, then it cannot be so in this sense. An all powerful and all knowing God could have done a much better editorial job! From the fact that such a God clearly failed in this sense, we can only conclude that God was not interested. The plain fact is that, in the manner of its origin, the Bible is a profoundly human enterprise. Like all such, however, it can embrace and communicate divine inspiration. We will now look briefly at how it does this in its account of the moral teaching of Jesus.

In the popular and pious imagination Jesus is not only the Son of God (this is problematic as we have seen), he is also an inspired teacher of a morality which was an integral part of his preaching and teaching. This imagination further supposes that we can read off the content of that morality and apply its detail to the circumstances of our own life and times. Seen in this way, Jesus is not only the Messiah, he is also seen as a great moral teacher. This moral teaching, moreover, is widely respected even by many of those who do not accept the wider Christian message. But, did Jesus actually teach a moral message of this kind? Did he, that is, teach morality in such a way that he legislated on moral issues in detail and for all time? If that is what he intended then he too surely could have made a better job of it. Christians are generally as morally perplexed as anybody else when it comes to facing issues of the day. They are, moreover, often noted for their sincere but differing moral opinions. If the teaching of Jesus did contain detailed moral instruction which was applicable for posterity, then somehow and somewhere it is got muddled, to say the least. Not so, some reply, Jesus left us with one profound answer to all our moral dilemmas: that of love. The injunction to love God and our neighbours in the preaching of Jesus is, they claim, nothing less than a new commandment. In the Gospels of Mark (12: 28–34) and Matthew (22: 34–40) Jesus formulated this in the last week of his life. It can also be found in Luke's Gospel but there it is located much earlier in Jesus' ministry. In all three, the commandment is associated with Jesus' preaching about the imminent arrival of the Kingdom of God. It enjoins his hearers to prepare themselves for this soon to be outpouring of God's love by sharing it among themselves in anticipation. The point of all this is clearly related to the imminence of the end of time. Love, so envisaged, is not therefore purported to be a humanitarian moral programme for all time. For that to be the case, the requirements of love would have to be self-evident. They are clearly not. Even a cursory knowledge of the history of Christian, let alone secular, morality is enough to show that this has seldom, if ever, been the case. What love requires in this situation or that is invariably something which love itself does not stipulate. When we think that it does it can put us seriously at odds with others who think differently and equally sincerely about love's requirements. What love, in fact, requires of us in the first instance is that we think out its detailed requirements for ourselves. It does not obviate the

And Morality

need for us to do this. This is what prevents love from becoming nothing more than a vague good intention.

Love can, however, do other important things. It can *motivate* us in the sense that it can make us compellingly aware that something must be done in this situation or that. This is no small thing for the simple reason that we invariably try to ignore moral problems which we know will be difficult to resolve. Love demands that doing this is unacceptable. It requires action. Even more than this it can also *inspire* us to be diligent in finding out what that action ought to be. It might, therefore, even be something quite innovative.

Even more than all this, love can *sustain* us when we find its requirements to be difficult to accept and even seemingly impossible to carry out. Moving evidence of this can be seen in the heroic lengths some people have to go to in caring for others in need. In these and other such examples love can sustain self-sacrifice to the 'nth degree.

These are the great works of love and they are to be cherished. They do, in fact, almost everything for us, except one important thing. They do not spare us the obligation to *think things out for ourselves*. This latter is the real key to understanding the place of moral teaching in the ministry of Jesus and in the Christian life.

People persistently asked Jesus for moral advice. Famously, the rich young Ruler asked of him '...what then should I do' (Matt. 22:35). Jesus replied that he should keep the commandments and the ruler replied that he had done that since his youth. Jesus then added that he should 'Sell all that you have and distribute it to the poor' (Luke 18:22). This was probably the nearest Jesus ever came to giving specific moral advice. It has been enough for some commentators to infer that he had a 'bias for the poor'.[8] This is a perfectly legitimate interpretation of what Jesus said in this instance which can be put to widespread economic purpose. More deeply however, he was also making a point about 'the poor' being those who might be materially affluent yet stood in need of God's love. So understood therefore, even this seemingly straight forward moral advice is couched in spiritual instruction which was always the real focus of his teaching. Get your spirituality right, he seems to say again and again, and all else will follow. Get it wrong and it will not. What that 'all else' might be in this situation or that is something we clearly have to think out for ourselves. The earliest Christian communities certainly interpreted his teaching in this way. Whilst they were initially not that interested in the detailed application of his message to everyday life, they were obliged to become so once it became clear that that life was going to last longer than they earlier thought. Once such concern was about divorce. Mark's Gospel responds to this in one way and St Paul did so in another. This is a central illustration of how these early Christians *developed* (the stress cannot be over stated) their thinking about morality. They knew that their discipleship required them to think things out or themselves. St Paul's and other letters in the New Testament along with the Acts of the Apostles show us something of all this in action. They reveal the exciting story of the Early Church coming to grips with the actual and ever changing circumstances of everyday life. St Paul, as we have seen, is particularly inspiring in this sense. His letters invariably take some theological aspect of Christian tradition, then develop it in ways appropriate to the task in hand and finally apply it to the actual circumstances of the lives of his addressees. This has, in fact, been the central model of Christian preaching, teaching and instruction ever since.

Even, therefore, in the New Testament Christian thinking about morality is dynamic and changing. This happens whenever individuals and groups respond to Jesus' insistence that they should think things out for themselves and throw themselves on the mercy of God. For this reason, he does not give a set formulae of detailed prescriptions about what always has to be done in this situation or that. His teaching about love leaves open rather than fore-closes questions about what actually has to be done.

All this, of course, is quite the contrary to what it is commonly supposed that Jesus said about morality. But there are even more startling things about it. One is that Jesus went on to point out that if we want examples of how to go about all this then we must be mindful to look for them in unexpected places. 'The religious authorities', we might appropriately think. Certainly not, Jesus replies again and again. Woe to the Scribes and the Pharisees and to all such groups who confidently thought that they always knew exactly what to do. The various religious establishments were repeatedly attacked by Jesus rather that held up by him as examples for others to follow. As if this were not bad enough for them, further humiliation was at hand. Jesus did point to exemplars of what he was saying and they were the very people the religious establishments despised! (e.g. Luke 10:33) These were the outsiders and even the outcasts of society who were thought to be beyond redemption. These were not the just-not-very-nice-people, they were explicitly the actually despised. The more despised they were the more likely Jesus was to laud their moral and spiritual virtues. Does this mean, for example, that in our own time we should look even to the most despised for moral wisdom? Mean that in spite of our revulsion for them and their deeds, they might yet be capable of being moral exemplars. This is seemingly incomprehensible, but Jesus' teaching really is as shocking as that. All this was and still is, nothing less than the subversion of spirituality and morality as it was commonly understood. Modern Novelists have also made much of the often startling nature of love's requirements in this situation or that. Thomas Hardy, for example, knew this to the cost of his popularity as a Victorian novelist. He believed that he had shown why Tess was morally exemplary, in spite of her being guilty of adultery and murder. His readership abreacted to this to such an extent that he never wrote another novel. Dostoevsky and many others have explored the same theme with similar reactions.

Love's requirements are, therefore, not always as self-evident as we might at first think. We have to work at discovering what they are. This calls for a complete open-mindedness, a total humility and, above all, an ever-willingness to be creative to the point of being radically innovative in our moral understandings and actions. In this way Jesus did not preach *a* morality at all. He did something much more profound and perennially relevant. He showed how moral virtue could be created, but only by those who earnestly and sincerely sought it *for themselves*. This last emphasis is the key to it. Such virtue has to be owned, period. It cannot be borrowed, copied or learned by rote. This requires personal and collective creativity and courage. Little wonder that it did not result in even more moral anarchy than it did. The reason why it did not is because, along with this incredible stress on individual moral autonomy and creativity there went an equally emphatic stress on communal sensitivity and responsibility. All actions however mundane they may be on the one hand, or innovative on the other, had to stand the test of whether or not they built up the body of Christ. Jesus was, as we have seen, not particularly interested in this implication because he clearly did not think that what he was preaching and teaching was anything other than a preparation for the imminent arrival of the Kingdom of God. It was meant, therefore, as the means to acquire the righteousness necessary for its entry. The delay of that event, as we have also seen, meant that what he said had to be modified into a form which would maintain its spontaneity on the one hand and yet become institutionalised on the other. This created an obvious tension which has been a feature of Christian morality ever since. Individuals had to be true to themselves but true also to the communities in which they lived, worshipped and in which they tried to do the right thing. None of this has changed. Nor will it ever do so this side of the Kingdom of God.

This dynamic view of Christian morality is rooted in the interaction of human righteousness and the righteousness of God, it never changes with the years or the circumstances. These are what we have to think out for ourselves. This is the only alternative left us when we reject recourse to moral certainties. Invariably, when we do this thinking we do not discover certainty. What we do is so much more profound than this. We learn *to cope with uncertainty* for ourselves and collectively. This is a dynamic view of Christian morality. Contrary to the popular belief that it stands for the *status quo*, or the *status quo ante*, it demands that even these things be re-examined if necessary. It also wants us to look forward rather than backward, to embrace innovation and novelty and to flinch in the face of nothing that life's vagaries can throw at us. Understood in this way, Christian morality is far more relevant to our own ever changing and challenging times that one would ever be likely to suppose from hearing the ways in which it is commonly and as we have shown, mistakenly, understood. It is part of a wider vision in which the biblical faith is not seen as having been made and set in parchment by the people of the Bible in their times once and only once for all time. On the contrary, the biblical faith is still as much in the making for us as it ever was for those who wrote and read it in the first place. We cannot make it by copying them. At their best, they did not copy each other anyway. They can clearly be seen to be thinking things out in ever changing circumstances. We have to do the same thing. We have to cope with applying the integrity of faith in the actual situations in which we find ourselves. In this we should no more expect others who follow to copy us than we have felt obliged to copy those before us. This is an ever ongoing and innovative task. It is nothing less than that of creating value in the midst of life's ever changing circumstances. At its best, the Christian Church has always known and practised this. It has done this perhaps most profoundly when it has had to realise that it has previously been mistaken about something. We will look at just two examples of this.

For, amazingly, about two millennia the Church morally accepted two things it has now had to change its mind on. These are the acceptability of slavery and the superiority of males over females. The story of the repeal of the first of these is well known. Towards the end of the eighteenth century William Wilberforce and others campaigned to have slavery made illegal in England. They were opposed, not so much because it was by then still extant in English society, but because England had great economic stakes in the international slavery as a 'third leg' of trade across the Atlantic on which a great deal of the national wealth depended. The other two legs were from Liverpool to West Africa and from America back to Liverpool. Vested interests were, therefore, formidable but the abolitionists prevailed against them. A whole raft of social assumptions which underpinned slavery and which were supported for so long by the Christian Church were swept away forever. The Church, like the wider society of which it was part, had been terribly wrong for nearly two millennia.

The second momentous recent change has been expressed in feminist theology. It emerged in the last half of the last century and is of growing importance. It is premised on a general view which was expressed by Liberation Theologians. Namely, that that traditional theology frequently takes the dominant form in which the interests of the politically and economically powerful prevail over the interests of those who are not so. Feminist theologians argued that much of traditional theology suppresses feminist interests in the same way. There are many different emphases and traditions in feminist theologies. What they all have in common with liberation theology is that they stress that theology should begin with a bias for representing the interests of those who are thus oppressed, rather than with the, however ostensibly well meaning, oppressors. The results of all this, as is well known, have been dramatic. Like the liberation theologians, the feminist ones have made their point repeatedly and cogently. Theologians should no longer ignore it. Christianity has for centuries been responsible for at least a part of and in truth a large part of, male dominance of Western culture. Indeed, some feminist theologians think that it is irredeemable at this point and they have a strong case. So much of what still prevails as theological orthodoxy is laden with sexist assumptions. The still widespread use of the male pronoun for God is an example. Avoiding this, as here throughout, sometimes requires the use of a not terribly elegant neologism, 'Godself', but this in infinitely (no pun intended) to be preferred.

The feminist criticism of traditional incarnational theology is a simple one. How is it, they ask, that God could be completely incarnate in only one of the sexes? There are, of course, traditional answers to this. Women are central to the Gospel story and this is epitomised in the cult of the Virgin Mary, and so on. The trouble here is that trotting out these answers simply makes matters worse. They are prejudiced and that is that, however uncomfortable it might be for some to face the fact. Christianity came out of cultures in which women held second place in so many ways and it did nothing to redress that. Exclusive focus on the 'Fatherhood' and 'Sonship' of God is, therefore, no longer acceptable in the light of the cogency of the feminist protest.

Both of the changes we have briefly looked at, slavery and male domination, took centuries, even millennia, to occur. Of course, other changes took place much more rapidly in this period, some of them in the New Testament itself as well as others we have noted in passing. For reasons we have also seen, it is self-evident that the pace of change is an ever accelerating feature of modern life. If the Churches are to maintain their credibility they have to respond to this. To achieve this they will need to make it clear that their natural stance on any particular issue is to look outwards and to the future, rather than inwards and to the past. This is easy to state as a general principle, but it is difficult for Churches to achieve. One reason for this is because, for the most part, they are institutions under siege for their very survival. So much of what they say and do in relation to everyday issues reflects this. The real sorrow of this is that the dynamic of the faith they try to communicate is, as we have repeatedly seen, far more relevant to modern life and times than they often seem to purport.

The foregoing claim to biblical certainty has been made mainly, but not exclusively, by Protestant Christians. By contrast, the claim that the source of moral certainty is the Church itself is classically Roman Catholic.

The teaching office of the Roman Catholic Church is called the Magisterium. It sees itself as the custodian and articulator of orthodoxy in doctrine and morality. Moreover, it claims that it is authoritative. Infallability has been claimed by the Pope, but only since the First Vatican Council in 1870. The Second Vatican Council of 1963–1965, seemingly mindful of the enormity of his claim, mitigated it to include the whole College of Bishops working with the Pope. This Council was convened after Pope John XXIII acceded at the age of seventy eight and was expected, therefore, effectively to be a caretaker Pope. Startlingly, only three months after his election on 25 January 1959 he announced that he was to convene 'an ecumenical council for the universal church'. He intended this to achieve two things. First, to bring the Church up to date (*aggiornamento*) with the period of rapid social change in which it was engulfed. Second, to enable the Church to be of ecumenical service to the wider Christian Church. To this end, the Pope also created a new Secretariat for Promoting Christian Unity. One of its first responsibilities was to nominate official observers to the Council from other Christian Churches. They were to attend closed as well as open sessions of the Council. In his opening address the Pope made it clear that the desire to serve the people of God the better was to be the pastoral motivation for all that the Council was to attempt. Pope John XXIII then died on 3 June 1963, as unexpectedly as he had come to office. The Council was suspended, Pope Paul VI was then elected and the Council re-convened. He made it clear that it was to continue in the spirit of his predecessor. As a result, high hopes of a new dawn for the Church were maintained. At the close of the Council sixteen documents were produced. These have been the subject of scrutiny and debate ever since. Their tone is both reformatory and conciliatory. The Decree on Ecumenism was promulgated on 21 November 1964.[9] This recognised that real degrees of ecumenism did exist, but claimed that that they are imperfect. The hint in all this is that the Roman Church had come to see this imperfection as embracing itself as well as other Churches. Some saw this as a new humility which could be expected to lead the way to dramatic reforms. These, frankly, have not happened. Paul VI and his successor, John Paul I, did not show sustained enthusiasm for serious reform. Nor did John Paul II. Pope Benedict XVI does not now appear to do so either. The Roman Catholic Church, at an official level, is nowhere as up to date and reformed as the Second Vatican Council clearly intended that it should by now be. Unofficially, of course, things are often very different as groups of Christians take ecumenical initiatives of their own. Even these, however, are invariably frustrated by a lack of official support. In fact, they are often officially prevented. All this is part of the background story of the modern relationship of the Roman Catholic Church to the rest of Christendom.

The craving for and claiming to achieve certainty in the Christian tradition does not come any more stridently than it does in the Roman Catholic Magisterium. It at least matches the parallel Protestant claims made for the biblical text. Like them, however, it is mistaken. This is more the pity because so much of what the Magisterium achieves is otherwise of high quality. The Encyclicals it publishes on behalf of the Pope have been phenomenally numerous in recent times.[10] Moreover, they contain much which has been well received and is more than worthy of wider attention. This, however, has to be understood as an ongoing contribution to wider debate rather than in the spirit that it is offered, as the infallible word of God. To see why it is manifestly not this, one only has to ask the rather obvious question: where does the Magisterium get its infallibility from? It is self-proclaimed of course. This is obvious enough, but it also purports to be nothing less than the sole custodian of all Christian truth for all time. Little wonder that so many otherwise even loyal, devout and scholarly Roman Catholics frequently admit to embarrassment about it. This engenders for them a commonality with those Protestants who demur with equal embarrassment from the same sort of extremes claimed in their tradition for the Bible. This creates a liberal 'common ground' which is fruitful of both scholarship and practical insight, not to mention also of fellowship, friendship and mutual respect.

Neither of these ways of establishing Christian moral certainty in the face of uncertainty are at all credible. In truth, for the most part they are but peddling prejudices of one sort or another. For this reason they can be counter-productive in the wider and more serious quest to discover the relevance of the Christian tradition to contemporary moral life. That their proponents, when so accused, deny this as implacably as they invariably do, does nothing but both compound the problem and impede the real work of the Churches. None of this criticism is to gainsay, however, that both of these traditions do not have their part to play in the wider witness of the Christian Churches. Biblical witness and the vast and accumulated experience of the Churches both have to be properly respected in any serious quest for moral integrity. This is why each of these traditions have contributions to make to wider debate. All we have pointed out is that neither of these approaches completely represents the whole truth about Christian morality in the manner their proponents invariably claim. That they, so to speak, stay in business as they do can only be explained by the fact that there are still significant enough numbers of people who want their religion to deliver moral certainties in these ways.

The third Christian response to moral uncertainty has become increasingly influential in recent years. It claims that Christian morality only makes sense in the framework of a Christian view of the world. The corollary of this is that to be virtuous in a Christian sense, one has first to join and share the outlook of the Churches. Non-Christians have made similar claims about the importance of understanding their views of morality in the light of related world-views. These approaches have been dubbed 'virtue ethics'. They are making an important point, albeit one which originated in protest at the supposed failure of the secularisation of modern, utilitarian, views of morality. The most influential such protest was made by Alasdair Macintyre in *After Virtue*.[11] Virtue ethicists reject the possibility of there being one world-view for morality to which all religions and value systems contribute. What they claim is that we all occupy discrete and effectively closed value systems, though they may well overlap from time to time. Therefore, for example, the moral teaching of the Bible has to and can only be interpreted by the Bible-believing community. Or, again, the Magisterium only has credibility to those who accept its authority as a matter of ecclesial discipline. Put in this light, these claims perhaps have more credibility that we have just allowed them. Virtue Ethicists who defend them in this way can rightly claim that they are re-locating our understanding of morality back into its classical roots. These stressed that questions about what we ought to do are bound up with questions about the sort of life-styles our wider belief systems require of us. Such a view has found able apologists in recent writings about Christian morality and is not to be rejected lightly. It points to something which cannot be gainsaid. In what we might call its 'weak' version it is acceptable enough. That can be expressed in the claim that there is *a* connection between our wider belief systems and our moral judgements. In its 'strong' version, however, it is not so easily acceptable. This claims that understanding that link is the *sole* defining key to discovering moral virtue. This imposes severe restrictions on our understanding of that virtue. These, in turn, cause the proliferation of discrete moralities which then vie with each other. This is a serious difficulty with virtue ethics. It alone should inculcate caution, particularly when we live in a world which should be more and more interested in what human beings have in common than in their differences. So, even if there is apparently some ground for understanding the relationship between morality and wider belief systems it should be treated with extreme caution. The moral project we now engage is nothing less than one which includes the whole of the human race. That is not to say that discrete systems of morality will have nothing to contribute to the wider debate. It is but to say that they should be prepared to join in it with more humility. When they do this, of course, they will encounter the sorts of uncertainty we have been discussing. They then face the test of whether they can sustain and contribute to ongoing debate with others, or whether they retreat into the private worlds of their own certainties. If they do the latter they will have helped to create is a world in which discrete moralities become a mosaic of moral systems which are effectively immune from each other. Whilst this might well provide them with certainties and comfort, it limits the scope of their moral responsibility and deprives wider debate of the benefit of their wisdom.

Rather than retreat into their shells, the Christian Churches must find every way they can to serve the common good. At their best they do this. They have a distinguished modern record of producing sustained reflection on matters of public concern. One simple reason why the Churches achieve all this is because they are well organised for the purpose. They are a networked part of academic and other debating forums. To further this work most of the mainstream Churches have their boards for social responsibility, or whatever, and these are answerable to synods or committees who both commission and receive their deliberations. If these are well-timed, they are often eagerly awaited and even receive national attention. All this has the effect of putting the Churches, often working together under ecumenical aegis, at the centre of the national and international political life. Overall, it must and can be said, these contributions are often of a high quality and carry their weight and influence in wider debate. One reason for this is because they invariably draw on the wider expertise of relevant professionals who appear ever willing so to engage. Military and medical professionals are often at the forefront of this sort of activity. Church members, be they theologians, philosophers or whatever, have invariably welcomed and taken part in these discussions. This is the main formal way in which modern Christian engagement with morality takes place.

In this chapter we have looked at some of the ways in which the Churches engage with and minister to their wider communities. In doing this we have only glimpsed at examples of a wide range of activity. It is a patient and sustained work both at the formal and informal levels of Church life. The central point of this discussion has been to show at least something of the practicality with which the Churches engage the world around them. In doing this they are, whilst at times intransigent, also responsive, do sometimes change their minds and invariably help to bring articulation and clarification to wider debate. At their best, they encapsulate a reciprocating vigour which is generated between their grass roots life and the official levels of their engagement in public opinion forming. This latter cannot exist without the former. Unless the Churches are strong at their roots in living Christian communities they cannot for long also be strong elsewhere. This has always been recognised and stressed since the days of their origin. St Paul, again, was the original visionary in all this. He saw well that the lives and preoccupations of the Church had to engage with those of the wider community. This vision is as relevant to the life of the Church now as it ever was. Church communities provide the nurture and the sustenance for the Christian way of life. In turn, that life is makes its contribution, with all people of good will, to the common good.[12] If we want that to happen, however, we must equally desire the vigorous life of the local churches in some form or other. In the next chapter we will look at some of the implications of that.

CHAPTER EIGHT

Being Christian

Throughout the foregoing we have shown why Christianity needs to reform itself if it is to remain the power for good that it can be in individual and collective life. We have also shown that there are ways in which it can achieve this. These demonstrate that it can be professed with modern intellectual integrity. We have also examined, in the last chapter, something of the way in which it engages with the actual circumstances of our lives.

We have also seen how Christianity helps us to face up to and live with radical evil. This is of immense importance. It enables us to go on living with composure and confidence in the knowledge that, even and particularly when all the evidence is to the contrary, life is blessed with knowledge that in the end all manner of things shall be well. This knowledge is not just for our own comfort. It requires of us an active engagement with the world around us. In this we have the privilege and opportunity to participate in the ongoing divine work of the world's redemption. When we experience even a glimpse of that we see evidence of God's grace revealing itself in the heart of human life. That this happens so frequently as it does is a cause for constant thanksgiving. This, in turn, is the reason why Christianity is centrally a religion of thanksgiving for the goodness of life and for its manifest blessings. It enables us not only to cope with life, but to do so with joy and thanksgiving. This is no abstract thing. It is what sustains our active and practical engagement with the world around us. It does this, moreover, with discernible results because its practical wisdom is so widely applicable to life's central concerns. This is its proper work. That of labouring with all others of good will to make the best we can of our own lives and those of others.

We have also seen how it is possible for Christianity to respond to the conflict of religions as well as how to use the Bible responsibly in the modern world. We have understood why Christian faith is, initially, a human response to God's love as it is encountered it in the teaching of Jesus. God's gift of faith follows this. Seen in this way faith is not of human creation Though it is, as we have seen, initially a human disposition that alone is not what comprises faith. Faith is, rather, the experience of the reality of the gift of God's love in personal and social life. This, in its turn, creates a life of trust and thanksgiving. The next most important thing to notice here is that none of this comes packaged with set beliefs, doctrines or propositions of any kind. Such things are often, so to speak, smuggled in at this point. When this happens nothing is, in effect, created except unnecessary and seemingly ever increasing baggage. The intellectual and other complications this then presents very soon become obstacles to, rather than facilitators of, faith itself. It is by far the better to travel light at this point. Keep it simple. Faith is the free gift of God in response to God's love. Of course, our understanding of faith only *begins* here. Once it is experienced it requires many other things of us. The first is that of living a vigilant and reflective life. One, that is which is ever alert to finding and engaging with its challenges and opportunities. We discussed this in the previous chapter. Beliefs serve their limited purpose at this point by enabling us to keep aspects of the faith in focus. This faith enables us to put our lives right with God and with each other. It is what properly be called righteousness. It is a gift of God and precious for that reason. It is also extremely vulnerable to *self*-righteousness. Of believing in all things that one is on the side, so to speak, of the angels. Self-righteousness is dangerous and ugly enough, religious self-righteousness is absolutely dangerous and never more so than when it causes religious people imperviously to impose their will on others in this issue or that in the face of uncertainty and confusion. Nothing in the nature of faith, as we have here understood it, can justify its perversion in this way. Here faith is, rather, seen to be more compatible with ignorance and open-mindedness than with such certainty. It is a loving trust in a God who transcends both human knowledge and love. It shines the more, therefore, when it humbles itself both before God and the world. Faith, in other words, does not proffer short cuts to religious knowledge and virtue. All it provides is the starting point from which to seek these things.

This understanding of religious faith is based, as we have seen throughout, on the understanding of faith found in the writings of St Paul. For him, faith and the righteousness it facilitates create a 'new creation' in the life of the faithful (Galatians 6:15). By this he meant that the life of faith was a life of liberation from religious constraint, one which put the believer right with God and left all else to be achieved thereafter. His great writing on this is to be found in his Epistle to the Galatians. All this heralded one of, if not the, most central development in the early Christian traditions. Primitive Christianity, as it is called, the Christianity, that is, which we can trace closest to its source in Jesus was effectively a new, though probably not always that novel, form of Jewish spirituality. Its home was in Jerusalem and its subsequent leader was James, Jesus' brother. From this point of view, Paul was seen as outsider and upstart. This was principally because he had had never met Jesus and could not, therefore, claim any of the authority of those who had done so. Following his famous conversion on the road to Damascus (Acts 9:3ff.) he was inspired to create something new out of the earlier forms of Christianity which were more closely modelled on Judaism. This newness focussed on the one simple thing we have been discussing. This was Paul's insistence not only on the fact that faith could not be justified, but also that it did not need justification at all (Romans 3). It was alone sufficient for salvation. The emphasis on the 'alone' here was at the time explosive. James and the so-called 'Judaisers' were still insisting that Christian justification still required circumcision and meticulous law keeping. Historically, all this came to a head in the First Apostolic Council in Jerusalem in 49CE. Paul and his companion Barnabas were literally summoned there by James and the Jerusalem party. Amazingly, Paul and Barnabas won the day and the so-called Christian Mission to the Gentiles began in earnest. Were it not for this single momentous event, Christianity would probably have died out just as that of the so-called 'Jerusalem party' in fact did. It would then have been nothing more than yet another Jewish Messianic sect which perished with its unfulfilled expectations. Who could have even imagined in 49CE that something had then begun which was to have such momentous consequences for both the history of religion and even for secular history itself? This something, justification by faith alone, has effectively been unstoppable ever since. It was the central motif of the

Protestant Reformation in the sixteenth century and it still reminds us that no human merit can displace the central work of God in human salvation. St Paul described faith, so understood, as one of the three paramount virtues along with hope and love (1 Corinthians 13:13).

This is the essence of the Christian religion. It is essentially simple, has endured for two millennia and is still as relevant to understanding and enhancing the human condition as it has ever been.

If we now see Christianity as being able to respond to the modern conflict of religions, meet the intellectual challenges of modernity and able to contribute to the incessant quest for moral virtue, that still leaves one last question to be answered. That question is, *how* can we be Christian in ways which make all this possible?

For some this is answered by their upbringing and, if so, it is not necessarily the worse for that. For others who are starting out with a genuine sense of enquiry and no such background, the question is not that easy to answer. Many, of course, think otherwise. They invariably suppose that being a Christian is primarily a matter of being a 'good person' and leading, thereby a certain sort of life. Anyone with even a little experience of Christian ministry will know this phenomenon well. Communities are full of people who think like this. They sincerely identify themselves with Christianity to the point of thinking that they actually do come to church to worship. Even coming once now and then over the years under constraint of some necessity or other is more than enough to create this self-delusion. This can also be maintained by supporting the Church financially and being well disposed and supportive in other ways towards its various doings. The term 'Folk Religion' is often used to describe this phenomenon.[1] It is not, of course, a wholly bad thing. It often brings out the best in people and can be a force for good in any community. More than that, it can stand folk religionists in good stead in their hours of personal need. Traditionally at least, even if awkwardly at times, they know where to turn for example for rites of passage, birth, marriage and death. Although this is now changing as in our increasingly secular societies alternative provisions for even these life-defining experiences are made and taken up. All this, however, is not what worship in traditional Jewish and Primitive Christian communities was only about. There it was a matter of central obligation. Something which had to be *done* and done regularly. People either identified with this or they did not. This understanding still, rightly, prevails. It does not mean, of course, that people who do not confess Christianity are not good people or that they are not blessed in the sight of God. To the contrary, many exemplify God's love. Following the Christian way, however, as we have been describing it, requires a conscious choice.

There is no single and definitive way of being a Christian. Different people have done, do and always will do so in different ways. In spite of the outrageous claims some often make for the supremacy their understanding of Christianity, no single manifestation of it is able to express its complete profundity. The imitation of Christ, as it is often technically called, requires a variety of interpretations. None of them are complete in themselves. They all contribute to a greater whole.

Some believers, for example, have emphasised the importance of its affect on the lives of individuals and have gone to great lengths to demonstrate this. They have often withdrawn from everyday life to deny the flesh and even done bizarre things to illustrate their integrity. The so-called Stylites which existed from the fifth to the tenth century were classic examples of this. They lived strict ascetic lives, often literally up pillars in the desert and had little contact with others beyond perhaps teaching and engaging in controversy. Less extremely, the monastic movements of Western Christianity also emphasise, at least initially, the importance of the withdrawal of the life of faith from everyday life. Some of these orders have also been noted for their work in social welfare. These, though numerically depleted, remain immensely important manifestations of one interpretation of the spiritual life. For most, however, living up a pole or in a religious order are not attractions. Not much fun there! For most of us the Christian faith has to be sustained and exercised in the midst of life's everyday concerns.

Living the Christian life consciously to the full cannot be a casual undertaking. Baptism by water is the universally recognised facility for initiation into all the Christian denominations. Broadly, they differ only in administering it soon after birth, as a sign of God's free and unconditional grace, or they administer it in adulthood as a response to a freely chosen mature decision. Increasing numbers of people now do this because they were not baptised as infants. The Baptist Churches, of course, epitomise this. The question about whether infants were baptised in the Early Church is one of the unresolved questions of New Testament study. Some believers there delayed baptism until their deathbed because they did not want to fall from the grace it bestowed beforehand. By the third and fourth centuries, however, infant baptism became the norm in the mainstream Christian Church and it has remained so ever since. Once begun, there are two main ways in which the Christian life of faith is then facilitated and we will discuss them in turn. They are worship and prayer.

The Christian faith is a shared activity. Worship is the central means by which it achieves this. Its Christian manifestations are so diverse that they defy general description. In some instances it is unstructured, but in most it entails ritual of one kind or another. This enables individuals to express formally what they have in common. These rituals have unchanging central cores but these are embellished according to the changing seasons or whatever. In all, they express adoration, prayer, praise and thanksgiving.

Christianity inherited from Judaism that religion's sheer genius for worship. The Jewish people centre their whole lives on the Temple and the Synagogues to such an extent that attending them is as natural as any other human activity. It embraces neither awkwardness nor strangeness. The rituals and their regularity are part of the central rhythm of life. All this can still be observed as a striking feature of Jewish liturgy and worship. It shows that Jewish people have nothing less than a natural talent for sharing and sustaining the religious life. They bequeathed this to both Christianity and Islam. It has two main emphases, initiation into the worshipping communities through rites of baptism and the ritual sharing of meals. (Through the discovery of the Dead Sea Scrolls in 1947 and 1956 it has also now been established that such rituals were equally common to other contemporary Jewish Messianic sects such as those at Qumran.) Sharing meals in ritual was as natural as sharing them in everyday life. All this illustrates that religion is first and foremost about what people regularly and ritualistically *do* together. This doing is as protean to religion as it ever was. It is what facilitates the 'confession' of faith and what it means to call Christianity a 'confessional' religion. It requires that something is done. In the first instance that something is worship.

This was clear enough in the first two centuries or so in the life of the Christian Church. It changed, as did so many other things, when in 312CE, under the Emperor Constantine, Christianity became the religion of the state. This created a tension at the heart of Christian worship which has, effectively, never been resolved. On the one hand, one could now effectively 'be' a Christian by dint of one's citizenship and on the other the older view persisted that more than this was required. That more being, for example, actually belonging to some worshipping Christian community or other. In the history of Christian worship these two views have reflected themselves most prominently in the denominational traditions. So-called established Churches like the Church of England have represented the Constantinian position. Alternatively, the non-conformist Churches which have been 'free' of this state relationship have represented pre-Constantinian forms of the so-called 'gathered church'. These alternatives are more or less reflected in different countries where the Christian Church is closely identified with the state or not so. Needless to say, this is a topic of ever ongoing debate which involves those inside and outside the Churches. Some inside the established Churches want their own freedom from state control, particularly to have the last word in the choice of their own leaders. Some outside the established Churches either want the state to be equally free of denominational association or they want it to include their own.

There are two broad views of the rightful focus of worship in Christian Church life. The first has been more focussed on the life of the Church itself and on the way that life is reflected in its sacraments of Baptism and Eucharist. The second, particularly since the Protestant reformation, has been more focussed on the Bible and its exposition. This is, of course, for the simple reason that in the Reformation the biblical texts were widely used to subject ecclesiastical practices to critical evaluation. These different emphases are reflected in church architecture and they are just one reason why its study can be so historically and sociologically interesting. For some Christians these centuries old differences and debates remain of central importance and concern. Others, however, now accommodate to a more centralist position where both the institution of the Church and the importance of the Bible and its exposition are held in creative tension. In the following discussion of Christian worship some such position as this will be assumed. Before resuming that, however, two other important observations about Christian worship briefly need to be made.

Choosing this type of Church or that is largely a matter of custom and habit. What, simply, one was brought up with. (Fortunate, in many ways, are those who have had more than one such tradition in their upbringing.) Now that more and more people are nurtured in families where there are no such traditions the likelihood is that, if they subsequently want to choose a Church, they will do so for reasons of either immediate personal circumstance or psychological preference. This latter will include either the desire for an intellectual emphasis or an emotional one. Most nonconformist Churches and many of the modern so-called 'house' Churches have reflected the importance of the emotional experience of faith in worship. Methodism is particularly interesting here because of the way in which, under the influence, of John Wesley it has invariably sought to reconcile, or balance, religious experience with mature intellectual reflection.[2] In contrast, the established Churches have mostly emphasised conformity and social permanence. All this is of the essence of the, historical, sociological and psychological study and analysis of Christian worship. It needs noting only as a background to our discussion.

To want to attend Christian worship is, first, to want to put oneself briefly aside from the ordinary concerns and preoccupations of everyday life. This is not to say that they are thereby ignored, it is but to say that in attending worship one wants to put them in a broader perspective. The perspective, that is, of the knowledge and the presence of God. Now, of course, Churches can only *aspire* to achieve this at their very best. For the most part, they fail to achieve it because they are part of and reflect our more earthly preoccupations. Equally, that knowledge and presence can thankfully, also be found outside them in aesthetic or whatever other experiences. To go to a church to worship, however, is to put oneself consciously in the position of wanting to seek these experiences. They might well still elude us because even in worship we, invariably, find it impossible to leave other and worldlier preoccupations behind. Happy and even blessed is our lot if just now and then we experience otherwise, even if we do so largely unconsciously. Perhaps we might just come away from worship with an inarticulate feeling that something about it resonated with our spiritual need and practical concerns. If that is so, then what it has achieved for us might well be more profound than we can ever fully either appreciate or understand. Perhaps, indeed, we might get more from it more regularly if we never do more that expect this from it. We are most commonly disappointed in life generally when we expect too much of things and this is never more true than it is of our expectation of worship. So, in attending worship we put ourselves consciously and deliberately aside with, advisedly, no inflated expectations. We do this, quite simply to wait on the knowledge and the presence of God. Some Christians reading this will react by saying that this is to expect too little. For them, nothing less than the full experience of spiritual things will do. Happy and blessed is their lot, I say! There is no quarrel here at all with that. The only point being made is that worship can be both rightful and rewarding far, far short of this. There might even be a deeper reward that comes from patience and persistence, even doggedness. This latter becomes particularly useful whenever we might suspect that all those around us are clearly getting something which is passing us by.

Most Christian worship is liturgical in some sense or other. This word is derived from two Greek ones for 'people' and 'work'. It literally means 'the work of the people'. What, that is, we do as human beings when we turn to worship. More generally, liturgy has come to mean 'form'. Here, yet again, we will see all sorts of personal preference being expressed. Some will prefer little or no such form. Quaker Christians are particularly noted and respected for this. They eschew formal ministry, sacraments and preaching and simply sit in silence waiting on the spirit of God. This reflects at the same time both a marvellous sincerity and confidence. Here the worshipper's offering is an expectation which will issue in a quiet inner confidence and peace. This latter is extremely important since Quaker spirituality prioritises the pursuit of peace and its making in a fallen world. Its pacifism has a significance and witness which has brought untold blessing to the wider Christian Church. For most, however, the pared down, even minimalist in modern jargon, simplicity of this sort of worship is simply too demanding. Some sort of structure to worship is necessary. This might be little or much and here again there is a wide range of practice and choice to be found. In what follows there is space only to look at the structure of traditional liturgical worship in the English Church. Even before we can do that, however, some little historical background knowledge is necessary.

Up to the late middle ages Christian liturgies had not been reformed for centuries. They were in Latin, as was the Bible and they focussed more on the priests who officiated them than on the laity who observed. The Protestant Reformation dramatically changed all that. As England asserted its independence from Rome under Henry VIII, the inexorable need grew for an English liturgy for the distinctive use of the newly independent English Church. This did not, in fact, happen until just after Henry's death. Two new Prayer Books then appeared in rapid succession during the two Protectorates of the young Edward I. Even the first of these was a radical revision of the Latin rites, but such was the clamour for reform that it lasted only a matter of months before it was succeeded by an even more radical version. None of this transition was smooth. It was *the* central political issue of the day. In some parts of the country it even gave rise to riots. In Cornwall for example, the locals resented the imposition of English language in their worship because they saw it as a political encroachment on the Cornish they spoke every day. It seemed to them that English threatened their native tongue as the liturgical Latin had long since ceased to do, if in fact it had ever done. They even further disliked the new rubrics (instructions) in the book for the distribution of the bread and the wine. It required them to come to the altar rail and stand to receive them. They likened this to 'a Christmas game'.[3] All this was heady controversy. It is always amusing to recall it, but it is also instructive to do so. Edward, tragically, died young and was succeeded by Mary who swept the reforms away and re-introduced the old Latin rites. When she died and was succeeded by Elizabeth in 1559, everyone rightly expected that the re-introduced Latin rites were again to be replaced by English ones. The only question was: which of the two available ones would it be? Would it be the first or the second book of Edward I? Was Elizabeth to show herself as a mild Protestant reformer with the use of the first book or a radical one with the use of the second? She rose amazingly to this occasion by, in effect – choosing the both. Her Book of Common Prayer of 1559 included options from both books which would reconcile both emphases. In this single act the abiding spirit of the English national Church, at its best, was born. Elizabeth had also thereby demonstrated her capacity for statecraft from the very beginning of her reign. The new Book of Common Prayer was to be inclusive, reconciling and above all tolerant. The insertion of the word 'common' in the title is important. Clergy were enjoined to use this book and non other. It was to be the focus of religious inclusion and harmony. (Clergy still have to swear oaths to the effect that they will use only the prayer books authorised. This is an undertaking, if ever there was, that is now more observed in its breach than its observance!) The 1559 Book of Common Prayer was also a masterly literary achievement. Archbishop Cranmer and its other authors made it a canon of English prose. It was revised again on the accession of James I in 1603 and again at the restoration the monarchy in 1662. It was revised again in 1928 and, though not then approved by Parliament, it entered widespread use. In recent years there have been a successive series of Alternative services which are now also in widespread use. These are lamented by many who draw critical attention to the frequent banality of their prose. A Society for the preservation of the (old) Prayer Book exists to counteract this. It appreciates the redolence of its prose and seeks to preserve its use and place in English history and culture. However, one welcome effect of modern liturgical reform has been the general convergence of liturgical style between the main Christian denominations.

The English Prayer Books all clearly suppose that their users will attend regularly more than one kind of service. They provide: the Eucharist, the 'offices' of morning and evening prayer and the occasional services, principally to mark birth, marriage and death. The modern alternative services, in contrast, are designed to cater for the fact that if people attend church at all, they will do so only once or so a week. Here a remarkable change has occurred in the Church of England in recent years. The main Sunday morning service for the majority used to be the office of Morning Prayer (Matins). Considerable numbers of those who had attended this would also attend Evening Prayer. This latter, set to choral music as Evensong, is a widely valued English cultural institution. Its weekly live broadcast from an English cathedral on a Wednesday afternoon is one of Radio Four's most long running popular programmes. It is impossible for those with any sensitivity for the relationship between liturgy and aesthetics not to be captivated by its timeless and haunting beauty. It is immensely to the credit of cathedrals and parish churches where this choral tradition is maintained.

The Parish Communion Movement began in the middle of the last century and has been so successful that the Eucharist, or Communion, is now the main Sunday service attended by the majority of regular worshippers. This, of course, is the central Christian act of worship derived from the Last Supper. It is *the* act of Christian thanksgiving which defines and sustains the fellowship of the Christian community. Four acts are central to the Eucharist: the taking of the elements and giving thanks for them, breaking the bread, consecrating the wine and distributing them both. This happens after introductory sections in which sins are confessed, the Bible read, the word preached, prayers made and the peace shared. Admission to this sacrament is traditionally restricted to those who have been through its initiation ceremony, Confirmation. However, making it open to all who wish to receive it is now a widespread practice in the Church of England. That is not so, however, in the Roman Catholic Church. It officially prohibits any but its own members from receiving the sacrament. Moreover, it also prohibits those members from receiving the sacrament in other denominations. This is a vexed point which bedevils much otherwise integrated ecumenical practice. This is, literally, the sharing of all things as it is done in one household of faith. The Eucharist enables the observation of the central Christian spiritual obligations. It also does so in a way which through the changing liturgical seasons brings forward this aspect of the faith or that. These seasons resonate with the natural ones in a way which is at the heart, still, of English life and custom. Country parish churches are wonderfully redolent of this. T.S. Eliot memorably captured it when he said of the church at Little Gidding 'this is a place where prayer has been valid'.[4]

There is, of course, one particular dimension of the spiritual and worshipping life which is central to it both personally and publically. It is that of prayer. Without prayer, the spiritual life as we have been discussing it cannot be sustained. For this reason alone it requires our concluding attention.

'Prayer' is a very general term for a range of human attitudes and activities. What they, perhaps, have in common is a disposition to something other than what is human. Being prayerful, in this sense, need be minimally nothing more than an awareness of a 'presence' (whatever that may be), other than our own. This reveals nothing less than the human capacity for awe and wonder. It can be experienced by something so simple as looking at the stars. Even this is ever increasingly more difficult for us to do as more of us live under refracted light than ever before. As a result, we can become oblivious to the eternal wonder of the heavens in a way unknown to our more remotely living contemporaries and ancestors. To contemplate the heavens, for example, from a small boat in a big ocean and see the stars as they have always been seen, can be a life enhancing experience. Less dramatically, prayerful awareness might be fleeting and even largely unconscious. It is what most of us will have experienced at some time or another. It might spring from some experience of a deep human emotion such as love. Or it might come from an aesthetic sensation. One such is the experience of the sublime found in the natural elements. Nature mysticism of his kind is, in fact, a universal human experience. At this level and so defined prayer, or prayerful experience, is a normal part of the everyday life of the human lot. It is, therefore, something that humans cannot not do. We are all capable of prayer in this sense. This is a profoundly redeeming feature of human experience. It makes human endurance possible whenever everything conspires to make it not so. Just as it has to do for too many human beings as they come face to face with the wretchedness of the human lot. It is also a part of our marvellous capacity for sensing awe and wonder. One which articulates our feelings beyond words by enabling us to become familiar with what is infinite and, therefore, beyond us. We might not know what this 'something' is though we do know that it is a powerful source of wonder and adoration which never fails to put our lives in a wider perspective. This is why it so often elicits from us responses which express our total surrender in silence. None of this is specific to any particular religion. It is, rather, one of the things which is common to them all, simply because it is common to the human lot. Its exercise at its best raises an awareness of one's limitations and of a presence which is not one's own. This innate human capacity for prayer is what opens human beings to the possibility of genuine religious experience. So understood, it is also a protean way in which human beings can share something with each other which they hold universally in common, regardless of their other differences. For most of us, however, such protean experience cannot remain inarticulate. Prayer needs its form and structure.

The central Christian prayer is, of course, the Lord's Prayer. It is found in the New Testament in two versions (Matt. 6:9–13, and Luke. 11:2–4). That in Matthew is the longer and most frequently used. In both, Jesus offers the prayer in reply to questions from his disciples about how they should pray. What is remarkable about it is not its content, much of which would already have been familiar to his enquirers. It is striking, rather, both for its sheer brevity and the way it interrelates the divine/human relationship. In this way it encapsulates Christian spirituality. The emphasis is on confession, forgiveness and the immediacy of the relationship to God which follows. This expresses the essence and simplicity of Jesus' central teaching about the immediacy of the human and the divine relationship. This prayer is used in nearly all Christian liturgies and by individual Christians as the basis of their private devotions. Prayer, in other words, requires its form no less than anything else in our lives. However, there is something even more fundamental about prayer to consider.

As we have understood it thus far, prayer is a human capacity for enabling us to come to terms with our humanity and our awareness of its limitations. It enables us to focus on what is infinite and awesome. For this reason it can be both reassuring, as we have seen it is in the Lord's prayer, or frightening because in it we expose the frailty of our human nature. This is also exposed by our common fears. Examples of this are: fears of the dark, of the unexpected, the strange, the unknown, confrontation with the power of the natural elements, or whatever. These will be no less fearful because we cannot articulate them, indeed they may be the more so for that very reason. (This is a perennial theme beloved of dramatists throughout the ages.) Here we have understood prayer as a human capacity which enables us to cope with all this. It is not the only one. There is another which, as we will see, has so much in common with prayer that it, in turn, can help us to throw light on it. It is not one commonly noticed for this purpose. It is humour. Humour, as William James (again) pithily observed, 'is a philosophic state of mind; it seems to say to Nature that we take her no more seriously than she takes us'.[5] So understood, it is the means whereby God allows us to come to terms with nature. As well as standing in awe of nature, we can also be scared and debilitated by it. A common way in which we cope with this is by laughter.

It is often observed that there are, in fact, only a very few good jokes and that all the others are variants of them. The reason for this is, quite simply, that there are only a very few things that we a human beings are actually afraid of. They are the things we have weak self-defences for. They are things like death, gender, defecation, sex, and race. We are so successful at managing our human condition that there really are but a very few such things we cannot come to terms with. This list is incomplete, but the point being made here is that it very soon runs out. Accordingly, whenever we laugh we are, in fact, exercising our instinctive human response to fear. On this view laughter is not funny. It is, rather, profoundly serious. Little wonder that it is so often identified as being essential to human well-being and flourishing. Laughter, so understood, is what prevents us from being screwed up by fear. There is something profound, blessed and redeeming about that fact that we can laugh as we do about the things we are afraid of. It provides us with an insulation from harsh and unacceptable realities and, above all, as we share laughter it binds us together. Binds us, that is, in the commonality of our human lot at the very point of our worst and most fearsome insecurities. When we re-discover our innate capacity for humour in the face of tragedy, we are discovering at the same time, our equally innate human capacity to deal with it. The greater the tragedy and the more personally we are affected by it the longer, of course, this might take. For example, humour has now, for some, only now begun to come out of 11 September 2001. By the same token, those old enough to remember the horrors of the Second World War remain ever delighted by and indebted to cartoonists like Carl Giles, of the *Daily Express*. The humour he made out of it, so soon after its horrors, was an early healing balm which still continues. His depictions of the funniness of it all are as endearing (and collectable) as they ever were. And they are still as important. Another enduring example of this is to be found, of course, in the antics of Captain Mainwaring and his confederates in their ever failing but magnificent attempts to protect Walmington on Sea, and all the rest of us to boot. These humours are particularly redemptive for those who remember the dire nature of the circumstances in which they are set. We can cope with things so much more effectively if we are not afraid of them and being able to laugh is the best evidence of that, even if we do so from time to time a little nervously. People of different religions and races who live closely together so often find that humour is the grace that makes all their differences possible. This is why too much, or maybe even just a little, political correctness in these and similar situations is a dangerous thing. To stifle humour is to stifle what is naturally human and redemptive. Laughing and being laughed at is of the stuff of human maturity. Shared humour is part of the fabric of social life. Enabling us to laugh at what we fear or are even just perplexed by, is of course, a serious business. The need for this is as great as it ever was. Satirical theatre and radio and television programmes and daily newspaper cartoons exist to meet it. We need them all.

Whenever we raise a smile, healing occurs. We are healed by it as are others who share it with us. Of course, there are distasteful jokes, just as there are distasteful works of art and perhaps these are necessary from time to time as they enable us to explore the boundaries of what is acceptable and necessary. Edgy humour is well named.

We do well to understand prayer in the light of this understanding of humour. Just as humour helps us to cope with the things we are afraid of, so prayer enables us to reconcile ourselves to those many things which bear upon us unacceptably. It also enables us to express our thanksgivings when we can find no other satisfactory way of doing so. Its dimension in our lives is, therefore, so much like the dimension of humour. It enables us to face things rather than turn from them. Even more, it enables us to live with them in the expectation of improving our own lot and, more importantly, that of others. This is why praying for others is so important. Just as humour gives a 'space' from our innermost fears, prayer envelops us with a healing balm which reconciles our personal anxieties and concerns for others with the God to whom we pray. The point here being stressed is that both humour and prayer enable us to be human in remarkably similar ways. Understanding that just might give us a better insight into both.

Happy is our lot if we have some innate ability in the art of prayer. Those who have no such facility can often, by skilful ministry, be brought to it in their times of need. The needs of the bereaved are a common example of this. Funeral services when conducted sensitively in response to the needs of the bereaved can be for them a surprising source of joy and comfort. There are many other such examples. They are, moreover, still widely recognised as being important even by those who would not normally think of themselves as being prayerful. Many often attend churches in response to sudden disasters and find surprising and unexpected comfort. As we have seen, like laughter, prayer is something all human beings have a natural capacity for. It may lie dormant in most of us most of the time, but it is always there. We may require help to recover it but that recovery is assured if we but respond. Prayer embraces us and restores our dignity and poise. To experience this and even more profoundly to observe something of it happening in others is to obtain a glimpse of the divine redemption of human need. The experience of prayer, then, and the experience of laughter are profoundly analogous. They throw light on each other. Prayer can be understood as humour, and humour as prayer. They both touch the essence of what it means to be human. Prayer is a part of the normal life of us all, just as laughter is. Perhaps even, we should learn to pray and smile more at the same time.

Prayer, so understood, meets our innermost human needs. This was widely acknowledged until comparatively recently. The need for and place of, public and private prayerful devotions was taken for granted. This is still sometimes the case. School assemblies are a good illustration. At their best they can be inspiring, but at anything less than this they can be the reverse. Too much is often expected of many of those who perforce have to conduct them. As a result they can degenerate into lessons in morality, folk wisdom or whatever. When this happens they can become counter-productive by serving as illustrations of the awkwardness and embarrassment of prayer, when they should serve the very opposite purpose. Just perhaps this is one of the simple and overlooked reasons why church schools are as popularly successful as they are. A school, and of course it does not have to be a church one, where prayer in practised with sincerity and understanding can give it an important foundation to education and self-awareness. It can do this, moreover, even if its participants are in the greater part unwilling and even antagonistic. Who knows what longer-term effect for the good it can have by laying foundations which remain. It is good to remember that the most formative influences in our education are so often the ones we are least aware of at the time of their being experienced.

Far from being a personal and public embarrassment, prayer, so understood is a normal and necessary part of life. For this reason all that can be done to encourage it should be done. Again, as we have so often observed throughout, there is nothing exclusively Christian about this. All religions make recourse to prayer in some form or other. When they share it together they also share their natural dispositions. Annual Remembrance Day services are a good and moving illustration of this happening as different religions and their denominations are seen to come together to remember and honour the fallen. So understood, the exercise of prayer is a touchstone of what it means to be human, both privately and publicly.

In this final chapter we have discussed briefly aspects of the practice of worship and prayer in the Christian life. Church membership, at its best, facilitates both of these things. Mainstream Christian Churches are broader than they even recently were. They have come to live with dissonance and just perhaps come also to see that it is a sign of vitality and creativity. All this means that one can be a member of such a Church without committing intellectual suicide. Active participation of the sort we have considered demands none of this. It positively cherishes differences which are held with integrity. All this is nothing less than the ideal of liberalism applied to the practice of religion.[6] There is, in fact, more dissident opinion in even the authoritarian Churches that they are prepared to admit. This dissidence is an important part of their strength and vigour. None of this is easy to maintain, as church leaders know well. They invariably have to preside over Churches in which disagreeing interests battle constantly for the soul of the whole. At the present, in churches like the Church of England they might yet lead to further schism and defection. Wise leaders, however, will know that everything needs to be done to prevent this from happening. Churches are the stronger by far when they achieve toleration and mutual understanding amid diversity.

In all these ways the life of the Churches is less than perfect. They are but earthen vessels which reflect human inadequacy as much as they do, at their best, divine inspiration. Whenever that is forgotten they fall victim to a spiritual pride which chokes the very purpose for their existence. At their best, however, they do serve to structure the life of faith. That is what most of us need if we are to live the Christian life. People can suffer from religion just as they do anything else, but they can also enjoy it as the central nourishing focus of their lives. One, moreover, which achieves this more completely than any other can. Even then, it carries no guarantees beyond those we have explored. Those, that is, of making the best sense and opportunity we can of life as we know it. More than that cannot be asked of us and, by the grace of God, it need not be. Make the most of religion and – above all – enjoy it.

Notes

Introduction

1. R. John Elford, *The Pastoral Nature of Theology: an Upholding Presence*, Cassell, London, 1999, pp. 9ff.
2. 'Always reforming' is a basic tenet of the Protestant Reformation.
3. *E.g.* Alister McGrath, *Dawkins' God: Genes, Memes and the Meaning of Life*, Blackwell, Oxford, 2007.
4. *Cf.* Marc Ellis, *Revolutionary Forgiveness*, Baylor University Press, Waco Texas, 2000.

Chapter One

1. Amir Taheri, *The Times*, 68768, 2 August 2006, p. 17.
2. R. Harries, *God Outside the Box: Why Spiritual People Object to Christianity*, SPCK, London, 2002.
3. *Ibid.* p. xii.
4. *Ibid.* p. 42.
5. D.M. Mackinnon, *Borderlands of Theology*, Lutterworth, London, 1968, p. 54.

Chapter Two

1. Edward Caird, *The Evolution of Religion, Vols 1 and 2*, James Maclehose and Sons, Glasgow, 1899.
2. *Ibid. Vol. 1*, p. xi.
3. *Ibid. Vol. 2*, p. 325.

4   *Ibid. Vol. 2*, p. 296.
5   Eds. Ian S Markham and Tinu Ruparell, *Encountering Religion*, Blackwell, Oxford, 2001, pp. 297ff.
6   Major Religions of the World Ranked by National Adherents, adherents.com/Religion, accessed 17 November 2010.
7   S.G.F. Brandon, *Man and His Destiny in the Great Religions*, Manchester University Press, 1962, p. 336.
8   Major Religions *op. cit.*
9   See p. 161 this volume.
10 *Encountering Religion*, p. 166.
11 E.g., Ben Witherington III, *Jesus the Sage: the Pilgrimage of Wisdom*, T & T Clark, Edinburgh, 1994.
12 Ed. Franklin Sherman, *Luther's Works*, Vol. 47, Fortress Press, Philadelphia, pp. 121ff.
13 Major Religions, *op. cit.*
14 *Cf.* Johannes Munck, *Paul and the Salvation of Mankind*, SCM Press, London, 1959, pp. 282ff.
15 Richard Hanson, *Christian Priesthood Examined*, Lutterworth, Guildford and London, 1979, p. 33ff.
16 *Cf.* Henry Bettenson, *Documents of the Christian Church*, Oxford University Press, Oxford, 1963, p. 22.
17 *Ibid.* p. 329.
18 R. John Elford, *The Pastoral Nature of Theology*, Cassell, London, 1999, pp. 16ff.
19 Wilfred Cantwell Smith, *The Meaning and End of Religion: a Revolutionary Approach to the Great Religious Traditions*, SPCK, London, 1978.
20 *Ibid.* p. 19.
21 *Ibid.* p. 50.
22 *Ibid.* p. 194.
23 *Ibid.* p. 195.

Chapter Three

1   G. Von Rad, *Genesis*, SCM Press, London, 1961, p. 95.
2   Marc H. Ellis, *Toward a Jewish Theology of Liberation*, SCM Press, London, 1988, p. 116.
3   Marc H Ellis 'On the Jewish Civil War and the New Prophetic' *Tikkun*, 16(4):24, 1st July 2001.

4   *Cf.* Naim Ateek, *A Palestinian Christian Cry for Reconciliation*, Orbis Books, Maryknoll, 2008.
5   David Martin, *Does Christianity Cause War?*, Clarendon Press, Oxford, 1997.
6   *Ibid.* p. 21ff.
7   *Ibid.* p. 25.
8   *Ibid.* p. 26.
9   *Ibid.* p. 31.
10 *Ibid.* p. 34.
11 *Ibid.* p. 35.
12 *Ibid.* p. 37.
13 Sydney Wignall, *In Search of Spanish Treasure*, David & Charles, London, 1982, pp. 91ff.
14 H. Reinhold Niebuhr, *The Nature and Destiny of Man, Vol. I*, Nisbet, London, 1941, p. 213.
15 *Op. cit.* p. 220.
16 For an excellent critical discussion of Dawkins' wider criticisms of religion see Alister McGrath, *Dawkins' God*, Blackwell Publishing, Oxford, 2007.
17 K. Ward, *Is Religion Dangerous?*, Lion, Oxford, 2006.
18 *Ibid.* p. 79.
19 *Ibid.* p. 73.
20 *Cf.* ed. Robin Gill, *The Cambridge Companion to Christian Ethics*, CUP, Cambridge, 2001, pp. 171ff.
21 Eds. Richard J. Bauckham and R. John Elford, *The Nuclear Weapons Debate: Theological and Ethical Issues*, SCM Press, London, 1989, pp. 188ff.
22 Ed. R. John Elford, *Just Reconciliation*, Peter Lang, Oxford, 2011, pp. 43–64.
23 R. Attfield, *The Ethics of Environmental Concern*, Basil Blackwell, Oxford, 1983, p. 83f.

Chapter Four

1   *Cf.* p. 124 this volume.
2   For a brief introduction see Bertrand Russell, *The History of Western Philosophy*, George Allen and Unwin, London, 1961, pp. 444ff.
3   Ed. L.A. Selby-Bigge, David Hume, *An Enquiry Concerning Human Understanding*, 2nd Edition Revised, Clarendon, Oxford, 1942, pp. 115–116.
4   *The Works of Alfred Lord Tennyson*, Macmillan, London, 1893, p. 261.
5   I. Kant, *The Critique of Pure Reason*, Macmillan, London, 1964, p. 606ff.

6   Ibid. p. 21.
7   Cf. Thomas Dixon, *Science and Religion: a Very Short Introduction*, Oxford, 2008, p. 63.
8   A. Plantinga, *A Study of the Rational Justification of Belief in God*, Cornell University Press, Ithaca, 1967, p. 271.
9   T. Altizer, *The Gospel of Christian Atheism*, Collins, London, 1967, p. 22.
10 D. Bonhoeffer, *Letters and Papers from Prison*, SCM Press, London, 1953, p. 280ff.
11 J.T. Robinson, *Honest to God*, SCM, London, 1963.
12 Cf. Walter P. Weaver, *The Historical Jesus in the Twentieth Century*, Trinity Press International, Pennsylvania, 1990, pp. 103ff.
13 G. Bornkamm, *Jesus of Nazareth*, Hodder and Stoughton, London, 1960, p. 26.
14 J.D. Crossan, *The Historical Jesus*, T & T Clark, Edinburgh, 1991, p. 422.
15 Ed. John Hick, *The Myth of God Incarnate*, SCM Press, London, 1977.
16 Ibid. p. 6.
17 Ibid. p. 29.
18 Alister E. McGrath, *The Future of Christianity*, Blackwell, Oxford, 2002, p. 133ff.
19 Eds. John Hick and Paul F. Knitter, *The Myth of Christian Uniqueness*, SCM, London, 1987.
20 Ibid. p33.
21 Ibid. p. 34.
22 Ibid. p. 53.
23 Ibid. p. 60.
24 Tr. F.M. Cornford, *The Republic of Plato*, Clarendon Press, Oxford, 1941, p. xxi.
25 Cf. Robert A. Duff, *Spinoza's Political and Ethical Philosophy*, James Mailhouse, Glasgow, 1903, pp. 221ff.
26 Ed. W. Stark, *Theodicy*, Routledge and Kegan Paul Ltd., London, 1951. p. 197.
27 Ed. R. John Elford, *Just Reconciliation*, Peter Lang, Oxford, 2011, pp. 87ff.
28 A. Camus, *The Plague*, Penguin, Harmondsworth, 1948.
29 Ibid. p. 186.
30 D.Z. Phillips, *The Problem of Evil and the Problem of God*, SCM Press, London, 2009.
31 Ibid. p. 272.

Chapter Five

1. David Knowles, *The Evolution of Medieval Thought*, Longmans Green, London, 1962, p. 319.
2. *Ibid.* p. 319.
3. Friedrich Schleiermacher, *On Religion: Speeches to its Cultured Despisers*, Friedrick Ungar, New York, 1955.
4. F. Schleiermacher, *The Christian Faith*, T & T Clark, Edinburgh, 1928, p. 11.
5. *Ibid.* p. 14.
6. *Ibid.* p. 46.
7. *Ibid.* p. 751.
8. H.L. Mansel, *The Limits of Religious Thought Examined in Eight Lectures*, John Murray, Oxford, 1859.
9. Ed. Roger Lancelyn Green, *The Works of Lewis Carroll*, Paul Hamlyn, London, 1965, p. 163.
10. *Cf.* See p. 127, this volume.
11. *Cf.* See p. 51, this volume.
12. *Op. cit.* p. 88ff.
13. *Op. cit.* p. 16.
14. Ed. H.W. Chandler, *H.L. Mansel, Letters Lectures and Reviews*, John Murray, London, 1873, p. 401.
15. *Cf.* Don Cupitt, *Taking Leave of God*, SCM, London, 1971, p. 29ff.
16. *Poems by Matthew Arnold*, Macmillan, London, 1888, pp. 63–64.
17. Tr. Norman Kemp Smith, I. Kant, *Critique of Pure Reason*, Macmillan, London, 1964, p. 450.
18. T.S. Kuhn, *The Structure of Scientific Revolutions*, 2nd Edition Enlarged, University of Chicago Press, Chicago, 1970, p. 206.
19. D. Emmet, *The Role of the Unrealizable: a Study in Regulative Ideals*, St Martin's Press, New York, 1994, p. 131.
20. John Macmurray, *The Self as Agent (SAE)*, Faber and Faber, London, 1957. *Persons in Relation (PIR)*, Faber and Faber, London, 1961.
21. *SAE*, p. 84.
22. *Ibid.* p. 85.
23. *Ibid.* p. 139.
24. *PIR*, p. 156.
25. *Ibid.* p. 222.

Chapter Six

1. R. Bultmann, *Theology of the New Testament, Vol. 1*, SCM, London, 1952, pp. 4ff.
2. Comp. Lord Birkenhead, *John Betjeman's Collected Poems*, John Murray, London, p. 188.
3. A.J. Ayer, *Language Truth and Logic*, Victor Gollancz, London, 1964.
4. L. Wittgenstein, *Tractatus Logico Philosophicus*, Routledge and Keegan Paul, London, 1922.
5. L. Wittgenstein, *Philosophical Investigations (PI)*, Basil Blackwell, Oxford, 1968.
6. A.J. Ayer, *The Central Questions of Philosophy*, Weidenfeld and Nicholson, London, 1973, p. 22ff, p. 33ff.
7. Ed. Henry Bettenson, *Documents of the Christian Church*, OUP, Oxford, 1963, pp. 6–7.
8. L. Wittgenstein, *Philosophical Investigations*, Basil Blackwell, Oxford, 1968, p. viii.
9. *Ibid.* p. 4.
10. *Ibid.* p. 4.
11. *Ibid.* p. 5.
12. *Ibid.* p. 20.
13. *Ibid.* p. 48.
14. Kai Nielsen and D.Z. Phillips, *Wittgensteinian Fideism?*, SCM Press, London, 2005.
15. *PI*, p. 19.
16. J. Dewey, *Essays in Experimental Logic*, Chicago, 1916, p. 63.
17. *Ibid.* pp. 303–442.
18. J. Dewey, *Reconstruction in Philosophy*, Mentor Books, New York, 1950, p. 157.
19. William James, *Pragmatism: A New Name for Some Old Ways of Thinking*, Longmans Green, London, 1907.
20. *Ibid.* pp. 45–46.
21. W. James, *Selected Papers on Philosophy*, J.M. Dent, London, 1917, p. 204.
22. *Ibid.* p. 210.
23. William James, *Pragmatism: A New Name for Some Old Ways of Thinking*, Longmans Green, London, 1907, p. 45.
24. Gay Wilson Allen, *William James: a Biography*, Rupert Hart-Davis, London, 1967, p. 205.
25. William James, *The Varieties of Religious Experience (VRE)*, Longman Green, London, 1904, p. 37.
26. Ed. R. Benton Perry, *William James, Essays in Radical Empiricism*, Longmans, London, 1962.
27. *Ibid.* p. 3.

28 *VRE*, p. 12.
29 *Ibid.* p. 45.
30 *Ibid.* p. 271.
31 *Ibid.* p. 272.
32 *Ibid.* p. 506.
33 *Op. cit. SPP*, p. 119.
34 *Ibid.* p. 120.
35 *VRE*, p. 163.
36 *VRE*, p. 163.
37 *Ibid.* p. 164.
38 *Ibid.* p. 165.
39 *Ibid.* p. 91.

Chapter Seven

1   R. John Elford, *The Ethics of Uncertainty*, Oneworld, Oxford, 2000, p. 107ff.
2   J. Bentham, *An Introduction to the Principles of Morals and Legislation*, Clarendon Press, Oxford, 1789.
3   J.S. Mill, *Utilitarianism*, Longmans Green, London, 1897.
4   *Issues in Human Sexuality*, Church House Publishing, London, 1991.
5   *Op. cit.* p. 71ff.
6   *Cf.* eds. D. Gareth Jones and R. John Elford, *A Glass Darkly: Medicine and Theology in Further Dialogue*, Peter Lang, Oxford, 2010, p. 46.
7   Richard B. Heys, *The Moral Vision of the New Testament*, T & T Clark, Edinburgh, 1996.
8   E.g. David Sheppard, *Bias for the Poor*, Hodder and Stoughton, London, 1983.
9   Walter M. Abbott, *The Documents of Vatican II*, Geoffrey Chapman, London, 1966, p. 336ff.
10 Intro. Michael J. Miller, *The Encyclicals of John Paul II*, Huntington, Indiana, 1996.
11 Alasdair MacIntyre, *After Virtue*, Duckworth, London, 1982.
12 For a recent discussion of the contribution of religious morality to human fulfilment see K. Ward, *Religion and Human Fulfilment*, SCM Press, London, 2008.

Chapter Eight

1 *Cf.* Paul C. Hiebert, *Understanding Folk Religion: a Christian Response to Popular Beliefs and Practices*, Baker Books, Grand Rapids, 1999.
2 *Cf.* Donald A. Bullen, *A Man of One Book?*, Paternoster, Bletchley, 2007, pp. 177ff.
3 *Cf.* A.L. Rowse, *Tudor Cornwall*, Jonathan Cape, London, 1941, pp. 253–290.
4 T.S. Eliot, *The Complete Poems and Plays of T.S. Eliot*, Book Club Associates, London, 1969, p. 192.
5 William James, *The Varieties of Religious Experience*, Longmans Green, London, 1904, p. 37.
6 *Cf.* ed. Ian S. Markham, *The Blackwell Companion to the Theologians, Vol. 2*, Wiley-Blackwell, Oxford, 2009, pp. 330ff. Eds. J'annine Jobling and Ian S. Markham, *Theological Liberalism*, SPCK, London, 2000.

Index

Abraham 35
Albert, St The Great 52
Amos 37
Anselm, St of Canterbury 96
Anti-Semitism 40, 80
Apostolic Council 179
Aquinas, St 53
Aristotle 52
Arius 127
Arnold, Matthew 130
Artha 33
Assyria 37
Augustine, St of Canterbury 143, 141
Augustine, St of Hippo 51, 96, 111
Avatars 34
Ayer, A.J. 40, 141

Babylon 37
Baptism 181, 183
Belief 126 ff
Bentham, Jeremy 158
Betjeman, John 138
Bin Laden Osama 13
Bonaventura, St 52
Bonhoeffer, Dietrich 101
Bohler, Peter 55
Brahma 34
Bridgewater, Duke of 88
Buddhism 27 ff, 154
Bultmann, Rudolph 103, 37, 137
Bush President 12, 39

Caird, Edward 19 ff
Certainty
    Religious 83

Chalcedon, Council of 50
Christian Uniqueness 107 ff
Clement, of Alexandria 96
Creation 65
Camus, Albert 112
Common Prayer, Book of 186
Conflict of religions 4, 41
Constantine, Emperor 50, 84
Constantinople, Council of 51
Crossan, John D. 104
Cupitt, Don 130
Cyrus, King 37

Darwin, Charles 19
David, King 36
Dawkins, Richard 76
Descartes, Rene 133
Devi 32
Dewey, John 148 ff
Drake, Francis 79

Ecumenism 56
Edward I, King 186
Eliot, Thomas Stearns 147
Elizabeth I, Queen 55, 186
Ellis, Marc H 69
Emmet, Dorothy 132
Environment 87 ff
Evil 108
Evolution 19 ff

Faith 126, 178
Feminist theology 169 ff
Fideism 143, 146
Filioque clause 51

Folk religion 180

Gentile Mission 49
Gnostic 111
God 94 ff
   incarnate 102 ff
   kingdom of 168
Gotama, Siddhatha 27

Hajj 44
Harries, Richard 14 ff
Hartshorne, Charles 100
Henry VIII, King 54
Hick, John 107
Hinduism 31 ff
Hirohito, Emperor 26
Hopkins, Gerard Manley 147
Hume, David 17, 97, 98, 121
Humour 190

Irenaeus, St 111
Islam 41 ff
Israel 9

James, Henry 148
James, William 148 ff
Jesus 105, 158, 163 ff
Jews of Conscience 69
Judaism 35 ff, 61

Kant, Immanuel 17, 97, 99, 123, 131, 132
Kami 25
Karma 28, 33
Kingdom of God 75
Kojiki 25
Krishna 34
Kuhn, Thomas S. 131

Leibniz 110
Liberation Theology 58
Lindsay, A.D. 140
Love 164 ff

Luke, St, Gospel 47
Luther, Martin 40

Macintyre, Alisdair 173
Mackinnon, Donald 14 ff
Macmurray, John 133 ff
Magisterium 171
Mansel, Henry 124, 130, 132
Martin, David 77 ff
Mark, St, Gospel 47
Matthew, St, Gospel 47
Mauice, Fredrick Dennison 114
Mecca 42
Merkel, Chancellor Angela 91
Messianic
   fulfilment 47
Metaphysics
   realist 125
Methodism 55
Milan, Edict of 50
Mill, John Stuart 158
Ministry, Orders of 49
Modernity 2, 119 ff
Monotheism, ethical 158
Mubarak, President 39
Muhammad 20
Multiculturalism 90

Nature 24
Nicea, Council of 51

Ockham, William 120
Ontological Argument 96

Pacifism 85
Palestine 9, 68
Paul, St 38, 48 ff, 128, 141, 144, 166, 179 ff
Phillips, D.Z. 113–114
Philo, of Alexandria 96
Pierce, Charles 150 ff
Plantinga, Alvin 100
Plato 110, 120

Index

Pope
  Benedict XVI 172
  John XXIII 171
  John Paul I 172
  John Paul II 172
  Paul VI 57, 171
Prayer 188 ff
Providence 71 ff
Puranas 32

Ramsey, Abp. Michael 57
Reason and commitment 147
Religion
  definition of 60 ff
  primitive 21 ff
Religious Studies 59
Renaissance, European 53
Robinson, John 101
Runcie, Abp. Robert 51

Saintliness 152
Salat 44
Sangha 28
Saul, King 36
Schleiermacher, Friedrich 17, 123, 129
Schools 91
Semper Reformanda 3
Sexuality 161
Shahada 41
Shari'ah 44
Shi'ites 41
Shintoism 25 ff
Shiva 34
Slavery 169
Smith, Wilfred Cantwell 59 ff, 107
Socrates 110
Solomon, King 36
Spinoza 110
Sunnites 41

Tantras 32
Technology 159 ff
Terrorism 10 ff
Tertullian 14, 144, 138
Trinity, doctrine of 95
Truth
  coherence theory 141 ff
  correspondence theory 141 ff
  regulative 131
  pragmatic theory 148

Umma 41
Uncertainty 158, 168
Unitarianism 56
United States 9, 13

Virtue ethics 173
Vishnu 34
Von Rad, Gerhard 66

War 76 ff
  Just, theory of 85
Ward, Keith 82 ff
Wesley, John and Charles 55
Whitehead, Alfred North 100
Wilberforce, William 169
Wiles, Maurice 105
Wisdom 38
Wittgenstein, Ludwig 141, 144, 146, 144, 146
Wordsworth, William 147
Worship 184
  Liturgical 185

Young, Frances 105

Zakat 44
Zedekiah, King 37
Zionism 39